CAREER OPPORTUNITIES IN THE FOOD AND BEVERAGE INDUSTRY

SECOND EDITION

CAREER OPPORTUNITIES IN THE FOOD AND BEVERAGE INDUSTRY

SECOND EDITION

B<small>ARBARA</small> S<small>IMS</small>-B<small>ELL</small>

Facts On File, Inc.

Facts On File, Inc.
132 West 31st Street
New York NY 10001

Library of Congress Cataloging-in-Publication Data

Sims-Bell, Barbara.
    Career opportunities in the food and beverage industry / Barbara Sims-Bell.—2nd ed.
      p. cm. — (Career opportunities series)
    Includes bibliographical references and index.
    ISBN 0-8160-4493-7 (hardcover : alk. paper)
     1. Food service—Vocational guidance—United States. I. Title. II. Facts on File's career opportunities series.

TX911.3.V62 S56 2001
647.95′023′73—dc21

                                      2001023267

Facts On File books are available at special discounts when purchased in bulk quantities for businesses, associations, institutions or sales promotions. Please call our Special Sales Department in New York at (212) 967-8800 or (800) 322-8755.

You can find Facts On File on the World Wide Web at http://www.factsonfile.com

Cover design by Nora Wertz

Printed in the United States of America

VB Hermitage 10 9 8 7 6 5 4 3 2 1

This book is printed on acid-free paper.

CONTENTS

For Carol Durst
teacher, colleague, and friend,
always a role model and mentor to culinary hopefuls.

INTRODUCTION

Day after day, willing customers enter restaurants, cafés, take-out food shops, and groceries trustful and confident they are buying and consuming food that will please their taste buds and nurture their bodies. The working millions who comprise the food and beverage industry today enjoy a singular level of trust from the people they serve, and they rigorously follow regimes of sanitation and food safety to deserve that confidence. There is pride and honor in being taken for granted this way, and it is one of the supreme joys of being a working professional in this industry.

The best news about the industry is that culinary jobs are among the fastest-growing in the United States. Income is also increasing, even doing a bit better than keeping up with inflation. In the process of reviewing and updating the 1994 edition, higher salaries and greater opportunity due to general growth in all areas of the industry bumped up every job profile in the book, save one.[1] Since there are more jobs than skilled candidates to fill them in some parts of the country, it is a very competitive time to market your services for top dollar—either by moving to another employer or by negotiating a wage increase in return for staying where you are.

New sectors in the industry have been added. The section titled Community and Social Service reflects the initiative taken by many compassionate leaders to deal directly with the needs of the hungry and the homeless outside the realm of government programs for the needy. Publicity, Public Relations and Marketing, recognizes the intensification of competition, going after every dollar to boost company profit. Professionals who succeed in these jobs almost always achieve higher income levels. Culinary Computer only touches on the dawning of Internet invasion into the food industry, an invasion that increasingly blankets every professional area.

Equal opportunity has been strengthened in the food industry. A decade ago there were ample stories of hazing and hard-core "teasing" of women employees in upscale kitchens by their male counterparts. Those stories have almost vanished, thankfully; now they are used as examples of what used to be. Women and other minorities in greater numbers are enrolled in vocational and academic schools, and after graduating they are being hired for the challenging jobs they seek. Female chefs are more frequently restaurant owners, and they have gained almost equal space with male chefs as celebrities. There are female role models in the food and beverage industry today. All of these changes have come about in the past few decades, and there are strong indications they will continue to grow.

Many immigrant refugee minorities—Thai, Vietnamese, Argentine, Peruvian, Turkish, Moroccan, Yugoslavian, Iranian, and Israeli are a few—brought their culinary culture with them. Many who were lawyers and doctors in their homelands could not afford the time or money to resume their original careers, but they enlisted family members to start small restaurants where they could enjoy the flavors and flavorings of home with others from their home country. It has not been surprising that their American neighbors discovered these small cafés with authentic ethnic dishes, became enthusiastic customers, and contributed to their popularity and their financial success.

In the segment of the food and beverage industry that consists of chefs, caterers, and cooks, workers are starting much younger and thus getting a head start on their careers that formerly was limited to European-trained chefs. Youngsters who very early latch onto the happiness associated with baking cookies for their families and friends have begun to learn that interesting careers are open to them as a pastry chef or a restaurant chef. In their after-school cruising of cable TV channels, they found the Food Network with the "Bam!" of Emeril Lagasse, the fast pace of Bobby Flay on or off the grill, and the show with the curious title of *The Naked Chef.* It isn't MTV, but it is entertaining, and the Food Network can probably be credited with attracting a generation of young workers to culinary and food industry jobs. Although they still enter the restaurant world as dirty dish bussers in the dining room and pot scrubbers in the kitchen, they are fearless about badgering the chef to let them learn and move up.

Another significant change is that smaller culinary academies now offer a liberal arts degree, at least an associate of arts (A.A.), and students have to satisfy general education requirements by taking courses in literature, communications, and finance. The kitchen no longer harbors people who can't get better jobs—it encourages workers to take courses that give them the knowledge to own their own business.

---

[1] Home economists in secondary education—the cooking teacher in 7th or 8th grade and the cooking classroom in high schools—have just about vanished. Sadly, cooking is rarely taught at home any more, certainly not by working mothers. Recent cutbacks in education costs, the same ones that eliminated or sharply curtailed music, art, and some sports programs in public schools, now show a fragile possibility they will be restored during the first decade of this century.

Finally, one of the first influences on many children, some even before kindergarten, is the Internet, and being computer savvy practically from toddlerhood has accustomed youngsters to a vast storehouse of knowledge and reference works. When the neighborhood library closes at 8:00 P.M., it's not a problem because the Web is "open" 24 hours a day. Culinary websites are abundant and growing in numbers and in size; all segments of the food and beverage industry have made a platform for themselves on the Web.

The changes explored in this second edition bode well for job seekers of every interest, skill, talent, and trait. They provide options for the general public that will elevate their daily lives with better health and broader choices, and bring delicious food to their tables.

INDUSTRY OUTLOOK
Insistent Issues Facing the Food Industry

Since biblical times, breaking bread and sharing food have been the symbols of friendship, peacemaking, and nurturing. This is the attitude we bring to work, studies, and community service. It creates an environment that is more than the way we make a living; it is how we make our lives. Now, as always, there are some conditions in our larger (global) workplace that raise concerns and the need to recruit volunteer warriors from our ranks to fight for change. None of these are particularly new issues, but they are vital issues that need advocates to change.

Literacy and Language

Throughout the United States, not just in Southern California, where I work, most minority employees are Hispanic—Mexican, Central and South American, and Caribbean, mostly—who have lived in Spanish-speaking environments their entire lives, first in their homelands and now in ethnic barrios in this country. In restaurant kitchens, food processing plants, and on farms, most employers have taken an easy route of learning Spanish instead of encouraging workers to learn English. The workers' day-to-day lives are frustrated by the language barrier they carry with them into the larger community outside the barrio, especially in banks, medical clinics, and government offices.

In very few workplaces, employers have made extreme efforts to help Spanish-speaking employees enter the English-speaking world by providing English classes accessibly scheduled at the end of their work shifts, by locating the classroom in the break room at the plant, and even by opening the program to workers' family members. Generous employers who initiate these programs are so few that little headway is made in the overall situation. If this could become commonplace, work advances for these people could be realized to everyone's benefit.

Language, though, is learned by ear. The other half of the need is literacy. A cook on the line in an upscale restaurant who cannot read must have customer orders read to him or her by the server. Posted notices in these kitchens, plants, and farms are routinely printed in English and Spanish, but when the worker can't read, the notices are useless. They may be safety warnings, required health practices, or even a benefit program. These employees are highly skilled, motivated, and hardworking, the mainstay of much of the food and beverage business. Without them, the products they pro-

duce would increase substantially in price while the business would suffer in terms of income. Someone must take steps to advance both literacy and language for these neighbors and coworkers.

Biogenetic Engineering Meets Slow Food International

Cross-breeding of plants and animals has been done for centuries, ever since humans freed themselves from hunting and gathering by settling in one place and inventing the practice of farming. Naturalist Charles Darwin (1809–82) and botanist Luther Burbank (1849–1926) set early scientific examples of careful research and development methods, but modern biogeneticists have scared the devil out of us by moving genes around seemingly as easily as one can rearrange paragraphs on a word processor. In earlier years of this science we didn't feel so vulnerable; we didn't think the science was invading our very bodies. After all, some genetic engineering can make plant foods more resistant to disease, thereby reducing the need for pesticide application. But when scientists talk about moving genes around to change a plant, our real fear is that they can move our genes around as well.

Today, two divergent points of view have captured the attention of food and beverage industry professionals, and it may seem at times that each side is fully involved in little more than nay-saying the other's beliefs. In fact, they are both strongly advocated points of view. Foremost is that everyone in both camps needs to pursue the available information to be well informed about both issues.

An Internet search for "food, genetic engineering" will result in a mountain of documents both pro and con, and trying to select objective reporting from that mountain isn't easy. The International Association of Culinary Professionals has developed a touring educational symposium with half-day sessions, initially in Los Angeles, New York City, Chicago, Portland (Oregon), Dallas, and Washington, D.C. Another source of reliable information is IFIC—the International Food Information Council Foundation—through their website: www.ificinfo.health.org. We need to learn more about it. A report titled "Food Biotechnology: Enhancing Our Food Supply," available from the IFIC Foundation (web address above) lists half a dozen other sites that are rich with information about modern food production.

An opposing position is that of Slow Food International, a grassroots organization that sprang in 1986 from Italian outrage at the building of a McDonald's in a historic location in Rome. By the end of 2000, Slow Food claimed 60,000 members in 35 countries. Anyone can join its free email distribution list by sending a request to majordomo@listserv.lynet.de. The group's web page is at www.slowfood.com. It includes membership information (U.S. dues are $60/year) and some unique publications, statements of philosophy, and its history.

From Slow Food's beginning the founders stated their aim to "promulgate a new philosophy of taste as a combination of knowledge and pleasure. The guiding principles of every initiative are still conviviality and the right to taste and pleasure." The statement continues: "Other key objectives are to disseminate and stimulate knowledge of material culture (every product reflects the scents of its place of origin and its age-old production rites and techniques), to preserve the agroindustrial heritage (defending the biodiversity of crops, craft-based food production and traditions) and to protect the historical, artistic and environmental heritage of traditional places of gastronomic pleasure (cafés, cake shops, inns, craft workshops and so on)." Many artisanal food producers are outspoken members of Slow Food: olive oil pressers, cheese makers, organic farmers, fruit growers, nut gatherers, truffle hunters, and winemakers are some whose work comes to our dinner tables at home.

It isn't always comfortable to read the other side of an issue, but the more we do it, and use that information to express our opinions, the more credible we can all be on the hot topics.

Learning, Practicing, and Promoting Food Safety

The U.S. Department of Health and Human Services, through its subagency the Food and Drug Administration (FDA), maintains the Center for Food Safety and Applied Nutrition. This is our bureaucratic path to learning about food safety practices, SafeServe Certification, and Hazard Analysis and Critical Control Point (HAACP).

Some of the training is as simple as always washing fruit that will be peeled, because when a knife penetrates the peel it can carry surface bacteria inside. Another is to take care that money (coins and bills) are never set on food handling surfaces in a restaurant or café—again, due to bacteria transfer dangers. We grumble at times about regulations and requirements that take us away from the workplace for training and to obtain required certificates, but these are protections for us personally and for our businesses. The government's website, at www.foodsafety.gov will give plenty of cause for our cooperation. Of the eight principles that introduce the subject, Principle 1 states "Prevention of microbial contamination of fresh produce is favored over reliance on corrective actions once contamination has occurred." Local public health departments do what they can to keep practitioners well informed and careful about the health of our customers and our families.

Responsibility for Community Hunger and Health

The annual fund-raising "Taste of the Nation" dinners held nationwide every May, with the leadership of Share Our Strength (SOS) and presented by American Express Cards, are initiated by prominent restaurant owners and chefs in each community. The entire cost of putting on the dinners is donated, and 100 percent of ticket proceeds are contributed to hunger relief programs in the local community, elsewhere in the United States, and in countries where starvation is a common cause of death.

Bill Shore and his sister, Debbie Shore, started SOS in 1984 in the basement of their home on Capitol Hill in Washington, D.C. The initial idea was to organize a handful of chefs to cook for fund-raisers—and they were hopeful their efforts would last and become one of the nation's leading antihunger, antipoverty organizations. They have succeeded in both goals. Their primary concern has been with the 39 million Americans who live below the poverty line, an enormous number of whom are children. Bill Shore believes strongly that "government, by itself cannot reach or save them. . . . because they need more than what any government can give." His message is that private individuals cannot assume that agencies are taking care of the problem—we have to offer our own healthy energies to eliminate hunger.

Bill Shore's first book on this subject, *Revolution of the Heart,* is a powerful argument for his point of view. Those of us who work in the food and beverage industry are surrounded by excesses of healthy food. We have the first responsibility to route this food to the people who need it.

Insistent Issues

The point is that you can make a difference. Each of the issues affects our individual working environment, and there is something we can do to improve each of them. For some of us, all we can do is read, study, visit, and learn, which in turn allows us to spread knowledge among our colleagues about these issues. As the current leaders in the food and beverage industry and as its future workers, we have a responsibility to care about them and, in caring, to alleviate the problems.

PREFACE
How to Use This Book

Purpose

The saddest person in the world is someone who knows what he or she wants to do but doesn't know how. The essential traits someone must have to join the food and beverage industry are an insatiable curiosity and a genuine love of food. If only that's all it took. What it takes to turn a dream into reality is knowledge. Learn how to study, learn where to meet people, learn how to break in at the entry level, and learn how to rise to the top. This book can help you do just that.

The food industry and the food service industry are growing faster than our population. Fewer people are cooking in their own kitchens; more are cooking in restaurants and food stores. Magazines, newspapers, radio, and television are stuffed full of advertising and articles about health, nutrition, food safety, and cooking. The food workers who aren't either cooking food or promoting it are busy selling food and all of its paraphernalia. There is a lot of work available, and anyone who aspires to be an insider needs only to be objective about his or her skills and personality traits in order to find an appropriate match. What you don't know, you can learn; what you have a talent for, you can develop.

Read this book any way you want: from beginning to end or by skipping through until something grabs your interest. When you find a profile that makes you say, "Golly, that would be fun!" spend some time with the profile, then explore your telephone book for local opportunities. If the work requires a certificate or a degree that you don't have, turn to Appendix I, Culinary Schools and Academies, for more direction. A good way to get a quick start is to find someone in your own area with a job that attracts you and write or phone them requesting a short visit to learn about their work. The more you know about a job, the more exciting it is to prepare yourself for it.

Sources of Information

The profiles in this book were written from my personal knowledge of the food industry and with the critical help of friends and acquaintances in every aspect of the field. To make sure the information was up to date, there was at least one interview or walk-through at the workplace for each profile. Rough drafts were sent to other food workers to confirm that nothing substantial was left out.

The appendix listings were compiled after hours of computer search on the World Wide Web. In Appendix I, schools listed are only those that are accredited by at least one of 10 recognized accrediting agencies: the Accrediting Commission of Career Schools/Colleges of Technology, the American Culinary Federation, the Accrediting Council for Independent Colleges and Schools, the Council on Occupational Education, and any of the six regional Associations of Colleges and Schools.

The Bibliography (Appendix II) and the Magazines and Periodicals lists (Appendix III) are to speed the reader's search for something more to read once his or her interest is piqued by a particular job. Neither list is intended to be comprehensive, but the books, magazines, and newsletters listed will be a gateway to further study.

The list of organizations, societies, and associations (Appendix IV) includes every one of the groups listed in the Unions/Associations section of each profile. If a particular profile catches your interest, phone, write, or make on-line contact with the related group. They will be glad to answer questions, provide career guidance, and offer additional resources. This book is a starting point.

Organization of Material

The profiles use a standard pattern that is easy to follow. The chart on the first page of each profile is a summary. The same headings appear throughout the text with greater detail. If you get excited by the salary number in the summary showing a range to $300,000 (it's probably a sales position), be sure to read the text to understand that those high incomes are reached after years of developing a sales territory and are based on commission. If the special skills summary calls for physical strength, believe it. Try picking up a 50-pound sack of anything in the supermarket and carrying it 50 feet; if you can, you've shown you're strong enough to be a baker and carry a bag of flour to your workstation. If you can't and you want to be a baker, start lifting weights to build your strength.

Read these profiles with an eye to your own lifestyle or how you hope to live your life. Look at the type of workplace a job entails. Look at whether the job is deskbound or is spent hurrying from one location to another. Look at whether weekends and holidays are always workdays. Look at whether there is hands-on work to satisfy your urge to make something. Look at whether promotions mean good-bye to cooking and hello to financial reports.

The Career Ladder may be misleading until you understand it tells only who is boss. The profile is always the middle step on the ladder; above is the boss and below is the direct report. The ladder is not necessarily the path that leads to the job. In the profile, and especially at the Tips for Entry section, you will read about skills, experience, training, and education needed to qualify for the job

in the profile. Loading yourself up with job qualifications is the path to getting hired, doing the work, and succeeding by promotions.

The food industry is a happy workplace. It also involves long hours, physical stamina, and good health. Except for commission-based sales work, it is not the road to wealth. But the people are sharing, friendly, helpful, and eager to welcome newcomers, and for most of us it doesn't get much better than that.

ACKNOWLEDGMENTS

My editor, Jim Chambers, has been a guiding voice from the beginning by first giving me leeway to explore many new aspects emerging in the food and beverage industry and by finally letting me have time without pressure to finish the work; he has my deepest appreciation for his calm contribution to a finished manuscript. Once again, thanks to Elizabeth Pomada for bringing me the opportunity to update my work of eight years ago.

This work has been aided and influenced by my colleagues in the food and beverage workplace. They have critically reviewed the old text and scrambled to find me contacts to provide information about newer job opportunities. Thanks to Donna Adams, Antonia Allegra, Michael Bergen, Lily Berrish, Cleone Grabowski Black, Diane Bock, Martha Casselman, Brian Conklin, Jerry Anne DiVecchio, Jessica Duncan, Carol Durst, Gerri French, Sherrie Springer Harris, Peter Jordano, Lynn Kerrigan, Suzanne LaCabe, Anne Luther, Christine Maii, David Maii, Robynne Maii, Jeanette F. Nadeau, Phillip Shaw, Mark Sheridan, Phyllis Vacarelli, Ignacio Vella, Nach Waxman, Jamie West, and at least one or two more whom I've unforgivably omitted.

CATERING, FAST FOOD, DELIS, AND TAKE-OUT

CATERER

CAREER PROFILE

Duties: Plans party with client; prepares cost estimate and contract; schedules cooking staff; shops for ingredients; preps for cooking; orders rental equipment; schedules the set-up, cooking, service, and cleanup

Alternate Title(s): Party Planner

Salary Range: $24,000 to $72,000 a year, or part-time at $17 to $25 per hour

Employment Prospects: Good to fair; many self-employed

Advancement Prospects: Limited

Best Geographical Location(s) for Position: High-income, socially active communities near major urban areas

Prerequisites:

Education or Training—Basic knowledge of cooking, menu planning, cost estimating, supervising staff, and customer relations

Experience—Professional culinary skills; business management practice

Special Skills and Personality Traits—Creativity; tact and diplomacy with clients; persuasiveness; organizational skills; flexibility; physical strength; love of people and parties

CAREER LADDER

```
┌─────────────────────────┐
│    Catering Manager     │
└─────────────────────────┘

┌─────────────────────────┐
│        Caterer          │
└─────────────────────────┘

┌─────────────────────────┐
│     Catering Cook       │
└─────────────────────────┘
```

Position Description

A caterer's work is to satisfy (and even exceed) the special needs and wants of the customer, providing food, decorations, and service for a party of any size from an intimate dinner for two to a spectacular wedding reception for 1,000 guests. Between those two examples is a variety of entertainments—social, business, and high-exposure media events—that impel a party-giver to hire a caterer.

The first step is usually a call from a client; the caterer sets up a meeting at the earliest time to learn what the client envisions, to picture the dream. While they talk, the caterer turns that dream into the details needed to supply a cost estimate to the client: the number of guests, location, date and time of day, sit-down service, buffet, or stand-up grazing, time length of party, decorations, musicians or entertainers involved, number of servers and their costumes. Soon the visual picture of the party comes together, and the caterer suggests appropriate food to be served.

The caterer comes to this first meeting with the knowledge and experience of what kind of food works in different situations. Will there be a kitchen at the party site where the caterers can finish various dishes and clean up or will this party require a camp-cooking set-up, hauling in stoves and ice chests to work outside? How much other equipment will be rented—tables, chairs, linens, umbrellas, tents, flower receptacles, cutlery and china? Is finger food appropriate for guests informally dressed for the outdoors or will guests dressed in their best clothes sit around linen-draped tables and tuck in their napkins before eating with knife and fork? Will the party go on for hours, requiring food to be held at safe temperatures for heat and cold? Or does the client want all 1,000 guests served simultaneously by a horde of waiters? The caterer will suggest specific recipes and menus for the client to consider, and by the end of the meeting the client will have turned over the anxious strain of party planning to the trusted caterer.

The caterer's next step is to prepare the cost estimate and the contract, spelling out everything he or she will provide and perform, and sometimes listing the exclusions that are still up to the client to provide: musicians, site cleanup, flowers and decorations, bartenders—it's different with every party.

The caterer schedules all the staff who will work on the party, including prep staff, cooks, set-up staff, and waiters. A vendors' (shopping) list is prepared with quantity orders of the food. The rental service order consists of equipment and decorations, as well as such cooking and serving equipment as steam units, trays, and showy serving dishes if the caterer or the client doesn't have them.

Putting parties together means the caterer has a network of temporary and part-time staff to hire only when they are needed. Some permanent staff can double as prep cooks one day and tuxedoed waiters the next.

Most parties involve some prep work done the day before or the morning of the party before packing everything up and moving it from the catering kitchen to the party site. Everything is timed so that guests are immediately pampered with delicious food, attentive service, and attractive surroundings.

Caterers try to be on the premises for every party they produce, but sometimes the schedule contains several events in a single day, and it's just not possible. During a party, it's not unusual for a guest to seek out the cooks and learn who is doing the catering. This is priceless advertising for the caterer, and often one or more new clients will surface as a result of the party they enjoyed. Next, the caterer follows up with the client the day after the event, or as soon as possible, to review their own performance, judge the client's satisfaction, and present the bill.

Salaries

As an employee of a catering company, with full-charge responsibility for selected events, a caterer can earn between $17 and $25 per hour. Annual income, of course, depends on the amount of work available; seasonal work is at its height during June for graduations and weddings and October through December for the holidays. As an independent contractor, a caterer can earn between $30,000 and $72,000 a year; location is a significant factor.

Employment Prospects

To some extent there are catering opportunities in any urban area, but catering is most dynamic where there are numerous charitable organizations relying on fund-raising parties and benefits to generate part of their operating income, affluent families who enjoy elaborate entertaining, and businesses that use open houses to advertise their goods and services. Any of these events call on a caterer to supply the food and more. Party rental shops are a good source of information about established caterers in any area; they often maintain a wall rack of caterer's business cards as a service for individual customers.

Larger catering businesses advertise in the telephone yellow pages and occasionally in the social section of the local paper. Most medium-sized caterers maintain an on-call list of workers for prep, cooking, and serving; larger operations have a full-time staff, from sales managers to clean-up helpers.

Advancement Prospects

As a catering company employee, your advancement depends on the size of the business where you are employed or the availability of jobs with larger catering companies in your community. As the owner of the catering business, advancement depends on how much your business grows, prices rise, and staff increases.

Best Geographical Location(s)

Big cities are better locations for catering businesses, but more often the key elements are affluence and social tradition.

Education and Training

Catering as a food service career is taught in culinary academies, vocational trade schools, community college culinary programs, and small private cooking schools.

A well-trained caterer usually has cooked in a restaurant or an institution and learned quantity cooking. (Multiplying a recipe for six to a production for 60 is never a simple matter of measuring out 10 times the ingredients. Seasonings and sauces require adjustments for bulk production.) Books for professional, large scale cooking are available through culinary schools or web-based book sellers.

Some caterers simply start out on their own, armed only with the experience of cooking for a large family or the love of entertaining friends. They acquire skills through trial and error, advice from colleagues, and reading.

Experience/Skills/Personality Traits

It is always advisable to work for a company before starting out on your own; larger catering companies usually have extra work in the busy seasons of June and December to justify hiring a novice. Even as a novice, to be worth a paycheck, the employee needs to know basic cooking language, knife skills, and sweet and savory sauces, and be familiar with the distinctions of roast, sauté, fry, steam, poach, braise, blanch, etc.

Because catering implies customized personal service—some of the synonyms for "cater" are coddle, humor, indulge, pamper, and satisfy—the work requires tact, diplomacy, flexibility, consideration, tolerance, and a genuine love of people and of providing for their creature comforts.

A successful caterer maintains an overview of the entire project and is sensitive to details at the same time. Organizational and management background is an invaluable asset. Although the client is clearly the host of the party, the caterer also assumes the attitude of the host and responsibility for every guest's pleasure at the party.

Unions/Associations

The International Association of Culinary Professionals (IACP) provides examination and certification of cooking professionals. Local culinary associations often exist in medium to large towns and cities. These seek as members cooking teachers, chefs, caterers, and food writers, creating a good network for a beginner. To find out if there is one where you live or work, call several caterers in your area for information.

Owners and managers of large city catering companies may benefit from membership in the National Association of Catering Executives (NACE). The association has local chapters, an annual conference in June, and a leadership conference in January.

The American Culinary Federation accepts caterers as members in the same category as restaurant chefs.

The umbrella labor union for kitchen workers, waiters, and bartenders is the Culinary Alliance and Bartenders Union. Check the yellow pages of your local telephone directory under "Labor Organizations" for a local branch. Depending on union influence in your area, the local organization may also represent catering company workers, especially in larger urban areas.

Tips for Entry

1. Offer to help in school cafeterias, church facilities, charitable organizations, or public institutional kitchens that utilize volunteers to gain experience in quantity cooking and use of commercial equipment.
2. Visit the local party rental and supply stores for business cards and information about the busiest and best caterers in your area and call them to learn of any current or future job opportunities.
3. If the local community college has a culinary program, their job counselors may also have information about work opportunities.
4. When you attend a catered party, arrange to meet the caterer, and follow up the next day with a call or visit to ask about working for him or her.

CATERING COOK

CAREER PROFILE

Duties: Working with preapproved recipes for a selected menu, the catering cook orders all necessary ingredients, lines up the appropriate equipment, schedules needed staff, and is responsible for producing the menu on time for delivery to the party; the cook may also accompany the delivery and supervise the final presentation, garnishing, and serving.

Alternate Title(s): Catering Chef

Salary Range: $10,000 to $20,000 a year or $10 to $20 per hour for part-time work

Employment Prospects: Good in the right geographic locations

Advancement Prospects: Good

Best Geographical Location(s) for Position: Large urban areas, high-income suburbs, and resort communities

Prerequisites:
Education or Training—Catering course at a culinary academy or vocational college; cooking on the line in a restaurant with a trained chef
Experience—Any professional cooking experience, especially garnishing and presentation
Special Skills and Personality Traits—Reliable; well-organized; team player

CAREER LADDER

```
┌─────────────────────────────┐
│          Caterer            │
└─────────────────────────────┘

┌─────────────────────────────┐
│       Catering Cook         │
└─────────────────────────────┘

┌─────────────────────────────┐
│       Assistant Cook        │
└─────────────────────────────┘
```

Position Description

A catering cook is responsible for the consistency and quality of food provided by the catering company. The cook may also be given responsibility for developing recipes or creating variations, and that work is subject to oversight by the caterer and becomes his/her property, since the product carries the catering company name.

As soon as a party is booked and the deposit check has been received, the cook receives the approved menu and begins to schedule all the actions leading up to the delivery of the food to the party site. Depending on the organizational structure of the catering company, the cook may also accompany the food to the site and be in charge—either in a hands-on or supervisory way—of actual presentation of the food at the party.

Working from the selected menu, the catering cook schedules every aspect of food production: collecting the recipes to be used, making the shopping list for ingredients and special orders, scheduling staff for pre-prep and preparation, and reviewing all food decisions, including presentation, with the caterer.

The catering company may have a vast collection of tested recipes that have been shuffled into many combinations for party and event menus, or it may use a well-stocked library of cookbooks to research new recipes. Computers have eased the work as much for caterers as they have in business offices; there is available software for determining the cost per serving of a recipe, for adjusting the individual ingredients for large volume cooking, for developing the cost estimate for a client, for making the shopping list for the complete party, and even for supplying nutritional data. Once the recipes for the party have been gathered, the cook has to determine quantities of every dish, place the ingredients order with the supplier, list the needed cooking equipment to make sure everything from special pots to unique appliances is available, estimate the time needed for preparation and cooking, and schedule any staff needed to assist.

The catering cook is responsible for the budget that has been established with the client; if menu changes cause the cost of the food to increase or decrease, the catering cook must inform the caterer, who will discuss the change with the client. In practice, the cost estimate for a party is usually developed in consultation with the cook and it usually includes a small contingency for unavoidable increases.

If the final cooking and assembly of the menu is going to be done at the party site, every step that can possibly be done ahead of time should be, and everything is packaged, labeled, and packed together to make the last-minute work simple. If all the cooking is done at the catering kitchen, then finished dishes are loaded into travel containers ready for final reheating, chilling, plating, and garnishing.

In large companies, a catering cook may work on a dozen or more parties at a time. The variety of occasions can include a birthday party for six toddlers and their parents, a grazing party for 50 friends to house-warm a new residence, working lunches for five consecutive days for a corporate retreat of senior executives, and a springtime garden wedding reception for 300 guests.

Salaries

The size of the catering company and the volume of its business influence the staff's salaries. Except for large companies in major urban areas, catering cooks are part-time employees who may work two 16-hour days one week and only four to five hours a day the next week. Wages differ across the country, but on average a cook can earn $10 to $20 per hour, or an annual income of $10,000 to $20,000 for half-time work.

Employment Prospects

A large number of catering businesses are one-person operations. But even these caterers sometimes hire an additional cook for an especially large party or to manage double-bookings (two or more parties the same day). Employment prospects are dependent on local circumstances, such as how many catering companies in town are large enough to use stand-by dedicated employees. Catering cooks often work regularly for more than one caterer in the area.

Advancement Prospects

Advancement in catering jobs depends on the amount of party-giving available to local caterers. If a company is able to substantially increase its volume of work, it will increase staff to provide the needed services.

Another means of advancement is to move to a larger city, where with recommendations and prior experience a catering cook can command a higher wage.

Many caterers start out working for someone for a few years to learn the business, and then set up their own company.

Best Geographical Location(s)

In resort areas with large second-home communities, in cities with a full complement of cultural activities, and in high-income communities with strong social traditions there are many large catering operations.

Education and Training

Vocational and technical schools teach catering as well as restaurant cooking; many small cooking schools and culinary academies have special courses for caterers.

Some caterers insist that restaurant cooking experience is invaluable in catering work. Cooking on the line alongside an experienced chef teaches organization, split-second decision-making, and speed, and it inspires confidence.

Experience/Skills/Personality Traits

As much cooking experience as possible—at home, at church suppers, at the school cafeteria, at homeless shelters or missions—provides basic knowledge and self-confidence. Reading both the recipes and the restaurant reviews in cooking, entertaining, and lifestyle magazines is an excellent way to get acquainted with current trends in food for entertaining. Catering is upscale food preparation, even when the event is a backyard barbecue, in which case the chili is bound to be made of black beans instead of common kidney beans.

All of the culinary skills—knowing knife techniques, sauce making, distinguishing between sauté, fry, braise, steam, roast, and grill, knowing freshness and peak flavor when purchasing produce, and familiarity with the widest range of herbs and spices and their uses—are an asset; the more an employee knows about cooking the more valuable he or she is to the catering business.

Reliability and responsibility are essential traits for a catering employee. The business is one of service to clients; any breakdown in providing the agreed menu at the agreed time is a black mark that will doom the business by word of mouth. The cook needs to have a dedicated sense of organization, always looking beyond the task of the moment, to keep the kitchen fully stocked for future assignments. In the end, catering is teamwork, and the cook needs to be a leader in sharing the workload to deliver the menu with flair and style to the party.

Unions/Associations

Local and regional culinary guilds and alliances are broad-based networks of caterers, teachers, writers, and chefs;

they sponsor educational events that are valuable for caterers, especially in staying abreast of new products and upscale menu styles.

The American Culinary Federation (ACF) is a membership association for skilled restaurant chefs, cooks, and pastry chefs, and it has local chapters in most large cities.

Tips for Entry

1. Local party rental and supply stores often display a rack of caterers' cards; help yourself to a sampling and start calling to introduce yourself and ask about job prospects.
2. At every catered party or benefit you attend, slip into the kitchen (after the major effort of serving has passed) to meet the caterer and ask about job prospects.
3. Locate the nearest cooking school or vocational training school and talk to the manager about job opportunities; they are often asked for recommendations for job openings.

CORPORATE CATERER

CAREER PROFILE

Duties: Provides all food service to the company employees on their premises. The work is the same as running a small café; the hours, as a rule, are weekdays only

Alternate Title(s): Corporate Chef; Company Cook

Salary Range: Full-time salary ranging from $21,000 to $42,000, plus insurance and vacation

Employment Prospects: Rare

Advancement Prospects: Promotions take the form of salary raises and bonuses.

Best Geographical Location(s) for Position: Large cities that are also financial centers with high-powered corporate offices

Prerequisites:
  Education or Training—Professional culinary training is beneficial, plus knowledge of nutrition.
  Experience—Catering company or restaurant cooking experience
  Special Skills and Personality Traits—Caregiver with special attention to health and fitness food; self-assurance and confidence; tact and diplomacy

CAREER LADDER

```
┌─────────────────────────────┐
│      Catering Manager       │
└─────────────────────────────┘

┌─────────────────────────────┐
│      Corporate Caterer      │
└─────────────────────────────┘

┌─────────────────────────────┐
│     Catering Assistant      │
└─────────────────────────────┘
```

Position Description

A corporate caterer is a full-time employee of the corporation and is in charge of all food service for that company. The workplace can be an on-premises kitchen, fully equipped as for a café or at home, cook and schlep from the caterer's workplace. Duties vary by the size of the company and food service needs. Food service may only be needed for an executive dining room, serving lunches to the senior staff, or it may be for a cafeteria for all employees. It will also include any corporate entertaining, such as special client lunches or dinners, open-house receptions, or the staff Christmas party.

One distinction of this type of catering is that the clientele is the same every day and every week. Like meal planning for a fussy family, the menus must be varied. Even so, certain favorite dishes will probably become regulars. Special food interests must also be catered to, such as diets with low fat, low salt, and high fiber; religious or personal restrictions for kosher, Muslim, or vegetarian diets; and popular food trends from northern Italian or eclectic Asian dishes.

The corporate caterer is running a specialized restaurant, requiring all the same work as done by an independent restaurant. This involves purchasing and maintaining the equipment, purchasing wholesale ingredients, inventory control, cost controls and, if a pay-cafeteria is part of the work, the pricing of menu items. Usually a company cafeteria and dining room are underwritten to keep prices low, and the cost control consists of breaking even, without any profit.

One advantage of corporate catering is the hours—daytime and weekdays, and only occasional evening work for receptions or special dinners.

Salaries

Depending on the hours of work and the number of meals served daily, corporate catering can be a full-time, 40-hour-a-week job or it can be part time. Annual salaries average between $21,000 and $42,000 and may include benefits (insurance and vacation) and bonuses.

Employment Prospects

These jobs are limited, and tend to be in the largest cities and only in certain businesses, such as law firms, investment firms, technology leaders with design secrets to discuss, or others where confidentiality of the discussion at business lunches is essential. A business might provide an employee cafeteria, a step up from vending machines, if it is in a rural location where lunchrooms and restaurants are not nearby.

Advancement Prospects

Advancement takes the form of salary raises and bonuses for outstanding performance in the culinary and/or financial aspects of the business. The Corporate Caterer will be treated like a middle-level executive, with annual reviews and work product assessment.

Best Geographical Location(s)

Cities that are major financial centers and technology centers are more likely to have a number of businesses that provide private dining rooms for their staff.

Education and Training

Training in a culinary academy or a vocational/trade tech school provides the basic food service and management knowledge required to run a private dining room.

Experience/Skills/Personality Traits

Catering experience, either in a small company of your own or as an employee in a larger catering business, is an ideal background to take on finicky eaters and corporate management families.

A broad-based understanding of food preparation, nutrition, and management skills all need to be accompanied by self-assurance and confidence in relation to the dining-room clientele and by tact and diplomacy in relation to the corporate management.

Unions/Associations

The American Culinary Federation (ACF) is a membership association for skilled restaurant chefs, cooks, and pastry chefs, and it has over 200 local chapters across the United States.

The International Association of Culinary Professionals (IACP) is a broad-based organization of professionals in all fields of culinary endeavor. It is also a source of information about regional culinary organizations in your geographic area, and membership provides an ideal way to meet other chefs and caterers to exchange sources and solutions to common problems.

Tips for Entry

1. If the area has a culinary association with a job hotline, contact them; you may have to join the organization to make use of this service. These jobs are filled by word of mouth rather than classified ads in the newspaper, making the membership dues well worth the investment.
2. Try making cold calls to the largest law firms, high-tech firms, and investment companies in your area, asking if they have a private dining room and for the name of the chef. Talk to the chef about an assistant job or other similar jobs the chef knows of in the area; perhaps one the chef has turned down might be just right for you.

CATERING OPERATIONS MANAGER

CAREER PROFILE

Duties: Books major parties; develops menus and specs; assigns chefs to events; monitors financial reports; schedules staff; maintains client relations

Alternate Title(s): None

Salary Range: $35,000 to $100,000+

Employment Prospects: Limited

Advancement Prospects: Limited

Best Geographical Location(s) for Position: Entertainment meccas; society enclaves; major cities

Prerequisites:

Education or Training—Culinary academy credentials and management training

Experience—Financial management to control direct costs and overhead expenses; team building to keep work crews motivated

Special Skills and Personality Traits—Creativity; leadership; adaptability; cost-consciousness

CAREER LADDER

```
┌─────────────────────────────┐
│  Catering Business Owner or  │
│       General Manager        │
└─────────────────────────────┘

┌─────────────────────────────┐
│  Catering Operations Manager │
└─────────────────────────────┘

┌─────────────────────────────┐
│   Catering Kitchen Manager   │
└─────────────────────────────┘
```

Position Description

The operations manager of a large-scale catering business is responsible for identifying potential clients, booking new and repeat business, developing menus and recipe specifications, assigning staff chefs to specific events or venues, reviewing the financial records of the business on a daily basis and on an account basis, ensuring that adequate staff is available for booked work, and maintaining relations with clients after each party or, in the case of ongoing corporate clients, periodically.

A large-scale catering business may have a permanent staff of chefs and sales representatives as well as an extensive on-call staff of cooks, servers, helpers, and clean-up workers. The challenge is to develop and maintain a steady flow of parties, spectacular events, and daily food service to afford the permanent employee payroll it involves.

Really big parties—the art museum fund-raiser for over a 1,000 guests or the debutante ball for several hundred—are the domain of these established catering companies, but to stay in business they need renewable, daily contract work. For the large blowouts, an on-call staff of hundreds of waiters and dozens of kitchen helpers is needed.

The operations manager coordinates with the sales representatives of the business to balance the schedule for months and even years ahead. Not only would it be a caterer's nightmare to have two major benefit events on the same night, it would devastate the fund-raising groups to have to divide up the guests on a given date. As soon as the party is booked and the menu is set, the operations manager schedules the head cook or chef in charge of the event, details all the staff needed for before and during the event, and determines what rentals are needed and reserves tables, tents, heaters, chairs, serving pieces, linen, china, and glassware for the party well in advance. Decorations for a major party get as much attention as the food; they must be planned with the host or hostess, suggestions offered, sketches produced, and on-call decorators scheduled to set up the event. The operations manager has to develop the budget as early as possible for approval by the client, and then has to be able to produce the party within that budget even if it's six months in the future. Contingencies, whether hidden or stated, go into every financial estimate for the event to protect the caterer against uncontrollable catastrophes, such as an untimely frost that damages every local

DELI/FAST-FOOD STORE COOK AND MANAGER

CAREER PROFILE

Duties: Selects menu; orders ingredients and supplies; hires and schedules part-time staff; supervises food preparation; records receipts and expenses, handles banking and payroll

Alternate Title(s): Deli Cook/Manager; Take-out Cook/Manager

Salary Range: $16,000 to $35,000

Employment Prospects: Plentiful

Advancement Prospects: Limited

Best Geographical Location(s) for Position: Urban areas with large work forces who need breakfast and lunch in a hurry

Prerequisites:

Education or Training—Vocational culinary and business programs are helpful but not essential

Experience—Working for a fast-food or catering company is good experience in both food handling and management.

Special Skills and Personality Traits—Human relations skills in hiring and developing teamwork; business and financial skills; a hospitality attitude toward customers

CAREER LADDER

```
┌─────────────────────────────┐
│        Store Owner/         │
│   Multi-Branch Supervisor   │
└─────────────────────────────┘

┌─────────────────────────────┐
│  Fast-Food Store Cook/Manager │
└─────────────────────────────┘

┌─────────────────────────────┐
│   Prep and Clean-up Person   │
└─────────────────────────────┘
```

Position Description

Take-out food counters are everywhere from upscale delicatessens with ethnic recipes, or grocery stores with prepared pasta, potatoes, and salad bars, to gas station snack bars with bargain hot dogs and burgers. There are hundreds of variations between those two extremes, translating to millions of employers across the country.

If the store has a visible sign and it is close to a highway, or if it is located in a cluster of office buildings, the customers want to select and walk out with their meals as quickly as possible. Establishing the menu depends on selecting foods that either hold well and look good in a refrigerated case, or foods that can be made quickly, such as sandwiches. A microwave is an essential tool for reheating foods such as soup or chili, or for melting cheese on a roast-beef-and-salsa sandwich.

The cook/manager picks the menu: salads, sandwiches, soups, muffins and small breads, cookies and desserts.

There may be a master list of the salads, soups, and desserts with a selection made fresh every day on a schedule that ensures variety for regular customers. Additionally, there may be racks of snacks, chips, and pretzels and refrigerated cases with soda, water, and beer. Everyday supplies need to be checked, orders made for ingredients, and kitchen assignments scheduled for all pre-prep food. The workday moves fast, beginning with breakfast when hungry customers want something they can grab and eat on the run, like a breakfast burrito, pastry, cappuccino or caffe latte.

From 9 to 11:30 A.M. is the cooking time for the lunch crowd. The day's salads and sandwich-making supplies of sliced meats, breads, tomatoes, lettuces, and cheeses have to be ready, and the soup warmer gets turned on. Part-time staffers are scheduled to arrive during the prep time, and all of them are in place by the time the lunch customers reach the counter.

Early afternoon is clean-up time; as well, the time is used for making soup and slicing meat and cheese that are needed for the following day, and for any on-premises baking of muffins, cookies, and desserts.

The cook/manager has to maintain a flexible crew of workers with a variety of skills. One speedy sandwich-maker may be a friendly favorite of the customers but may not be a reliable cook in the back kitchen after rush periods. Another sandwich specialist may be a whiz at clean-up when the rush is over but fails to perform well at keeping the racks and cases stocked. These employees are often at the bottom of the pay scale, at minimum wage or slightly more; many are students. The cook/manager has to create work assignments that get the most out of everyone.

The cook/manager's job includes all the money handling, workers' time cards, weekly paychecks, receipts from the day's sales, prompt payment of invoices to vendors, bank deposits, and monthly financial statements.

Salaries

The cook/manager is often the owner of the business if there is only one location. Depending on the size of the business, if there are several locations, the cook/manager is probably the only full-time employee of the business, relying on part-time and temporary help for all the necessary work. As an hourly employee, a cook/manager is paid from minimum wage to $15 per hour, depending on the volume of business and the store's geographical location; an annual income would be $16,000 to $35,000, with minimal benefits.

Employment Prospects

Millions of these businesses exist across the United States. An excellent way to get a cook/manager job is to start as a part-time worker for a company in your area that owns several fast-food take-out stores and is in a growth mode.

Advancement Prospects

Advancement is more likely if the business is one of a group under the same ownership. A promising employee in one location is likely to be tagged to manage the next shop to open.

Best Geographical Location(s)

Large and small cities that have a mass of office workers, construction crews, and students—anyplace where there is a daily mass of hungry customers clustered in a busy area—are ideal locations.

Education and Training

This work can be done successfully without formal culinary training. Vocational education programs provide important classes in cleanliness and sanitation practices for food workers and in business management, on controlling costs and maximizing the value of purchasing, whether it means buying lettuce by the case or purchasing a new meat-slicing appliance.

Experience/Skills/Personality Traits

A stint as an employee in a catering or fast-food business, observing what works and what doesn't, is the best experience for managing a shop. The knack for hiring good workers and promoting teamwork among the staff, the willingness to pitch in whenever needed, and the ability to keep costs close to the bone while providing a delicious product are the aspects that help a manager succeed.

Unions/Associations

The cook/manager of a small business may see a benefit from joining the local chamber of commerce or a booster's group of neighboring business owners.

To become part of a network of food workers, a local culinary guild will welcome owners and managers of small food businesses. This association will also be a source of employees and business advisers.

Tips for Entry

1. Visit as many of the fast-food shops in your area as you can to identify one or more that you'd like to manage. Follow up by talking with the owner or current manager about job opportunities.
2. Work for a caterer who specializes in delivering office lunches to develop the sense of the food these customers are seeking.
3. Check whether a shop manager is planning a major change in life, such as moving or going back to school. If someone is leaving a job, the owner will be looking for a replacement.

DELI PREP AND CLEAN-UP PERSON

CAREER PROFILE

Duties: Slices meats, cheeses, vegetables; cleans work surfaces constantly; assists the cook with specials; makes
sure all food products are properly wrapped and stored

Alternate Title(s): Assistant Cook

Salary Range: $10,000 to $12,000

Employment Prospects: Plentiful

Advancement Prospects: Very good

Best Geographical Location(s) for Position: Anywhere
in the United States, especially in cities with a large
workforce

Prerequisites:
   Education or Training—Good general education
   Experience—Any kitchen experience is valuable
   Special Skills and Personality Traits—Ability to take
direction; willingness to learn new skills; consistency
and reliability

CAREER LADDER

```
┌─────────────────────────────────┐
│      Deli Cook and Manager       │
└─────────────────────────────────┘

┌─────────────────────────────────┐
│   Deli Prep and Clean-up Person  │
└─────────────────────────────────┘

┌─────────────────────────────────┐
│             Gofer                │
└─────────────────────────────────┘
```

Position Description

Delicatessens, which provided urban take-out even before
Chinese food and pizza, offer a variety of prepared cold
food to tantalize the tastebuds of any tired shopper. Even
very small delis have at least two varieties of potato salad,
pasta salad, coleslaw, pickles, olives, and a choice of bread
along with cold cuts of meat and cheese. The prepared
dishes are made in a small quantity to maintain fresh flavors, and somebody has to keep working in the back of the
shop so they don't run out of a standard dish.

A beginner learns to use the electric slicer for meats and
cheeses, adjusting the thickness from see-through, paper-thin
prosciutto to generously thick rounds of mozzarella and, in
deli tradition, lays each slice precisely in a fan pattern on
paper. It's also the prep person's responsibility to maintain and
sharpen that slicer and oil it when necessary. Some soft
sausages, the wursts, are always sliced by hand, and so are soft
cheeses, ripe tomatoes, cabbage for slaw, potatoes for salad,
and beets for pickling. The prep person has to care for the
knives, knowing when to put on a quick edge and when to
send them out for professional sharpening.

Depending on the style of the delicatessen, it may serve
as a sandwich and sausage shop for the neighborhood or it
may provide upscale take-home combinations for nearby
office workers at the end of their workday. Whichever it is, a
conscientious worker with well-honed knife skills—slicing,
chopping, mincing—is an indispensable backup to the
counter person.

Between every ingredient that touches the chopping
board, the prep person has to be fastidious about sanitation,
scrubbing down the plastic board with an acidic mixture to
neutralize raw food bacteria that can generate intestinal dis-
comfort and lose a store's customer in the process. Every
kitchen should be certified by "SafeServe" training. Much
more clean-up work is involved—deli cases, glass, counters,
and containers all have to be sparkling for every use.

With the basic training of prep slicing and sanitation
well learned, a delicatessen worker can progress to a
wealth of knowledge about sausages, cheeses, and side-
dishes. If the shop is in an ethnic neighborhood—Greek,
Jewish, Italian, Mexican, Middle Eastern, German—the
food traditions are numerous. Some of the ingredients are
imported and merely set out for sale in stainless-steel trays
to be purchased by the ounce; these same ingredients can
go into delicious concoctions like dolmades (stuffed grape
leaves), fresh chopped chicken liver delicately seasoned

and cooked to a crumbly paste, lasagnas and tortellini, tamales, filo sheets made into savory and sweet finger food, and pork in many disguises as pâté.

An aspiring caterer or deli owner can learn the food side of the business by working for a variety of quality take-out shops. There is lore and history of food to be learned from many of the old-time shopkeepers that is in danger of being lost with the passing of apprentice systems. These jobs are an opportunity to learn the tastes of a wide variety of cuisines, develop a palate that recognizes authentic flavors, and gather ingredient knowledge that can spark the creative development of new dishes.

Salaries

This is minimum-wage work to begin and, depending on the degree of training the store owner will give to helpers, it may not go much higher. At best, annual income might reach $12,000, but by moving to better and better food shops, the worker can learn the traditional skills for a cook's position.

Employment Prospects

At the lowest level, sandwich shops, there are numerous jobs available, and they offer a start in the food industry. Many major grocery stores have developed large deli counters which offer further opportunity.

Advancement Prospects

This is a springboard for working up in the food preparation business, and the opportunities are unlimited. The more a worker learns about styles of food and his or her own taste preferences to chart a career path, the better he or she can aspire to a cook's position in better shops and restaurants.

Best Geographical Location(s)

These jobs are everywhere in the country, and most numerous in urban areas with dense office and factory neighbor- hoods where workers can be tempted to buy prepared foods to take home as well as the quick lunches to eat on the job.

Education and Training

Even a minimum education will be enough to qualify for a job as prep and clean-up. The advantage of these jobs is that they provide training to go on to better jobs.

Experience/Skills/Personality Traits

Any kitchen experience is valuable, especially in the care and use of knives. A strong practice of following sanitary methods is essential. Knowledge of weights and measures is basic. Being able to take verbal instruction, a willingness to follow direction, and consistency in performing the same work the same way repeatedly are important for success in these jobs.

Unions/Associations

Unionization does not apply to these jobs. As a prep person advances his or her skills into cooking, the same associa- tions listed for cooking jobs should be considered.

Tips for Entry

1. Visit or phone the specialty delicatessens listed in your local phone book to ask if they are hiring.
2. Check the classified ads in your local paper for sand- wich shop jobs.
3. Using a variety of chef's knives, practice slicing skills on meat, cheese (chill the soft ones first to firm them), and tomatoes until you are confident of your precision in maintaining identical thicknesses.
4. If there is a vocational trade school with a culinary program in your area, talk to the job placement officer about delicatessen training.

PARTY PLANNER

CAREER PROFILE

Duties: In charge of overall planning for elaborate, large-scale parties: works with client; schedules all subcontractors, including caterer; provides cost estimate; controls budget; supervises every stage of delivery and production

Alternate Title(s): Caterer

Salary Range: $70,000 to $200,000 a year; $25 to $225 an hour

Employment Prospects: Poor—most are self-employed business owners of very small businesses with very few employees

Advancement Prospects: Limited

Best Geographical Location(s) for Position: Urban areas; wealthy communities; party towns

Prerequisites:
    Education or Training—Catering and hospitality management courses from a vocational school or culinary academy
    Experience—Catering and business management
    Special Skills and Personality Traits—Communications and human relations; style and artistry

CAREER LADDER

```
┌─────────────────────────────────┐
│           Impresario            │
└─────────────────────────────────┘

┌─────────────────────────────────┐
│          Party Planner          │
└─────────────────────────────────┘

┌─────────────────────────────────┐
│   Assistant Planner or Caterer  │
└─────────────────────────────────┘
```

Position Description

The party planner is a resourceful coordinator who can bring together all the components of a major party: food, beverages, flowers and decorations, furniture and equipment rentals, musicians, waiters, bartenders, and valet parkers.

A party planner may also be the caterer and must be very knowledgeable about food, in terms of preparation and current trends. But for major events, large benefits, and social ceremonies such as weddings, a party planner would have full charge and be the only contact with the client.

If the planner has previously done work for the client or is highly regarded in the area, he or she may be given the job without competition from other local planners. If this is a first contact for the planner, the client may be interviewing more than one planner for the occasion. In this case the planner brings his or her portfolio—a display of photographs of especially successful parties and letters of recommendation from thrilled clients.

Once selected, the planner's first assignment is to meet with the potential client to discuss every aspect of the party: the number of guests, desired level of elegance or casualness, idiosyncrasies of the site, food, beverages, music, flowers or plants and decorations, and the rough budget.

The planner prepares suggested menus, estimates the cost and labor for the food and beverages and the cost and labor for the bar, determines the type and cost of rental equipment needed, contacts several appropriate music groups, dancers, or other entertainers for their availability and their fees, prepares sketches or descriptions of suggested decorations and their comparative cost, and sets a date to review this with the client.

Once these items have been decided upon and approved by the client, the planner submits a contract for services to the client and receives a deposit, usually 50 percent of the estimated cost. Some planners also require that the contract amount be paid in full the day prior to the event.

Using multiple worksheets, every detail of the party is listed and a timeline is established. If the site is a public, corporate building and the event is at the end of the work-day, it is unlikely that the planner will be able to set up many hours in advance. If the location is a private home, usually the rentals—tents, tables, chairs, buffet serving pieces, linens, vases, etc.—can be delivered the day before, the white wines, beer, and soft drinks can be chilled, and the set-up can start early the day of the event.

The planner is available at all times to consult with the client, listen to additional ideas, and incorporate extra touches. The day of the event, the planner is on site to check every delivery and the arrival of staff. The planner has the responsibility of seeing that the entire event is set up and ready for guests with the least inconvenience to the employees or family members where the event is being held. The party planner, properly dressed to blend in with the guests, stays at the event to deal with any glitches, communicate with the client, and help where necessary to keep everything at the most festive level.

Salaries

Depending on location, in major urban areas with heavy social schedules, a planner can earn between $75,000 and $200,000 a year. As the executive decision-maker for an event, a planner will charge from $45 to $200 per hour for his or her own time.

Employment Prospects

Most party planners are self-employed, and unless they are also a catering company they have minuscule staffs. An assistant to the party planner would have clerical/secretarial duties as well as the responsibility of following up with all hired services and products.

Advancement Prospects

Advancement most often takes the form of going into business in competition with former employers. In major urban areas, party planner companies who deal with multiple parties every week give assistants the chance to take full charge of smaller parties, working up to developing their own clients and bringing in new business.

The next evolution of a caterer is as an *impresario,* one who creates spectacular entertainments, the milestone parties that are remembered and talked about for years.

Best Geographical Location(s)

Major urban areas and wealthy communities where party giving is prevalent year-round.

Education and Training

Catering background, from a vocational school or culinary academy, is invaluable for moving up the ladder to party planning, but it is not essential. Business training to deal with contracts, payables and receivables, and public relations are essential skills whether learned in school or on the job.

Experience/Skills/Personality Traits

Catering experience is highly useful, especially in contracting with local caterers for jobs. Knowing food preparation techniques and current trends is essential. The planner has to have excellent skills in communication and human relations to keep everyone happy and hardworking, to maintain a party atmosphere in the face of hard work, accidents, and the unexpected.

He or she has to be flexible, and able to quickly devise solutions to sudden problems. Artistry and style are the hallmarks of a successful planner, so the events he or she plans are not rubber-stamp copies of previous parties.

Unions/Associations

The National Association of Catering Executives (NACE) has local chapters for networking and educational meetings, an annual conference every June and a leadership conference every January, and it establishes certification standards for caterers.

The International Association of Culinary Professionals (IACP) is a broad-based organization of cooking teachers, chefs, caterers, food writers, and related professionals and it holds an annual meeting every spring.

Tips for Entry

1. Contact local caterers who specialize in parties and apply to work in any capacity—cooking, serving, or cleanup—to get a full range of understanding of the catering business.
2. Offer to coordinate large parties and weddings for your friends to get experience.
3. Work as a volunteer on fund-raising social events for local charities or on membership parties for culinary organizations to get experience in the degree of detail control necessary for a successful event.

RESTAURANTS

RESTAURANT CHEF

CAREER PROFILE

Duties: The chef is in full charge of kitchen and staff; designs the menu; directs ordering and preparation; cooks to order; manages costs.

Alternate Title(s): Executive Chef

Salary Range: $38,000 to $450,000

Employment Prospects: Good to excellent

Advancement Prospects: Good to excellent

Best Geographical Location(s) for Position: Large urban areas and tourist/resort/recreational areas

Prerequisites:

Education for Training—Culinary academy education or vocational/trade tech certificate, an apprenticeship, or training with quality chefs

Experience—Restaurant kitchen work and small business management

Special Skills and Personality Traits—Trained palate to design flavor combinations; an artistic sense of arrangement; ability to lead a team of kitchen workers

CAREER LADDER

```
┌─────────────────────────────┐
│   Restaurant Chef/Manager   │
└─────────────────────────────┘

┌─────────────────────────────┐
│      Restaurant Chef        │
└─────────────────────────────┘

┌─────────────────────────────┐
│        Sous-Chef            │
└─────────────────────────────┘
```

Position Description

The chef is the "chief" in charge of the kitchen and all of its activities. Areas of influence in the restaurant are referred to as "front of the house"—the dining room—and "back of the house"—the kitchen. The chef manages the kitchen staff, consisting of the dishwasher, prep/pantry person, pastry/dessert chef, assistant, and sous-chef. In a very small restaurant every one of these jobs except the dishwasher's might be done by the chef. As the business grows, the chef adds to the staff to relieve himself or herself of work, but it means he or she has to train and supervise these additional workers.

The selection and planning of the menu is the chef's primary charge, and everyone else's work runs off the menu. A menu isn't static, either, but changes with the season or even by the week or the day. Even if the restaurant keeps a basic menu unchanged, it may be augmented by specials, particularly appetizers and entrees. *Soupe du jour* means "soup of the day," and "assorted desserts" means just that. The chef plans specials based on seasonal ingredients, a special price on an item from a supplier, or just the desire to create a new dish. The chef will usually be calling his or her suppliers,

hearing about fresh produce in the market, and learning of a fresh, unusual fish while the menu is shaping up on a scratchpad or in the chef's head. By the time the menu is set, the orders for all the ingredients have been placed.

Kitchen workers arrive hours before mealtimes, i.e., about 8 A.M. for lunch and about 2 P.M. for dinner. The chef assigns the day's work: vegetables are prepped and cleaned by the cooks, desserts are chosen so the pastry/dessert chef turns out one or more to add to the selection, the assistant or the sous-chef helps the chef prepare meats and birds—trimming, boning, shaping, browning—and cook sauces, side dishes, and whatever else needs preparation.

Once the kitchen is abuzz with activity, the chef can take care of desk work. If the chef is also the restaurant owner, receipts from the prior day have to be put in order, the money has to be counted and a bank deposit has to be made. Invoices come in with every order, and statements arrive in the mail; it's the chef's job to approve invoices and pass them on to the bookkeeper. (If a restaurant gets in arrears with vendors, the vendors may not issue credit but insist on COD [cash on delivery], a very troublesome way to do business.) Staple supplies are tracked by the assistant or sous-chef and reordered so nothing runs out.

As soon as the first customers begin to fill the front of the house, the chef is ready at the stove to cook the orders. The prep work all comes together: a mounded julienne of freshly steamed leeks, carrots, and celery waits to dress the plate under a moist fillet of fish; cooked and marinated shellfish is ready to garnish a spring salad or an appetizer of fresh pasta. Everything the chef needs is prepped and within reach. Even if the chef doesn't cook every order, he or she scrutinizes every plate before it is carried out to the customer, assuring the most pleasing presentation.

At the beginning of the next day there are timecards to be approved for the workers and more paperwork to be sent over to the restaurant bookkeeper. By then, the chef is planning the day's menu changes.

Salaries

Small restaurants are more likely to have chef/owners and in the first few years while the business is being built up, the salary may not be quite regular. If the restaurant owner is the front-of-the-house manager and the chef is an employee, salary will be strongly influenced by location, amount of business, and the chef's training and experience. The current range of salaries for chefs is $38,000 to $450,000 and up.

Employment Prospects

Opportunities for chefs are numerous, but there is also a growing work force of trained culinarians vying for every one of them.

Advancement Prospects

The restaurant news of "who is cooking where" is a constant game of musical chefs; as one moves to a larger, more prestigious kitchen, his or her place is taken by another on the way up or down.

Best Geographical Location(s)

Restaurant work is found everywhere—in major cities, small towns, resort communities, and recreational centers—where there is a customer base seeking fine food.

Education and Training

Restaurant chefs are trained in one of three ways: at a culinary academy or vocational trade school, in an apprentice program approved by the ACF and the U.S. Department of Labor, or by working at restaurants, moving up to work with better and better chefs.

Experience/Skills/Personality Traits

The experience a chef acquires from working in restaurants or in a culinary school covers more than cooking, because a chef has to manage every aspect of the kitchen—the human relations management of the staff, the financial management of supplies, and the culinary management of the menus.

A chef needs a natural as well as a trained palate for combinations of flavors and ingredients. Although people management and money management are essential for the restaurant to succeed, the requisite skill is creating delicious, beautiful, popular food.

To cope with the rigors of kitchen work, a chef needs great physical stamina, especially the ability to work 10- to 12-hour days. Restaurant work is heavier over holidays and weekends; it helps the chef to have an understanding partner at home.

Unions/Associations

The American Culinary Federation (ACF) is a professional association of chefs, cooks, caterers, and culinary educators with local chapters in cities and localities where there is a strong restaurant presence. The ACF also provides a highly regarded testing and certification program for chefs.

The National Restaurant Association (NRA) and its state chapters provide newsletters, educational programs, and trade shows.

Tips for Entry

1. Select a local restaurant whose food is personally preferred by you, and talk to the chef about an entry-level job in the kitchen.
2. Investigate vocational trade programs in your local community college for training to qualify you for restaurant kitchen work.

RESTAURANT PASTRY CHEF

CAREER PROFILE

Duties: Prepares all the regular desserts on the restaurant menu and designs and prepares dessert specials at the chef's request; makes pastry, meringues, cakes, sauces, glazes, and custards

Alternate Title(s): Dessert Cook

Salary Range: Hourly wage in small restaurants for part-time work ranges from $10 to $14. Large hotels with multiple restaurants and large dining rooms use a full-time pastry chef at salaries ranging from $30,000 to $50,000 + a year.

Employment Prospects: Good in cities or resort areas with lots of restaurants, hotels, cafés, and coffeehouses

Advancement Prospects: Fair, depending on opportunities to move to better restaurants with higher pay

Best Geographical Location(s) for Position: Major restaurant cities and resort areas known for fine food

Prerequisites:

Education or Training—Culinary education from an academy or vocational/trade tech school, a restaurant apprenticeship, multiple cooking classes from a number of dessert specialists, or self-taught from observation and cookbooks

Experience—Commercial pastry cooking in a bakery or restaurant

Special Skills and Personality Traits—Artistry; consistency; patience; pleasure in performing small details, constantly repeated

CAREER LADDER

```
┌────────────────────────────┐
│     Pastry Specialist      │
└────────────────────────────┘

┌────────────────────────────┐
│       Pastry Chef          │
└────────────────────────────┘

┌────────────────────────────┐
│      Pastry Trainee        │
└────────────────────────────┘
```

Position Description

The pastry chef is responsible for making all the desserts in the restaurant. If the pastry chef works for a hotel with multiple dining rooms, the job consists of making the desserts and specials for each of the menus. This covers tortes, tarts, *petits fours sec,* ice creams and sorbets, custards and flans, and constructed desserts that are assembled to order, such as *tuille* cups filled with ice cream and dressed with a warm sauce with another sauce on the plate scrolled by a colorful fruit puree.

The standard desserts are made on a daily basis, so items neither run out nor become tired or stale. If the restaurant changes the menu daily, and the dessert selection with it, this means preparing the listed desserts for the menu every day.

Some items are made in quantity to maintain supply: *tuilles* and other *petits fours sec* (carefully stored in airtight containers), custard-based ice creams, standard sauces such as chocolate, butterscotch or caramel, raspberry, and *crème Anglaise,* pounds of puff pastry, meringues, and layers of *génoise* ready to be filled, frosted, or glazed.

When the chef encourages daily specials for desserts, it is the pastry chef's job to choose the one or two to be made each day while keeping in mind the tastes of the house's regular customers. When specials are too complex for the servers to describe to the customers, they are unlikely to be ordered.

Seasonal specials make use of the first strawberries and blueberries in the spring, fresh cherries and ripe peaches in the summer, local varieties of apples and pears in the fall, and cranberries or chestnuts in the winter. Chocolate, of course, knows no season.

Whether the restaurant is a dinner house only or it serves lunch as well, the pastry chef's hours are usually early morning to midafternoon. The bulk of baking and sauce making is done first, to use the ovens and the stove when the other cooks don't need them. This is usually a friendly, slower-moving time of day in the kitchen, with the early prep workers checking in the produce order and cleaning everything to be stored for the cooks. By late morning, the pastry chef begins to assemble the specific desserts. Two layers of chocolate/ground almond cake separated by a raspberry filling, coated smoothly with a chocolate glaze, and decorated with chocolate curls or chocolate pasta threads and a few fresh raspberries strewn on top. A *pâte sucrée* shell painted inside with a jam glaze and filled with *crème patisserie* topped with a nautilus design of poached fresh apricots, glazed again with jam. Two circles of hazelnut meringue filled with white chocolate mousse and studded with fresh raspberries, dusted with confectioners' sugar. The variety is endless.

Salaries

The pastry chef in a small dinner restaurant may work only a few hours a week to maintain the quantity of desserts on hand. This is hourly work, paying from $10 an hour to $14 an hour. In a major hotel chain that offers fine dining in more than one restaurant on the property, the pastry chef is a full-time, salaried worker, earning from $30,000 to $50,000+ a year.

Employment Prospects

There are ample opportunities for pastry chefs, particularly in urban areas and destination resorts with lots of restaurants. The field is very competitive; the work is popular due to the ideal working hours, the availability of part-time jobs, and the rampant occurrence of sweet tooths.

Advancement Prospects

Since a restaurant usually employs only one pastry chef, the form of advancement is to move to a more upscale restaurant that will pay higher wages. This is common and limited only by the prevalence of restaurants in a given area.

Best Geographical Location(s)

Major urban areas and resorts are good spots for pastry chefs, particularly those known for upscale dining, such as New York, Chicago, New Orleans, San Francisco, and Los Angeles.

Education and Training

Pastry chefs are trained in culinary academies, vocational education/trade tech schools, and as apprentices in large restaurants or hotels. A pastry chef needs to know all the basic preparations: *génoise,* meringues, *feuilletage,* buttercreams, mousses, crèmes and custards, sauces, glazes, fruit preparations, ice creams, and sorbets.

Experience/Skills/Personality Traits

The innate talent that comes into play when designing a special dessert or finishing and garnishing a regular menu standby sets a pastry chef apart as an artist.

Pastry work is repetitive, so the chef needs patience and persistence to make bases, sauces, and toppings without deviating from a standard of quality. The product has to be consistent, not a dry cake one week and the raw taste of underbaked flour the next.

Unions/Associations

Union membership is usually a factor only in major hotel chains and in large cities where union influence is strong.

The American Culinary Federation (ACF) is a membership association for skilled restaurant chefs, cooks, and pastry chefs, and it has over 200 local chapters across the United States.

The International Association of Culinary Professionals (IACP) is a broad-based organization of professionals in all fields of culinary endeavor.

The National Restaurant Association (NRA) is a good source of information about training and career opportunities.

Tips for Entry

1. If you have a specialty dessert that you make, try peddling it to the chef or owner of one or more restaurants in your area that buy their desserts. (You can tell they do if their dessert menu is primarily cheesecake, ice cream, and frozen mousses.)
2. Locate any cooking school in your area for classes on pastries and desserts if you want to broaden your repertoire, or consider offering a class that you can teach there.
3. Whenever you taste a dessert you like, analyze what makes it special, experiment with your own version, and add those techniques to your own store of knowledge.

RESTAURANT SOUS-CHEF

CAREER PROFILE

Duties: Works as assistant to the chef; cooks alongside the chef and in his or her place, always cooking in the style of the chef; assists in kitchen staff supervision and business management details as assigned by chef

Alternate Title(s): Assistant Chef; Chef

Salary Range: $18,000 to $65,000

Employment Prospects: Very good to excellent

Advancement Prospects: Good to very good

Best Geographical Location(s) for Position: Major urban areas; wealthy communities; resort and recreation areas with numerous restaurants

Prerequisites:
    Education or Training—Basic chef training at a culinary academy or vocational school plus on-the-job training to cook in the style of the chef
    Experience—Any restaurant cooking experience
    Special Skills and Personality Traits—Flexibility and attentiveness to chef's style of cooking; good leadership qualities with the rest of kitchen staff

CAREER LADDER

```
┌─────────────────────────────┐
│      Restaurant Chef        │
└─────────────────────────────┘

┌─────────────────────────────┐
│         Sous-Chef           │
└─────────────────────────────┘

┌─────────────────────────────┐
│      Kitchen Assistant      │
└─────────────────────────────┘
```

Position Description

The sous-chef in a restaurant is the number-one backup for the chef, his or her right hand, stand-in, and reliable assistant. The sous-chef cooks alongside the chef or in place of the chef, depending on how busy the kitchen is with orders. This requires the sous-chef to cook all the restaurant dishes in the style of the chef. If he or she wants to experiment with some variations on the regular menu items, prior approval by the chef is needed.

The sous-chef takes on all the secondary duties assigned by the chef; this may include ordering, taking inventory, accepting deliveries, checking invoices, approving time records, training kitchen workers, conducting off-premises catering, and opening and closing the restaurant. If there is an apprentice program in the kitchen, the sous-chef will conduct much of the training and supervision for the chef. If the chef takes a vacation, the sous-chef takes full charge.

Although an overloaded plate of management duties may be one of the chef's major reasons for hiring a sous-chef, the essential talent he or she must bring to the job is culinary skill. The style of the restaurant is set by the chef; this means the sous-chef has to maintain and develop the chef's style of cooking so a perceptive, regular customer cannot tell which of them cooked the dish.

In large restaurants, there may be several sous-chefs, each in charge of specific operations, such as banquet or catering, lunch or dinner.

Salaries

Chefs' salaries range between $18,000 and $65,000 across the United States, and a sous-chef's pay is in the lower range. This varies depending on the size and quality of the restaurant.

Employment Prospects

There are unlimited opportunities for sous-chefs as the restaurant business increases nationally. A typical way for a sous-chef to chart his or her career is to identify talented chefs whose food they admire and pester their way into a job in one of those restaurants.

Advancement Prospects

Within a restaurant, advancement for a sous-chef occurs when the chef leaves for another job. Otherwise, the sous chef lets it be known that he or she is interested in advancing to a more responsible (that is, higher paying) job.

Best Geographical Location(s)

Top restaurant work is more plentiful in major urban areas, resort areas, and high-income communities.

Education and Training

Being a sous-chef is a form of training to work closely with the chef to replicate his or her style of cooking and sense of menu balance. To be qualified as a sous-chef, an individual must have either restaurant experience or culinary education in all the standard and classic techniques of food preparation.

To even be considered for a sous-chef position an individual usually has several years of experience as a line cook in restaurants. Then there is specific training to duplicate the flavors, balance, and presentation of the restaurant menu to become a counterpart of the chef.

Experience/Skills/Personality Traits

In addition to basic culinary experience, a sous-chef needs to be flexible and attentive to the chef's way of cooking and managing the kitchen. As the middleman or woman between the chef and the kitchen staff, the sous-chef functions as an interpreter, a teaching assistant, and a mediator.

Unions/Associations

In some very large cities there are restaurant workers' unions, but they are not found nationwide.

Sous-chefs may be members of the American Culinary Federation and benefit from the educational programs of local chapters.

Tips for Entry

1. Acquire a certificate of completion from the community college or nearby vocational training program for chefs, and with this as a reference apply for cooking positions at the best restaurants in your area.
2. Keep informed about your local restaurant scene and pick out the best chefs to work for. A sous-chef can work his or her way through an ever-improving range of restaurants, learning one chef's style after another.

RESTAURANT KITCHEN STEWARD

CAREER PROFILE

Duties: Responsible for all fresh, raw ingredients and staple preparations used in the kitchen; controls inventory and maintains quality

Alternate Title(s): *Garde-manger*

Salary Range: $7 to $10 an hour; $12,000 to $20,000 a year.

Employment Prospects: Excellent

Advancement Prospects: Good, depending on ambition

Best Geographical Location(s) for Position: Any city or town with restaurants of moderate size

Prerequisites:

Education or Training—Vocational schools teach basic ingredient selection and care, but on-the-job training ensures the work is done to the chef's liking.

Experience—Any restaurant kitchen experience

Special Skills and Personality Traits—An insistent concern about sustaining the quality of ingredients and an interest in learning about new produce and products

CAREER LADDER

```
+-----------------------------+
|            Chef             |
+-----------------------------+

+-----------------------------+
|          Steward            |
+-----------------------------+

+-----------------------------+
|  Prep and Clean-up Person   |
+-----------------------------+
```

Position Description

The restaurant kitchen steward is responsible for the condition of all the fresh, raw ingredients used in the menu: cartons of vegetables, lettuces, shallots and garlics, herbs, fruits and berries, as well as sufficient supplies of staple preparations such as stocks, sauce bases, puff pastry and *pâte sucrée* pastry bases, fruit purees, and shelf-stable ingredients such as dried fruits, spices, and dried pastas.

Many of these ingredients must be cared for twice—when they are first received and when they are being prepared for the day's menu. The kitchen steward is responsible for seeing that everything is first-quality when it is received, and that it is washed, trimmed, and properly stored to protect its appearance and flavor until use.

When the menu is decided for the day the kitchen steward is given instruction about which items to prepare for cooking. While vegetables are prepped, trimmings are reserved as well—carrot, celery, onions for meat stock and others for soups. Salad greens are washed and spun dry.

Salaries

Depending on the size of the restaurant, the kitchen steward may be an entry-level chef learning the background work before being trained to go on the line or an hourly worker who has moved up from dishwasher. Pay rates range from minimum wage to $10 an hour. Annual wages range from $12,000 to $20,000 depending on experience, training, and responsibility.

Employment Prospects

In a small restaurant, the duties of a kitchen steward may fall to the sous-chef or be combined with a salad maker and prep cook; the combination of duties varies depending on the size of the kitchen staff.

Advancement Prospects

This job is a stepping stone: It can be a promotion for a dishwasher and it can be the launching pad for a chef-in-training.

Best Geographical Location(s)

Large cities with medium-to-large restaurants and upper-income communities with lavish restaurants are the best locations for this work.

Education and Training

The kitchen steward's work is whatever the chef wants done, and since it has to be done the chef's way, training on the job is normal. When a steward moves from one restaurant kitchen to another, or if the chef changes, the steward may go through radical retraining to satisfy the chef.

Experience/Skills/Personality Traits

A sense of caring about the quality of the ingredients to the level of the chef's concern is vital. The more open to learning the steward is, the more likely he or she is to be promoted.

Unions/Associations

In major urban areas, a local of the Culinary Alliance and Bartenders Union will recruit kitchen workers to union membership. Unions rarely exist or have much clout in smaller communities.

Tips for Entry

1. The first level of training for a kitchen steward is available in hotels or other institutional kitchens, and jobs are routinely listed in the classifieds. Take your first job in the best kitchen available.
2. A three-month or six-month catering program in a vocational trade/tech or community college will cover the skills needed by a kitchen steward.

SERVER

Duties: Supervises and assists in the set-up of dining room station; is familiar with menu and special dishes; greets customers; explains menu as needed; takes orders and serves meals; creates a mood of comfort and ease for the customer

Alternate Title(s): wait person

Salary Range: Minimum wage up to $12 an hour, plus tips

Employment Prospects: Unlimited at entry level to scarce at top of the range

Advancement Prospects: Fair to good—mostly by changing to another restaurant, some by advancing to management

Best Geographical Location(s) for Position: Cities, resort towns, and vacation destinations with numerous restaurants

Prerequisites:

Education or Training—On-the-job training as a server or front-of-the-house training in a restaurant management program

Experience—Prior serving experience in increasingly better restaurants

Special Skills and Personality Traits—Bright, quick, and friendly with a real concern for the pleasure and comfort of others; appreciation of good food, particularly of the style of food at employing restaurant

```
┌─────────────────────────────┐
│        Maître d' or          │
│   Dining Room Manager        │
└─────────────────────────────┘

┌─────────────────────────────┐
│          Server              │
└─────────────────────────────┘

┌─────────────────────────────┐
│  Assistant Server or Busser  │
└─────────────────────────────┘
```

Position Description

A server is a specialized salesperson, who touts the unique food that comes from the restaurant kitchen and cinches the sale by taking the order from hungry customers. As in all sales work, the server must be well-informed about the product to be able to lure customers to order the higher-priced dishes or to eat one more course than they planned. With every notch the bill goes up, the tip for the server increases proportionately.

The server's work starts with checking the dining room before the restaurant opens. Usually, the tables are set before the restaurant closes the night before. In some houses, the servers start the day by giving the napkins their special fold or by polishing glasses and cutlery. Salt-and-pepper shakers and sugar containers are checked and filled. Flowers must be fresh; anything that droops gets discarded

and replaced. In some restaurants, where flamboyant dishes are cooked or finished at the table, the server's set-up includes special preparation. For example, a Caesar salad requires the server to peel the garlic, put out containers of anchovies and mustard, grate the cheese, and check for crispy croutons and clean cruets of vinegar and oil.

Once the house is open and customers start to fill the tables, the server is host and teacher and wizard of moods, creating an atmosphere of comfort and ease, and making the meal a memorable event. Regardless of how much staff a particular restaurant has in addition to the servers—usually a maître d' or a manager, a wine steward, and busboys for a fully-staffed, white tablecloth place and sometimes only a host or hostess in a small café—the warm greeting from the server can make all the difference in the customer's mood.

The server answers menu questions: Is it very spicy? What kind of mushrooms are served with that dish? Is the salad mostly chicken or mostly lettuce? What's the sauce like on that? Is it a terribly big serving? What's gravlax? As the order is decided upon, the server asks how the customer wants something cooked: rare, medium, or well-done. The order can be turned in to the kitchen in a variety of ways—verbally, in writing (clipped up to a metal ring or a metal strip for the cooks to read easily), or on a user-friendly computer monitor where the server indicates the order by pressing codes on a keypad.

The computer menus range from the cocktail order (stemmed glass or tumbler for a martini "up" or "over") through to dessert (pie wedge, ice cream mound, parfait glass), and the most sophisticated systems can handle special orders. Such a system can do far more than just communicate the orders to the bartender and the kitchen; it is also used by the management for inventory control and purchasing, cost control and pricing, sales figures by the day, week, month, or year, to predict business highs and lows, and for the server's own information.

While the meal is in progress, the server keeps an eye on the table to offer another drink, to grind fresh pepper on the salad or entree, to get more bread, and to clear the table promptly. There's a fine line that has to be drawn between interfering too much in the customers' meals and being inattentive to their needs. If there is any sign of displeasure with the food, depending on the restaurant policy the server will offer a substitute, strike the cost from the bill, or have the kitchen recook the item. The goal is a happy and satisfied customer who rewards the server with a tip for service.

Salaries

Servers are most often paid the current U.S. Labor Department minimum wage, but their share of tips may put them in a much higher income tax bracket.

Restaurants that value skilled employees because they are known moneymakers, generating repeat business from their cluster of preferred customers, will give these servers a higher pay rate, even a monthly salary, and sometimes employee benefits such as insurance, sick leave, and paid vacations.

Employment Prospects

There are unlimited numbers of jobs available for servers, but the cream, as always, is for the very few. Trendy, big-city restaurants tend to prefer youthful servers; classic and elegant restaurants hire more experienced and mature servers. A server may start at a hotel or a chain with several restaurants and cafes to get training and move up the ladder to exclusive houses where turnover is very rare. It has been estimated that by the time they are 25 years old, 85 percent of Americans have put a plate down in front of someone. These jobs are available to high school and college students

and to people with erratic employment—actors, musicians, and artists; it's a lifelong career for those who want it.

Advancement Prospects

The most common form of advancement for a server is to move to a better restaurant, one with greater demands on the wait-staff and higher-priced food that generates larger tips.

A server may also aspire to management. Maître d' is the French term—master of the house—for a headwaiter. On a slow night the headwaiter might work the room alone and on weekends bring in a crew to serve the crowd. In a larger establishment, the dining room manager is responsible for all front-of-the-house duties and oversees the headwaiter, and wine steward and hires and fires at every position.

Best Geographical Location(s)

Cities and resort communities with numerous upscale (white tablecloth) restaurants offer more opportunities for ambitious servers, but there is less employee turnover for the available jobs. It is often necessary to start as a busser or lunch server and work up.

Education and Training

Server training is commonly given by the restaurant. Even a seasoned server is trained in the quirks of the house, such as flashy touches like flipping the cloth napkin and draping it on the customer's lap or serving all entrees under silver domes and lifting them simultaneously for each person at the table. Training can also merely be being shown where you turn in orders and where you pick them up.

Community colleges and vocational training schools that have Hotel/Restaurant Management programs train students for front-of-the-house management. First-semester students usually do a stint of waiting tables at the school-run café and proceed through classes and on-the-job training in dining room management. Some schools have a management course that is separate from culinary training.

Experience/Skills/Personality Traits

In all forms of sales work, an out-going, friendly person will make a customer comfortable and make the exchange pleasant, even fun. A server has to be knowledgeable about the menu and the make-up of dishes. If a customer asks what kind of mushrooms are in a *risotto di funghi* and the server isn't sure, he or she had better hot-foot it to the kitchen to ask the chef before the customer decides to order something else. A good memory, or a consistent system in writing orders, is helpful when serving a large table where every order is different. Interrupting their happy conversation with "Who has the sea bass?" isn't professional. Being naturally attentive to people's needs—for more water or for picking the right time to clear the plates and offer dessert—makes the customer feel properly pampered.

Unions/Associations

Unions for restaurant servers are only common in major cities and hotels, and usually a new employee can join the union immediately after being hired.

Tips for Entry

1. Bussing—clearing dishes and pouring water, iced tea, and coffee and generally serving as assistant to the wait-staff—is the entry-level job in food service. Some restaurants will promote busboys to server status and some won't; if promotion is your goal in taking a bussing job, ask about advancement before you start.

2. As a customer in the restaurant where you would like to work, observe the wait-staff; if your serving person isn't too busy, engage him or her in conversation by asking for advice on how to get started.

WINE STEWARD

Duties: Selects, orders, and maintains wine selection of the restaurant in consultation with the chef; trains staff in fine points of wine service and characteristics

Alternate Title(s): Sommelier

Salary Range: $25,000 to $65,000

Employment Prospects: Fair, with limited opportunities

Advancement Prospects: Fair to good, by moving to a restaurant or hotel with a larger wine program

Best Geographical Location(s) for Position: In states where wine is an accepted accompaniment to dining; major urban areas

Prerequisites:

Education or Training—Wine appreciation courses, wine and beverage management courses in vocational schools, wine tastings and winery tours, as much background as possible

Experience—Any job in the wine industry, e.g. at a winery, brokerage, or wine shop

Special Skills and Personality Traits—A discriminating palate and an exceptional palate memory; an orderly system of reference

```
┌─────────────────────────────┐
│       Maître d'hôtel         │
└─────────────────────────────┘

┌─────────────────────────────┐
│       Wine Steward           │
└─────────────────────────────┘

┌─────────────────────────────┐
│       Wine Trainee           │
└─────────────────────────────┘
```

Position Description

The wine steward is in charge of the entire wine program for the restaurant. This program consists of consulting with the chef about appropriate pairing of food and wine; tasting, selecting, ordering, listing, storing, and inventorying the wine; training the wait-staff in the proper handling and service of wine; and managing the restaurant's budget and income for wine.

The range of wines the steward must select and keep on hand extends from aperitif or preprandial wines, such as domestic sparkling wines and imported Champagnes, vermouths, sherries and popular cocktail wines; the variety of red and white dinner wines, such as French, Italian, and German regional wines and domestic cabernets, pinot noirs, gamay, Syrah for the reds and sauvignon blanc, Chardonnay, and pinot blanc for the whites; and after-dinner ports, Madeiras, Sauternes, and cognacs.

The wine steward's knowledge of wines must be constantly updated as each year's harvest is bottled and released to buyers. A bad year for reds might nevertheless produce some spectacular vintages from a few wineries. A popular winery might change ownership, lose its winemaker or suffer a localized natural crisis in its grape production, and any of these changes would have a major impact on their wines in succeeding years. The steward who is maintaining a large cellar and wine list has to constantly read to keep informed about winery and wine news since it affects his job.

Wine tastings are another way the steward keeps up-to-date. In a wine-producing area such as California and Oregon, the steward may make an annual visit to particular wineries that have major selections on the restaurant's list. In the rest of the country, the wineries send out their distributors to set up local tastings for restaurant owners, chefs, and wine stewards; most often these are in the early months of the year and the winemaker is present to discuss his new bottlings. There are one or two major conferences about wine held annually, and the wine steward might arrange to attend at least one of them.

If the restaurant's menu changes seasonally, the wine list may need to be changed to offer some especially appropriate bottles to pair with the food. The steward and the chef spend time together tasting wines, discussing the menu changes, and tasting new dishes with specific wines, looking for an ephemeral symbiosis to enrich the flavors. This is a prelude to the seasonal training of the wait-staff on the new menu and the wine list.

Wine storage space in the restaurant is carefully selected for temperature and humidity factors. If an expensive wine is improperly stored, it can diminish rapidly in quality and value. On the other hand, every available inch of the restaurant is traditionally dedicated to the front of the house, the tables, because that's where the income is. This allocation of space can limit the amount of wine the steward can order and store at a time, and it seriously affects his or her flexibility in taking advantage of sales and discounts.

Restaurants are judged by their wine lists, and sometimes the award-winning wine list is a greater draw for wine buffs than is the chef's food. The more the wine steward knows about current and historic wines, the better he or she can purchase the balance of wines to enhance the cellar.

Depending on the size of the restaurant, there may be more than one wine steward on the staff, and the head steward may be expected to train the wait-staff in the proper handling and serving of wines. The wait-staff is usually instructed to call a steward to the table to guide the customer's selection and answer questions about particular bottles on the list. If the wait-staff does participate in wine selection and serving, the steward may arrange for tasting sessions to train their palates, at least to sample the most popular wines on the list.

As with all management assignments, the wine budget is the responsibility of the steward. How much the wine is marked up varies by restaurant—$1^1/_2$ times, 2 times, or $2^1/_2$ times retail—but the restaurant buys wholesale at a case price and thus the markups can generate large profits. The wine steward has to keep on top of costs, watch what wines are selling, determine which wines to sell by the glass to move them out of the cellar and which to store, and take advantage of sales and discounts for regular listed wines.

Salaries

As a manager, the wine steward will be paid a salary and an annual bonus depending on the restaurant's profits. The work is full-time, at least, and annual salaries can range from $25,000 to $65,000, plus insurance benefits and bonus.

Employment Prospects

Midsize restaurants—those places with 30 to 50 tables that are open for lunch and dinner, which turn each table over one-and-a-half times a night—are likely to employ a wine steward. These jobs are not plentiful; there are less than a thousand such jobs nationwide.

Advancement Prospects

The wine steward, with very specialized knowledge about wines, can advance by moving to a larger, more expensive restaurant, or by moving up to *maître d'hôtel* and assuming the entire management of the front of the house.

Best Geographical Location(s)

States and communities where wine is especially appreciated as an accompaniment to meals are most likely to have exceptional wine lists and the wine stewards to manage them.

Education and Training

Courses in wine are given, primarily in wine-producing areas, by local community colleges. Intensive courses in wine knowledge are given in the major wine-making areas. Keep in mind that the information given on wine in books is affected by the books' publication dates, since wine is a product that changes annually. Training in wine knowledge, tasting, and serving is also an on-the-job learning experience.

Experience/Skills/Personality Traits

A wine steward must have an excellent palate to recognize the component flavors of a single wine, and a palate memory to bring forth a description of a wine, even though it was last tasted several years before.

The matrix of data that a wine steward deals with consists of the varieties of wines and producing wineries in the United States and abroad as well as the vintage years and their characteristics. It requires an orderly system of data for reference, whether it is in human memory or computer files.

Unions/Associations

The Society of Wine Educators publishes a newsletter and a journal and holds an annual summer conference. Some vintners associations encourage associate memberships which give members newsletters and a network of information sources.

Tips for Entry

1. Read a variety of wine publications (both magazines and newspapers) for news, and books for overviews, to get a sense of the vocabulary of wine appreciation.
2. Locate the nearest fine wine store, get acquainted with the owner/buyer to learn as much as you can about their most popular wines, taste as many of these as you can, and keep records.

3. Check for a local chapter of the American Institute of Wine and Food to attend any of its wine-tasting events and make the acquaintance of professionals in the wine industry who might give you guidance for jobs or training.

4. Assess your local restaurants for the quality of their wine lists and get acquainted with the wine steward to ask about job opportunities and career advice.

DINING ROOM MANAGER

CAREER PROFILE

Duties: Influences the style of the dining room; manages the dining room; trains, schedules, and supervises wait-staff; may double as the wine steward

Alternate Title(s): Headwaiter; Maître d'Hôtel

Salary Range: $30,000 to $60,000+

Employment Prospects: Limited

Advancement Prospects: Limited

Best Geographical Location(s) for Position: Major urban areas; affluent communities with high-quality restaurants

Prerequisites:

Education or Training—Dining room management, wine service, and hospitality courses from a vocational culinary program

Experience—Any dining room serving or managing work

Special Skills and Personality Traits—Attentiveness to the comforts of others; leadership skills in team building

CAREER LADDER

```
┌─────────────────────────────┐
│     Restaurant Manager      │
└─────────────────────────────┘

┌─────────────────────────────┐
│    Dining Room Manager      │
└─────────────────────────────┘

┌─────────────────────────────┐
│           Server            │
└─────────────────────────────┘
```

Position Description

The maître d' or headwaiter creates the style of service in a fine dining room. The French term means "master" or "manager" of the hotel; in historic times, hotels had the only public dining rooms. The maître d' trains the wait-staff and their helpers and supervises the dining room during service, at the same time greeting diners and assisting some servers with the wine orders or even with table service for large groups. In a moderate-size, white-tablecloth restaurant, the maître d' manages the front of the house and reports to the restaurant manager or owner. Depending on the size of the restaurant, there may also be a wine steward and even an assistant manager reporting to the maître d'.

The maître d' checks the advance reservations scheduled to determine the number of wait-staff that will be needed. If it is early in the week and a very quiet night is anticipated, he or she may work the room alone or with only one other waiter and some bussers. As the weekend approaches and the book fills, the additional prospect of walk-ins means that a full staff had better be on duty.

Service starts several hours before the restaurant opens when the wait-staff arrives, checks the set up of the dining room, and completes the individual preparations for table service. If the restaurant offers some tableside dishes, say Caesar salad or crêpes suzette, the wait-staff checks that all the necessary ingredients for finishing these special orders are in place. The headwaiter has already ordered the flowers, and the bussers make sure candles, salt and pepper, and any other tablesetting items are in place. If the restaurant features a fancy folded napkin, there are always piles of linens fresh from the laundry service that need to be folded into the signature shape.

Often the maître d' doubles as wine steward in a moderate-size restaurant. In this role, he or she is responsible for ordering and maintaining the wine list, training the wait-staff in the characteristics of the house's wines and their significant components for matching wines with food. Even though the servers are trained, on a busy night the maître d' will probably consult with the diners about the wine list, recommend bottles based on the evening's menu, and serve the wines. This allows the servers to concentrate on the food orders and service, creating a smooth division of duties.

During service the maître d' must seem to be everywhere at once—greeting incoming guests and escorting them to their tables, chatting about specials or appetizers if they want something ordered right away, attending to the wine order, supervising everyone in the dining room, assisting a server if needed and, finally, gathering coats and umbrellas and ushering the guests out with the conviviality of a host seeing off good friends.

The maître d' has an essential role to fulfill that gives the customers the sense of being welcome and important as the staff proceeds to serve them and please them during their meal. The style the maître d' imparts may be informal and friendly or a bit more distant but always with a desire to please.

Salaries

The maître d' may be the only full-time, front-of-the-house employee of the restaurant, with a reliable group of servers and bussers guaranteed a minimum number of hours of work per week but on-call as needed. In this case his or her pay rate would be at the top of the servers' pay range, but instead of a higher salary, it is more likely the restaurant will periodically pay a bonus based on total dining room sales, including wine and spirits. This translates into an annual wage in the range of $30,000 to $60,000 and up in major cities.

Employment Prospects

Restaurant management jobs exist at every level of restaurant, but the best ones rarely turn over, as they are usually held by a long-term employee for decades. An area with an active restaurant population, meaning there are new places opening all the time, will have job opportunities for experienced managers.

Advancement Prospects

Promotion is possible in a restaurant chain by moving to a larger property; in an individual restaurant, advancement can happen if the house is enlarged physically by adding tables, so there are more meals served and thus more income to pay a manager's salary. Otherwise, advancement may depend on moving to a better or larger restaurant when the opportunity arises.

Best Geographical Location(s)

Major urban areas, upscale resort communities, and affluent communities have a higher incidence of white-tablecloth restaurants with formal service, which offers employment to trained maîtres d'.

Education and Training

A few culinary academies are planning service courses to train maîtres d' and sommeliers—that is, headwaiters and wine stewards—and almost all vocational culinary programs give first-semester students training in the front of the house. This is an area of training that has been ignored until now, and it is beginning to get more attention as service is assumed to be the missing ingredient in many top restaurants.

Experience/Skills/Personality Traits

Any experience waiting on customers, especially in a dining venue, is valuable in moving up to maître d'. The essential attitude is understanding hospitality, making the customer a guest, and emphasizing the welcome. Primarily, a maître d' needs to be attentive to people and to make them to feel comfortable. In terms of staff management, building teamwork is the key ingredient.

Unions/Associations

There are no specific unions or professional groups for maîtres d', but they are welcome in the associations of lovers of fine food and wine—such as the American Institute of Wine and Food.

Tips for Entry

1. Take any serving work in the best restaurant in your area to be trained to high standards, and let your manager know you are interested in becoming an assistant manager.
2. Check with the job placement office of the nearest community college with a culinary program and learn what local restaurants require for dining room management; perhaps there is a short course that will help you get a first job.

BAKERIES

BAKERY MANAGER

CAREER PROFILE

Duties: Decides the amount of baked goods to be made daily; schedules shifts and assigns tasks to bakers; trains staff; orders ingredients and supplies; prices all baked products; enforces sanitation practices

Alternate Title(s): Head Baker

Salary Range: $40,000 to $60,000

Employment Prospects: Numerous

Advancement Prospects: Very good

Best Geographical Location(s) for Position: Everywhere in the country

Prerequisites:

Education or Training—Culinary academy, cooking school, or vocational trade/tech school baking course

Experience—All baking experience, including self-taught from cookbooks; work in financial and personnel management

Special Skills and Personality Traits—Consistency; attention to detail; concern for a quality product

CAREER LADDER

```
┌─────────────────────────────┐
│        Bakery Owner         │
└─────────────────────────────┘

┌─────────────────────────────┐
│       Bakery Manager        │
└─────────────────────────────┘

┌─────────────────────────────┐
│   Bakers and Counter Staff  │
└─────────────────────────────┘
```

Position Description

The manager of a neighborhood bakery is responsible for producing just the right amount of goods every day, to ensure that customers are not turned away disappointed because there aren't enough goods or that products aren't discounted or discarded because there is too much. The variable factors in the bakery business include time of the year, weather, advertised specials, and holiday traditions.

A typical neighborhood bakery offers a wide range of sweets in addition to a variety of breads. The sweets category consists of cakes, cupcakes, muffins, Danish pastries, pies, tarts, cookies, and sometimes donuts. Breads may range from sliced white sandwich loaves through egg, whole wheat, rye, multigrain, and special shapes including braids, rolls, and buns. A few tables and a coffee maker often add the feeling of a cafe, but the basic business is baking and selling the goods.

The workday starts at 5 A.M. or earlier. The manager starts the first shift with yeast breads that need an hour or two of rising time before they go into the ovens. The next process, using a sweetened yeast dough, is to form the assortment of Danish pastries—crescents, snails, bear claws, braids, rings—to be finished with fruit or sweetened cheese filling and glazed with butter creams and sugar icings. The Danish, which are a popular early-morning purchase, are time-consuming to shape and fill so the baker has to get them in and out of the oven before the shop doors open, usually by 7 or 8 A.M.

The manager's workday ends in the early afternoon when everything has been baked and is in the cases for customers. As soon as the breads are underway, cakes, cookies, and pies have to be produced. Even in the smallest bakery, there is usually an assistant baker who may work a later shift or fewer hours, measuring ingredients, mixing doughs, tending the ovens, beating cream frostings and stirring custard fillings, washing and peeling fresh fruits for pies, and taking trays of fresh goods out to the counters.

Some items—at least some components—can be made ahead of time in batches and then frozen, to be baked when needed. Pastry, both *pâte sucrée* and puff pastry, benefits from a chilling rest after blending, and extra batches can be made ahead, limited only by the amount of refrigerator space available for storage.

The number of special orders fluctuates with the seasons. Wedding cakes take anywhere from six to 14 hours to decorate. Perhaps this is a specialty of the bakery manager or, alternatively, there may be an on-call employee who comes in just for this painstaking work. The bakery must be careful not to take more orders for wedding cakes than the decorator can produce. At Thanksgiving, pumpkin and mince pies are ordered in multiples for large family feasts; it's at these times the manager has to decide whether or not to use a shortcut, like ordering commercial pastry shells or hiring an extra baker. *Bûches de Noël* at Christmas have to be planned, preordered, and ready for pickup on December 24 for traditional French family fetes.

The manager is responsible for setting the retail prices of the baked goods; this is done with careful attention to the price of ingredients, cost of additional labor, and other overhead factors. With simple computer software or old-fashioned pencil-and-paper arithmetic, each item has to be priced so the monthly income covers the cost of doing business.

Knowing what to bake and how much of it to prepare are skills that come with experience. For example, when a heat wave hits, sales of rich cakes fall off, but it is a good time to produce a variety of savory quiches, selling them by the slice or the whole to customers who welcome a premade dinner. In the early summer, the charm of fresh, seasonal fruit pies is strong. On blustery winter days, a rich dessert or hearty bread added to the menu is appealing. It is the manager's job to sense what is likely to sell best in the coming days and provide the right quantities of baked goods to satisfy the customers.

As with all management jobs, careful hiring and training is essential to a smoothly operating business. Counter workers need different skills than kitchen workers, and it's the manager's job to see that both sides function as a team. Public health and sanitation are another concern, and standards have to be maintained. When the health inspector comes calling it should not be a reason for panic; the manager needs to keep a sharp eye out for the same problems the inspector will notice.

Salaries

The baker/manager for a neighborhood business will earn about three to four times the hourly wage of assistant bakers and counter workers. Their pay will start at United States minimum wage and rarely go much higher. The manager will be paid $18.00 to $29.00 an hour, and there may be benefits such as insurance, paid vacation and sick leave, and profit sharing. The range is between $40,000 and $60,000 a year, depending on the volume of business of the bakery.

Employment Prospects

There are ample opportunities throughout the country for a well-trained baker to manage a neighborhood business.

Even the smallest town usually has one bakery patronized for its cookies, cakes, pies, and breads.

Advancement Prospects

If the manager can substantially increase the volume of business by enhancing the bakery's reputation or attracting more customers, this merits a pay raise, even though the job title doesn't change. A baker with a stellar reputation may be courted by nearby bakeries trying to hire him or her away to their own shop. Another way to improve one's job is to develop a popular specialty—Danish yeast doughs, hearty ethnic breads, or open French *tartes*—that will pay well in a larger, departmentalized bakery.

Best Geographical Location(s)

Good bakery jobs are available throughout the country. Whether it is a family area or a locale populated by singles and working couples, sweet tooths seem universal.

Education and Training

A bakery manager needs culinary skills that can be acquired at an academy, vocational trade/tech school, recreational cooking school, self-taught from cookbooks, or trained on the job. The more a baker knows about flours and leavening and the ideosyncracies of sugars, fruits, and chocolate, the more creative he or she can be in production baking.

Experience/Skills/Personality Traits

Any job experience in making desserts and breads in a restaurant, cafe, bakery, or institutional kitchen will give a baker the credentials for being hired. Knowledge of the other aspects of management can be gained at a community college or on the job.

A baker must accept the limitations that ingredients and weather conditions impose on commercial baking—flour, yeast, humidity—and understand their idiosyncrasies enough to control them.

One of the hardest lessons to learn is to leave the kitchen, even if there is more to do; 5:00 A.M. will come around again the next morning.

Unions/Associations

The American Institute of Baking has an educational program of short courses, correspondence classes, and seminars in the science of baking, bakery management, and allied sciences, especially food hygiene and nutrition.

Tips for Entry

1. Look for any cooking school program that features baking. In addition to the learning experience, it is a good place to meet employed bakers looking for additional workers.

2. Talk to a few owners of local bakeries, timing your visits for mid- to late-afternoon when business is likely to be slow, and ask them what skills they look for in a manager. What you don't already know, you can learn.

3. Take a job as a counter worker just to get on the payroll, and let the kitchen manager know you want to learn baking.

BAKERY SALES MANAGER

CAREER PROFILE

Duties: Develops annual marketing plan approved by bakery management; supervises all advertising; makes sales calls on restaurants and retail stores; attends trade shows; generates mail-order brochures and inclusions in catalogs; contacts department-store buyers; supervises sales staff; works with bakery production manager to schedule sufficient product to meet sales demand

Alternate Title(s): None

Salary Range: As a beginner with a salary/commission arrangement, starting annual salaries are in the range of $20,000. With experience and working only on commission, a salesperson can earn $100,000 or more a year.

Employment Prospects: Unlimited

Advancement Prospects: Good

Best Geographical Location(s) for Position: Urban areas with high density of customers providing top sales volume

Prerequisites:

Education or Training—Sales training is provided by the best companies. A college or university degree helps a worker gain promotion into the executive ranks of a company.

Experience—All sales experience is valuable, even if it was door-to-door selling of chocolate bars to help the high school's team.

Special Skills and Personality Traits—Knowledge of the product, credibility, closure, liking people, willing to work extra hours

CAREER LADDER

> **Bakery Manager**

> **Bakery Sales Manager**

> **Bakery Sales Assistant**

Position Description

The sales manager of a bakery business is in charge of all advertising; sales calls on local customers, such as restaurants, coffee houses, and retail stores; contacts with customers out of the area, such as direct mail orders, catalogs and retail stores; and supervises all additional sales staff.

The extent of sales opportunities depends entirely on what goods the bakery makes, the size of the business, and whether the product has an extended shelf life and can be shipped without damage or spoilage. Some cookie bakeries make an immense volume of their product and

package it in boxes, tins, and bags that keep it fresh and unbroken (ideal for shipping all over the country); some cookie bakeries make only enough product for their local, walk-in customers.

The sales manager starts by developing a marketing plan for the year ahead. He or she will work with the bakery manager for attainable goals, with the production manager to schedule sufficient quantities of goods on hand for peak sales periods (like holidays), identify potential and repeat customers to buy the goods, and contract with distributors to sell and deliver in specific regions.

National trade shows that are held annually or semi-annually, such as the National Association for the Specialty Food Trade (NASFT), and regional shows, such as the Pacific Northwest Restaurant Show, are good showcases for both established businesses and for newcomers. Handing out samples at the booth and talking to potential customers is half the benefit; among the many passersby may be a major mail-order clothing catalog representative who is looking for some holiday foods to include in the next mailing, a buyer from a national department store chain who is looking for holiday foods to augment their deli or food boutique, and owners of small gift stores, coffee houses, and cafés who are always alert for new items to sell. The other benefit of these shows is seeing what other companies are selling, meeting distributors who can expand the sales range of the company, and looking at different types of packaging for new and inventive ways to present the product.

The rest of the year the sales manager is in constant contact with potential large-order customers, encouraging repeat customers to increase their orders, calling on local customers, making sales trips to areas where sales are increasing to meet new customers, working with the advertising people who design ads and sales pamphlets, keeping the production manager aware of new orders, and tracking sales against the year's marketing plan.

Salaries

Salespeople are usually paid with commissions on the volume of merchandise they sell or with a combination of commission and salary. A straight commission is usually 40% of sales, and a starting salary combination begins at about $1,000 to $2,000 a month plus 10% commission. Usually, a sales employee can negotiate his or her basis of pay.

To understand the advantages of either payment system, look at this example: If the salesperson sells $1000 worth of product in a month, the commission would be $400, and the salary/commission would be about $1,600. When the volume of sales increases to $15,000 a month, the commission is $6,000, and the salary/commission combo would be about $3,000. A sales manager can earn between $20,000 to over $100,000 a year, depending on the product volume and the extent of marketing activity.

Additionally, a manager is also paid a percentage on orders taken by sales assistants reporting to the manager, and often meeting or exceeding a marketing plan for the year means a cash bonus for the manager.

Employment Prospects

Sales jobs are plentiful; good sales jobs consist of top-quality products and a company that provides constant training opportunities for their sales staff. Believing in the product that you sell and respecting the company you work for make selling a comfortable occupation, but not necessarily an easy one. One of the largest groups of newspaper help-wanted ads is for sales employees, at every level.

Advancement Prospects

A successful salesperson is a moneymaker for the company. Rewards consist of an assignment to a better (higher volume) territory, a promotion to district manager to supervise a group of salespersons in several territories, and bonuses for meeting sales goals.

Another form of advancement is to join a larger company with the potential for a higher sales volume, thereby creating opportunities for larger commissions.

Best Geographical Location(s)

The best territory for sales work is one with the highest volume of customers: usually a densely commercial urban area. Cities where more companies are headquartered are not the only locale for their sales jobs; with a nationwide marketing program the sales staff is assigned to specific geographic locations. A career in sales often requires moving, to shift to a better territory or to work a period in the corporate office as a prerequisite to promotion. Starting out in sales work often means working on the road and affects the amount of time spent at home with a family.

Education and Training

Top companies train their sales staff in their own style. A college degree in business and marketing provides a background in sales techniques and traditions. Sales jobs do not require a degree or certificate in a related program, but having one will facilitate advancement in a top company.

Experience/Skills/Personality Traits

Having a knack for sales work is identifiable but it is usually not something that can be consciously acquired. Experience is the most effective training; even selling Girl Scout cookies is valuable experience.

The most essential trait to successful selling is knowing the product inside and out and being believable when answering the customer's questions. That includes saying "I don't know," but getting the answer and reporting back. Another essential is having closure: knowing the instant to stop promoting the product and make the sale. Being friendly and outgoing, if those characteristics are controlled, is an asset, but many top salespersons are very reserved in manner. To consistently serve the company's clientele, the salesperson can't be a clock watcher.

Unions/Associations

In most cities there are informal organizations that promote product marketing and build presentation skills. In many industries there are trade associations and marketing meetings that provide educational programs.

Tips for Entry

1. Go to any nearby trade show to cruise the aisles, assess the products, and talk to company representatives about job opportunities.

2. Watch the business section of your local newspaper for stories about new companies or companies experiencing strong growth; call them about sales openings.

BREAD BAKER

CAREER PROFILE

Duties: Specifies ingredients to be ordered; supervises ordering and inventory; overseas all bread production; trains bakery workers; develops new bread products

Alternate Title(s): None

Salary Range: $22,000 to $37,000, depending on size of bakery and volume of production

Employment Prospects: Plentiful to limited, depending on size of city or town

Advancement Prospects: Limited

Best Geographical Location(s) for Position: Major restaurant cities; resort and recreation areas

Prerequisites:
    Education or Training—Vocational trade school certificate as a baker or apprentice
    Experience—Basic understanding of the chemistry of bread making gained either through education, training, or reading
    Special Skills and Personality Traits—Physical stamina to work long hours, mostly standing, and to lift and move heavy ingredients

CAREER LADDER

```
┌─────────────────────────────┐
│       Bakery Manager        │
└─────────────────────────────┘

┌─────────────────────────────┐
│        Bread Baker          │
└─────────────────────────────┘

┌─────────────────────────────┐
│      Baker's Assistant      │
└─────────────────────────────┘
```

Position Description

The bread baker in an exclusively bread-production bakery or in a general bakery is responsible for daily production of all varieties of fresh bread. The baker also specifies the quality of ingredients and supervises ordering and maintains inventory.

Bakers start work in the darkness of morning to ensure fresh bread is available for customers when the store opens. The hours and length of a baker's day depend on the types of breads that are made, i.e., whether they are yeast-risen, use sourdough or other starters, require a sponge to be set first before mixing the doughs, etc.

The baker sets the schedule based on the variety of breads to be made, and the details of making them—rising, forming, second rise, and baking. Oven capacity even in a well-equipped bakery is an infuriating tyrant that drives the baking schedule. Whether or not the bakery has proofing equipment—temperature-controlled receptacles wherein bread rises reliably in a predicted time—also affects the schedule. As the day's work proceeds, there

has to be enough staff on hand to weigh or measure and shape the loaves after the first rising of large batches of dough.

Specialty bread bakeries have a distinctive menu of breads. A French bread baker produces a variety of crusty loaves by controlling steam inside the oven. A German bakery offers breads made from a selection of classic flours, such as rye, unbleached and whole wheat, many of them hearty and dark. A natural foods bakery produces robust loaves rife with nutritious seeds, nuts, and dried fruit, made from organically grown and certified ingredients.

General bakeries have a line of sweet goods—cakes, pies, and cookies—in addition to the breads, and some crossover items like Danish pastries. They also offer quick breads and muffins, leavened by baking soda and baking powder. These other products ease the rigidity of the work schedule by giving the baker other tasks to be performed during the down time while bread is proofing.

In some areas, restaurant chefs will purchase directly from a small production bread baker in order to get a fresh, quality product.

Salaries
Depending on the size of the bakery and the volume of production, a full-charge baker can earn between $22,000 to $37,000 a year.

Employment Prospects
Bakeries are everywhere from small villages to huge cities, providing unlimited opportunities for entry-level jobs, training, and promotion. Trained bakers, either with a certificate from a vocational school or with experience from another bakery, are in constant demand by bakery owners.

Advancement Prospects
Bakeries tend to be small, neighborhood stores where advancement is limited. Multi-branch bakeries, supermarket in-store bakeries, restaurant supply bakeries, all of which are mostly found in larger urban areas, provide opportunities for promotion to management jobs.

Best Geographical Location(s)
Major restaurant cities—Los Angeles, San Francisco, New York, Chicago—with upper-income residents that know and appreciate good bread will have a demanding clientele for good bakery products, especially bread.

Education and Training
Vocational trade/tech schools, culinary academies, and all kinds of cooking schools teach bread baking. Trade/tech schools are likely to have a separate program for baking careers. The American Institute of Baking in Manhattan, Kansas, offers training courses and a certificate program.

Experience/Skills/Personality Traits
A well-trained baker knows the chemistry of baking and the effective factors involved in all the ingredients (flour, yeasts, leavening agents, sweeteners, nuts and seeds, herbs and spices). This experience may be gained through hands-on baking, reading, and training.

A baker needs reliable conditioning to work extended work shifts, ability to lift and carry 50-pound bags of flour, and stamina for long hours of standing and moving large baking trays.

Unions/Associations
In major urban areas, the bakers union is very prominent, governs hiring practices, and also provides training and promotion in rank from apprentice to journeyman, with attendant pay scales. Elsewhere, baking jobs are unrestricted.

Tips for Entry
1. Check with the nearest community college for culinary programs and baking courses, or any small local cooking schools for professional baking courses. A course as short as three months will provide enough basic training to apply for a job.
2. Contact the American Institute of Baking for job opportunities and career advice.
3. A talented bread maker who lives in an area unable to support a small commercial bakery can offer home baking for local restaurants. This can be developed to a profitable level, depending on the size of the baker's home oven and the volume that he or she can produce.

PASTRY AND CAKES BAKER

CAREER PROFILE

Duties: Determines quantities of dessert goods produced daily; supervises ordering and inventory of ingredients; responsible for making all dessert items; trains bakery workers; creates new desserts

Alternate Title(s): Dessert Baker; Pastry Chef

Salary Range: $18,000 to $45,000, depending on size of bakery and volume of production

Employment Prospects: Fair to good, depending on size of city or town

Advancement Prospects: Limited

Best Geographical Location(s) for Position: From small towns to large cities

Prerequisites:
  Education or Training—Vocational trade school certificate as a baker or pastry cook
  Experience—Basic understanding of the chemistry in cake baking and principles of emulsions in frostings, fillings, and glazes
  Special Skills and Personality Traits—Good health and physical stamina to work long hours, mostly standing

CAREER LADDER

```
┌─────────────────────────────┐
│      Bakery Manager         │
└─────────────────────────────┘

┌─────────────────────────────┐
│   Pastry and Cakes Baker    │
└─────────────────────────────┘

┌─────────────────────────────┐
│      Baking Trainee         │
└─────────────────────────────┘
```

Position Description

The pastry and cakes baker is responsible for all the sweet preparations in the bakery; this covers cakes, frostings and fillings, pies, turnovers, cookies, cupcakes, and muffins. Most bakeries divide the production between breads and other products because they are two very different kinds of baking.

Unless the bakery is a new business, the menu of pies, cakes, cookies and other sweets will already be established. The regular customers are also established, and they want their own standbys unchanged, but they will try new goods, especially if bite-sized portions are put out for a few weeks as each new item is introduced.

Certain items must be customer-ready at the moment the bakery opens for business, so the baker starts the day early. The bread baker will produce Danish pastries made from yeast doughs at the same time the first breads are coming out. Muffins and donuts are the cake baker's job; loaves of sweet breads made from batters similar to muffins can be mixed and baked early.

The bakery may have one or more employees who do only cake decorating, and they come in after the first cake layers are out of the ovens and cooled enough for frostings and glazes. The decorators make batches of butter creams, boiled frostings, and small quantities of colored frostings for decorating with roses, scrolls, and lettering.

Custom-made cakes are usually ordered and paid for at least a day ahead to guarantee they will be picked up. Elaborate scenes for children's birthday cakes, many-tiered wedding cakes, and theme sheet cakes for holidays require the special scheduling of decorators, and perhaps extra workers who are on call because of their finely-honed skills.

A retail bakery may also do a wholesale business to restaurants, coffee shops, and small take-out delicatessens where the cook doesn't have the time or the skill to make desserts. These orders are placed in advance and are a guaranteed sale.

Salaries

A full-time cake baker in a retail/wholesale bakery earns in the range of $18,000 to $45,000 a year. The assistant or number-two baker can expect to earn $16,000 to $35,000.

Employment Prospects

Even a town of under 100,000 residents will support several dozen bakeries, so ample jobs can be found everywhere in the country.

Advancement Prospects

A full-charge baker, who supervises decorators and other kitchen workers, can advance to manager for a higher salary or seek a similar job in a larger bakery.

Best Geographical Location(s)

Larger cities with sizable populations have a greater number of bakeries, but these jobs are everywhere.

Education and Training

Most vocational trade culinary programs have a separate course for bakers, and baking is taught in all culinary schools and academies. It is important to understand the chemistry of cakes, pastries, and baked goods to be able to develop original desserts, which can draw customers from a great distance.

The American Institute of Baking in Kansas provides training in baking, bakery management, and allied sciences, especially food hygiene and nutrition, in short courses and seminars and it even has a correspondence program.

Experience/Skills/Personality Traits

Having a well-indulged sweet tooth seems to be common among pastry chefs and bakers, and since this trait is shared by their customers it provides a harmony that contributes to their success.

An artistic eye and a sense of design, color balance, and decoration are assets the baker brings to the overall look of the baked goods, demonstrating special care with glazes, shaping, and sizing.

Unions/Associations

The American Culinary Federation is a national association of chefs, cooks and pastry chefs with local chapters wherever there are sufficient restaurant chefs to support an educational and networking program.

Tips for Entry

1. Contact your community college or the closest vocational trade school for their culinary program, especially baking classes. Ask the program counselor about job placements.
2. A vast amount of baking knowledge can be gained by reading professional baking texts and by experimenting in your own kitchen (learning by trial and error).

INSTITUTIONAL (LARGE-SCALE) FOOD— FROM RESORTS AND COUNTRY CLUBS TO HOSPITALS AND PRISONS

HOTEL CATERING MANAGER

CAREER PROFILE

Duties: Represents the hotel in negotiations with clients, both private and business, for special events including food, beverages, meeting rooms, decorations, and services; solicits customers through community channels

Alternate Title(s): Sales Manager

Salary Range: $25,000 to $61,000 with performance bonuses

Employment Prospects: Excellent

Advancement Prospects: Excellent

Best Geographical Location(s) for Position: Large urban areas where major hotel chains are clustered

Prerequisites:

Education or Training—College degree or certificate in marketing or communications

Experience—Sales experience working with customers for luxury and upscale purchases

Special Skills and Personality Traits—customer service skills, detail oriented, and staying well-informed about the property, the chef, and menu options

CAREER LADDER

```
┌─────────────────────────────────┐
│   Food and Beverage Manager     │
└─────────────────────────────────┘

┌─────────────────────────────────┐
│    Hotel Catering Manager       │
└─────────────────────────────────┘

┌─────────────────────────────────┐
│     Hotel Catering Trainee      │
└─────────────────────────────────┘
```

Position Description

The hotel catering manager books all the special events at the hotel, such as weddings, anniversaries, business retirement parties, office holiday parties, conferences, workshops, management meetings, balls, and many more.

The catering manager coordinates the many services of the hotel for a single event, including lodging, meals, private party rooms, and any extra food services. The manager negotiates all prices and serves as the primary liaison with the client.

For a business conference, the catering manager's duties would include arranging all meeting rooms, breakout rooms, in-room coffee and snack service, meals, and audiovisual equipment.

For a family event such as a wedding or anniversary dinner, the job includes planning for the flowers and decorations for the wedding and reception or for the banquet preceded by the reception. Details that have to be painstakingly planned include the menu, service of all beverages with either a set-up bar and bartender or waiters, valet parking and security for gifts.

Sometimes a client is considering several locations in the city for the event; other clients may pick a particular hotel for its known culinary excellence and negotiate the price aggressively. The hotel catering manager has to be completely familiar with the chef's capabilities, aware of the ingredients used in standard menus, and able to suggest combinations to the client. For a business meeting, the menu must be highly nutritious and energizing to keep the attending executives awake during what may be a long workday. For a family fete, the menu must be balanced to offer both light entertaining and rich delights. Special requests are likely to be made: my mother is allergic to scented flowers, so we have to decorate very carefully; my father's family is vegetarian, so the hors d'oeuvre can't contain any hidden sausage or meat broths; two of our general managers eat kosher, so we need special meals; after the meeting, everybody needs to relax so the dinner room should have a full bar and accommodate a bit of rowdiness. The catering manager has to treat every request seriously and provide a solution.

Unless the arrangements are being made from out of town, the client usually walks through the hotel's accommodations with the catering manager. This allows many of the details to be decided, such as whether or not to tent the outdoor reception area in case of bad weather, or how elaborately to decorate with plants and flowers. Every detail carries its own price, so the catering manager has to have the cost in mind while suggesting which amenities can be handled within the budget.

The catering manager consults with the chef if special food is requested and mediates between the chef and the client until the client is satisfied. All of the work orders must be complete in every detail and approved in writing by the client in advance. Credit-card charges must be set up in advance so billing can be put through without bothering the client during the event. Following an event, many hotels provide a questionnaire asking the client to rate their services; others make a phone call several days after the event to discuss whatever aspects the client considers either critical or complimentary.

Salaries

Large hotel chains pay between $25,000 and $61,000 per year with performance bonuses based on the volume of work done during the year. Properties in major urban areas and destination resorts may pay more than smaller ones. An individually-owned hotel will set a salary in proportion to the amount of business the catering department can expect to do in a year.

Employment Prospects

Hotel chains employ thousands of catering managers and provide training in their own style. Owners of small properties may do their own catering management or hire one person as the business grows. Most hotels with over 50 lodging rooms and more than two banquet rooms have a catering manager to solicit additional business.

Advancement Prospects

Hotel chains promote skilled managers horizontally as well as vertically, moving them to a larger property with more business or up the next ladder step. A catering manager working for a small, individually-owned hotel or inn can successfully seek a job with a bigger volume of work and more pay at a larger property.

Best Geographical Location(s)

Major urban areas, commercial centers, and destination resorts have the most hotel business and on-site catering, and provide the greatest number of related jobs.

Education and Training

A vocational course in catering is helpful but not essential. This work is more in the category of sales and marketing than in cooking. College courses in communications or tourism would be particularly useful. Large hotel chains provide training for their catering management staff.

Experience/Skills/Personality Traits

Since this job involves front-line interaction with customers, the catering manager must have very sensitive skills in communicating the client's needs and desires to specific hotel personnel who will be providing the service. Listening carefully to the client, especially one who may not know exactly what he or she wants or what the property can provide, is essential. The best catering managers are intensely detail oriented.

A catering manager must constantly update his or her knowledge about the chef, the kitchen, and the price lists of the hotel. A smooth and amiable presentation of what the hotel offers will set a client at ease, thus establishing confidence.

Unions/Associations

The American Hotel and Motel Association (AH&MA) provides ongoing educational opportunities for employees of member hotels through their Educational Institute.

Tips for Entry

1. Call the General Manager of some hotels in your area to ask if they offer catering services and describe your interest in a job.
2. Take any job selling services (rather than products) to develop marketing and customer relations experience.

HOTEL EXECUTIVE CHEF

CAREER PROFILE

Duties: Responsible for all food service operations in the hotel: develops new recipes and creates menus; manages sous-chefs and pastry chefs; in charge of apprenticeship training (if any); represents hotel at food-related benefit events

Alternate Title(s): None

Salary Range: $50,000 to $120,000, depending on size of hotel operation

Employment Prospects: Excellent and growing

Advancement Prospects: Very good, either up the ladder or to a larger property

Best Geographical Location(s) for Position: Wherever large hotel chains have their properties—cities, resorts, and hub airports

Prerequisites:
    Education or Training—Professional culinary training, including management
    Experience—About 10 years of chef's experience
    Special Skills and Personality Traits—Well-trained sense of taste and smell; excellent physical condition; innate sense of organization

CAREER LADDER

```
┌─────────────────────────────────┐
│    Food and Beverage Manager    │
└─────────────────────────────────┘

┌─────────────────────────────────┐
│         Executive Chef          │
└─────────────────────────────────┘

┌─────────────────────────────────┐
│           Sous-Chef             │
└─────────────────────────────────┘
```

Position Description

The executive chef in a hotel is responsible for all food service operations in the hotel, as well as at public appearances and community benefits. Depending on how many food venues are in the hotel (coffee shop, dining room, banquets), the chef may rely on separate chefs to manage food service for each operation. There will be a pastry chef for all dessert preparations, and if the hotel participates in an apprenticeship program, it will be managed by the executive chef.

The executive chef is in charge of the menus for all operations. The chef's public reputation will primarily be based on the signature dishes he or she creates for the fine dining room that change seasonally to showcase fresh foods. The coffee shop's menu may change less often, mainly to reflect lighter foods in the summer and richer comfort foods in the winter. When the hotel is advertising a theme promotion, such as Caribbean or jazz, with special entertainment and discounts, the executive chef creates special menus to add to the fun. Banquets and private room catering have their own menus for the customer to select from, but they may also be custom-designed in consultation with the chef to satisfy the customer's expectations. Weddings are other special events with distinctive menus.

Once the menus for all the operations have been created, the chef is responsible for developing recipe specs for each dish and training the sous-chefs in the dishes; the sous-chefs train their lead cooks in the new menu and pass it on to station cooks and the apprentices, if there are any. Most hotel kitchens are arranged pyramidically, with dishroom workers and porters on the widest base, more skilled cooking staff further up and the executive chef at the top.

The chef works with the hotel's purchasing manager to order ingredients on a daily basis and then with the chief steward to ensure that produce, meat, and staples are delivered in a timely manner and stored properly for premium shelf life.

When the hotel agrees to participate in a benefit event that showcases many local chefs, the executive chef—with the approval of the hotel's food and beverage manager—accepts the invitation, determines what signature dish to serve, arranges preparation of the dish by the banquet sous-chef, and represents the hotel at the event.

Even though the executive chef is not cooking on the line at every meal and plating and garnishing dishes, he or she is prominent in the kitchen, tasting dishes at various stages of preparation, observing the work of the chefs and the apprentices, and correcting anything he or she thinks should be done differently.

Salaries
An executive chef's salary depends on the size of the property, the volume of business, and the number of meals served; the range is from $50,000 to $120,000 a year.

Employment Prospects
Tourism and business travel are both increasing steadily, and with that trend more hotels are being refurbished or newly built, steadily creating additional jobs for executive chefs.

Advancement Prospects
Advancement for an executive chef is either further up the ladder into management, as food and beverage manager, or to a larger hotel property with a larger business.

Best Geographical Location(s)
Wherever major hotel chains have their properties—in large cities, resort communities, and major airport hubs—there are ample opportunities for chefs to advance their careers.

Education and Training
An executive chef must have the best possible education in culinary practice, from an academy, a vocational school, or through an apprentice program, and it must include management training.

Experience/Skills/Personality Traits
An executive chef should have at least 10 years' experience as a restaurant or fine dining room chef to be promoted to executive chef. In addition to cooking skills, he or she should have a thorough knowledge of management for front-of-the-house human relations, including hiring, personnel policies and practices, teaching skills for training his or her direct reports, and knowledge of business finances, especially cost controls.

The chef must have a well-trained sense of taste and smell to be able to judge his or her own cooking and that of others in the kitchen. As with all kitchen workers, a chef must be in excellent physical health and have sufficient strength to work long hours and lift and carry heavy items.

Unions/Associations
The American Culinary Federation is a national organization of professional chefs, cooks, pastry chefs and culinary educators. ACF has local chapters in most cities and large towns that produce educational programs and provide a network of peers.

Many chefs will also join one of the broad-based culinary groups such as the International Association of Culinary Professionals, a regional guild if there is one, or the American Institute of Wine and Food.

Tips for Entry
1. Get acquainted with the executive chef at a large hotel—preferably one that is well-known for excellent cuisine—and make an appointment to discuss career opportunities with him or her.
2. Contact the American Culinary Federation about a chapter in your area and call the chapter chairperson for an appointment to learn about any local training programs, including apprenticeships.

HOTEL FOOD AND BEVERAGE MANAGER

CAREER PROFILE

Duties: Responsible for the quality and profitability of all food and beverage service throughout the hotel; hires and supervises all food and beverage unit managers

Alternate Title(s):F&B

Salary Range: $40,000 to $120,000

Employment Prospects: Good and growing

Advancement Prospects: Excellent

Best Geographical Location(s) for Position: Large cities, commercial capitals, resort communities, and tourism destinations where hotel chains have properties

Prerequisites:

Education or Training—Classic food preparation plus front-of-the-house management education at a culinary academy or vocational trade school, with additional courses in human relations management, marketing, and business

Experience—Broad and varied background in every aspect of hotel management

Special Skills and Personality Traits—Teaching skills are valuable for training and motivating next-level management

CAREER LADDER

```
┌─────────────────────────────┐
│      General Manager         │
└─────────────────────────────┘

┌─────────────────────────────┐
│  Food and Beverage Manager   │
└─────────────────────────────┘

┌─────────────────────────────┐
│      Executive Chef          │
└─────────────────────────────┘
```

Position Description

The manager of all food and beverage operations in a hotel is responsible for the quality of service, the profitability of all departments, and the managers of each department. It is often a huge job, as there may be more than one public bar in a large hotel, and there will surely be more than one restaurant. In addition the F&B supervises catering arrangements for food and beverage service in meeting rooms, conferences, receptions, and room service operations.

The number of managers reporting to the F&B varies according to the size of the hotel and the management style, but it might be as few as seven or as many as 15 managers as every bar, food outlet, and catered service operation has its own manager. One of the most time-consuming activities of the F&B is staff meetings, which are held at least weekly to review every aspect of the hotel's services, and explore ideas for improvement, cost cutting, and profit enhance-

ment. A change resulting from a staff meeting might be something as simple as buying custom-designed bicycles with hot boxes so room service waiters can deliver orders hotter and faster to outlying bungalows.

The F&B expects each of the unit managers to meet certain goals and objectives during the year, and during annual salary reviews and midyear performance reviews the F&B will check the manager's progress against them. Objectives may include profit percentages, amount of business, training programs for the staff, and long-range improvements in the service areas.

Working with the hotel's sales manager, the F&B sees to it that planned promotions (often with alliterative names like Jazz in June and Caribbean Cruises month) are fully supported by every unit. It means special menus, drink names, happy hour games, and even special wait-staff uniforms related to the advertising being placed in travel magazines and placards in the hotel elevators. Special sales goals are set for promotions, and the F&B checks revenue reports daily to see that the objectives are being met.

An F&B manager is rarely found in his or her office. Except for meetings, much of the day is spent on rounds through the property. It's like a military white-glove inspection, but it is conducted all day long. Rounds are conducted first thing in the morning to make contact with every manager, to get an informal status report, and for early warning of any expected problems. Each manager can take care of late deliveries, dissatisfied guests, electric failures, or most of the foibles fate throws, but keeping the boss informed is part of good managing.

The F&B's most valuable tools are his or her managers, their ability to hire and train staff and run their units profitably. If the management pyramid is working as it should, every unit is straining to be the best in the hotel.

Salaries

In major hotel chains, the food and beverage manager of a medium-sized hotel (of about 300 rooms) earns between $60,000 and $120,000 a year plus benefits and bonuses. In out-of-the-way towns, a small hotel food and beverage manager may earn $40,000 a year.

Employment Prospects

Tourism and business travel are big businesses, with every indication that they will continue to grow. New hotels are being built and old hotels restored, all providing additional jobs for food and beverage managers. The opportunities are growing.

Advancement Prospects

Advancement to general manager of a hotel is one possibility; moving to a larger, more profitable property in a major hotel chain is another promotion. Opportunities for advancement up this career ladder are excellent.

Best Geographical Location(s)

Large cities, commercial capitals, resort communities, and the destination areas for tourism are the locations where large and small chain hotels have most of their properties.

Education and Training

Education should include classic food preparation either at a culinary academy or as an apprentice. Front-of-the-house management is equally essential. Training in human relations, marketing, and business management may be acquired in a combination of school and work experience.

Experience/Skills/Personality Traits

This work is primarily managerial, but built on a career working in food service. A step or two down the ladder, most food and beverage managers have been the executive chef at the same property or another owned by the same chain. The more experience an individual has in every aspect of hotel food service, the better qualified he or she will be as food and beverage manager.

Unions/Associations

The American Culinary Federation is a professional organization of chefs, cooks, pastry chefs, and culinary educators. They hold an annual meeting with educational programs, support local chapters that offer a meeting forum, and manage a national apprenticeship program.

To develop and maintain an association with local residents who are avidly interested in fine food and wine, the food and beverage manager may also be an active member of such organizations as the American Institute of Wine and Food, the Chaîne de Rôtisseurs, and Les Toques Blanches.

Tips for Entry

1. Investigate the local community college for hotel and restaurant management programs, and ask the course counselor for suggestions about a fast-track program.
2. Contact the F&B managers at the larger hotels in your area and discuss the possibilities of a limited internship. An internship is a good way to learn if you will enjoy the detailed responsibilities of management.

INSTITUTIONAL CHEF

CAREER PROFILE

Duties: Creates and schedules regular and special menus for residents or inmates requiring specific nutrition; designs and manages kitchen systems; hires and trains all kitchen staff; manages food service budget for the institution

Alternate Title(s): Executive Chef; Managing Chef

Salary Range: $30,000 to $60,000 depending on institutional size

Employment Prospects: Numerous and varied

Advancement Prospects: Good

Best Geographical Location(s) for Position: Well distributed throughout the country; better where there is high-density population

Prerequisites:
    Education or Training—Vocational training or culinary academy, or in-service training in an institution kitchen
    Experience—All volume-cooking experience is beneficial
    Special Skills and Personality Traits—Good leadership skills to manage the staff of a large kitchen operation

CAREER LADDER

```
┌─────────────────────────────┐
│    Food Service Director     │
└─────────────────────────────┘

┌─────────────────────────────┐
│            Chef              │
└─────────────────────────────┘

┌─────────────────────────────┐
│            Cook              │
└─────────────────────────────┘
```

Position Description

The chef at an institution such as a hospital, school, prison, retirement residence, professional sports league—any kitchen that serves a large volume of food every day to the same people—has greater demands to provide variety and to meet specialized nutritional needs than does a restaurant chef.

An elderly hospital patient who has difficulty swallowing might expect to get a batch of small bowls filled with the equivalent of baby purees; an imaginative chef will cook and mince well-flavored food and shape it into a re-creation of its origins. Minced string beans can be mixed with mashed potatoes for binding and extruded through a pasta machine to look like slant-cut beans; cooked pork or chicken can be minced, blended, and shaped to resemble a chop or a drumstick. Hospital patients have to be encouraged to eat, and attractive food is more welcome than mush.

The chef in a hospital faces the greatest range of restrictions due to standard diets (liquid, bland, pureed, low-salt, low-fat) prescribed by the doctors, and sets of menus must be developed for each restriction. A chef for a retirement residence faces a similar challenge because of restrictions

due to health conditions (high cholesterol, high blood pressure, ulcers, diverticulitis, undergoing chemotherapy, poor appetite) or ethnic diversity, requiring individual menus. In a school kitchen the growth needs of young people need to be met with ample choices of protein and dietary minerals. In many of these work places there is also a staff nutritionist to provide input based on medical, lifestyle, sports activity, or age factors.

The chef hires and trains all the kitchen staff, which usually consists of two shifts. From the prep work before breakfast to the clean-up after dinner, the workday spans about 14 hours. The breakfast crew may do lunch prep, and the second shift may work both lunch and dinner. Kitchen workers in institutional kitchens have one characteristic that is unusual in restaurant kitchens: They stay for decades, moving up in job classification from dishroom to line cook over the years.

Such a large kitchen, preparing 3,000 meals a day or more, has to have a system; one system would be divided into bakery, salad prep, hot food, cafeteria, tray line, cold prep, and desserts. Menus are usually repeated on a three-week cycle or less, a one-week cycle for hospitals. One of the chef's first duties of the day is the production meeting to review any menu changes, inform cooks about new or discontinued dishes, and touch on essential standards—cleanliness, time schedule, controlling grease, using too much detergent—that may need reinforcement.

The chef is responsible for budget management; in addition to food costs there are labor costs, and equipment maintenance and replacement. The cost of meals per person per day can be very difficult to control if the number of people eating fluctuates widely, as in a hospital. Taking deliveries of fresh and staple ingredients is an all-day job, and it is one of the most important for cost controls.

Still another difference between institutional and restaurant cooking may be the involvement of a major food service company that manages the kitchen, imposes systems, and supplies most of the food; in this case the chef manages the workers and the service but does not have full authority over the quality and cost of the food.

Possibly the greatest difference, at least one that is touted by institutional chefs, is that the working hours are likely to be family-friendly daytime hours, 7:00 A.M. to 5:00 P.M.—even though it is still a 10-hour chef's day.

Salaries

Chefs' salaries range between $30,000 to $60,000 a year. An institutional chef's salary will be affected by the number of meals served a day and by length of service.

Employment Prospects

This area is a rich source of jobs. Although there is only one chef's job in each institutional kitchen, there are schools, boarding schools, colleges, universities, hospitals, rehabilitation centers, medical centers, country clubs, camps, retirement homes, and residential care communities everywhere.

Advancement Prospects

Since these jobs are coveted, they are not abandoned as freely as restaurant chefs switch kitchens. There is a security in seniority that is lacking in restaurant and hotel work, but advancement is more commonly accomplished by moving to a larger institution.

Best Geographical Location(s)

There are no blackouts on these jobs. They exist everywhere, and the more dense the population, the more institutions there are to serve it.

Education and Training

In addition to culinary training, a chef needs management skills. Culinary academies and vocational training schools provide both aspects of a chef's training.

Experience/Skills/Personality Traits

Any variety of kitchen experience is valuable—restaurant, club, camp, or church—especially if it involves volume cooking rather than cooking to order. In some parts of the United States, kitchen workers may be recent arrivals from non–English speaking countries, and rudimentary knowledge of the kitchen vocabulary in these second languages is helpful.

Unions/Associations

The American Culinary Federation is the professional group for chefs and apprentice trainees. In addition to local chapter meetings where the chef can become acquainted with other chefs in the community, ACF holds an annual meeting with educational workshops and seminars dealing both with culinary topics and business management.

The American Society of Hospital Food Service Administrators is a branch of the American Hospital Association with a support program for food service professionals in health care institutions.

Chefs in higher education facilities, colleges and universities, may be encouraged to join the National Association of College and University Food Service (NACUFS), especially if the school is active in that organization.

Tips for Entry

1. To develop an aptitude for volume cooking, volunteer to work in any church, school, or camp kitchen, and apply for the first job opportunity.
2. Investigate the nearest vocational training or community college culinary program; some schools have short-term courses to give workers a head start.
3. Locate the highest quality institutional kitchen in your area and ask the chef if he or she will consider training you in an ACF apprenticeship program.

INSTITUTIONAL HEAD COOK

CAREER PROFILE

Duties: Supervises each kitchen station and fills in gaps caused by vacations or illness; learns the work at every station; trains all new hires and cross trains where appropriate at additional stations; manages schedule and menu cycles; maintains sanitation and safety conditions.

Alternate Title(s): Head Cook; Kitchen Manager; *Chef Tourant*

Salary Range: $32,000 to $40,000 plus benefits

Employment Prospects: Plentiful

Advancement Prospects: Limited

Best Geographical Location(s) for Position: Everywhere in the country

Prerequisites:

Education or Training—Vocational trade/tech culinary certificate or on-the-job training in an institutional kitchen

Experience—Full understanding of culinary practices and techniques; personnel management experience

Special Skills and Personality Traits—Attention to detail; consistency; appreciation of well-prepared meals

CAREER LADDER

```
┌─────────────────────────────┐
│           Chef              │
└─────────────────────────────┘

┌─────────────────────────────┐
│         Head Cook           │
└─────────────────────────────┘

┌─────────────────────────────┐
│        Station Cook         │
└─────────────────────────────┘
```

Position Description

An institutional cook—in a hospital, school, country club, prison, camp, or retirement home—supervises the cooks at all the stations and is able to fill in for any of them in the case of vacation or illness. The variety of food preparation work ranges through salad preparation, sauces, cold food preparation, hot food preparation, bakery, cafeteria, tray line (hospitals and cafeterias), and desserts.

As the head cook or kitchen manager, he or she reports to the food service director of the institution, who is responsible for deciding the menus and their rotation (such as a five-week cycle) and who probably approves all the hiring and firing of kitchen staff.

The day-to-day operations of the kitchen are in the hands of the head cook. This starts with ordering and receiving all menu ingredients and supplies and supervising their proper storage. Food costs are directly impacted by the care taken to store food products properly, rotating stock so older items are used first, and vigilantly guarding against waste. In some kitchens, the lead cook calls staff meetings to review

policies and changes; if the executive chef calls these meetings, the head cook attends and is responsible for implementing any new decisions.

The head cook supervises the daily work of all the cooks and intervenes if anyone's work is not satisfactory, either by retraining or replacing the worker. The head cook is at every station with a fresh tasting spoon before any food goes out to the dining room to assure that the specs for each dish have been followed. For example, the surprise flavor of garlic in the tartar sauce has to be caught before it hits the plate and the palate; it gets thrown out and remade. Training the staff to follow standard sanitation procedures is a constant concern. Chopping blocks have to be correctly cleaned with acidulated water (vinegar, lemon, or chemical) after each use, and especially after cleaning or cutting fresh fish or poultry. Garlic can get in the tartar sauce if the board isn't cleaned thoroughly after crushing garlic and before the pickles, onions, and capers are minced for the sauce.

Health department inspections can happen at any time, and the kitchen must operate daily in a manner that will pass the most rigorous scrutiny for sanitation, safety, and food storage standards. Any equipment that is malfunctioning has to be serviced and repaired promptly or replaced, another responsibility of the head cook.

The head cook creates a smooth working environment for all the cooks, cleanup workers, and servers. Sometimes an institution provides food service in more than one location: dining room, cafeteria, snack bar, and tray service. Each of these areas may have a different menu and different food preparation specs that need to be followed. As new hires are integrated into the kitchen, the head cook trains each one in the systems and standards of the institution, even if the new hire is a very experienced cook or kitchen worker from another job.

Salaries

Pay levels vary depending on the size of the institution and the number of meals served each day. Geographic influences between low-income areas and more affluent communities are also reflected in the salaries. In a moderate-to-small institution that feeds 200 to 300 residents, inmates, patients, or students the head cook earns between $32,000 and $40,000 a year with paid vacation, sick leave, and insurance benefits.

Employment Prospects

There is a wide variety of jobs available in residential institutions, including schools, hospitals, homes, prisons, hotels, spas, some resorts, and country clubs. The culinary level will differ depending on the customer, but the work is substantially the same.

Advancement Prospects

With adequate training and work experience, advancement is possible, but many institutional cooks remain at the same work station by their own choice for decades.

Best Geographical Location(s)

Institutional cooking is in demand by businesses and major food service companies everywhere in the country.

Education and Training

Vocational trade schools with culinary programs provide a solid education in all aspects of institutional cooking. These schools are a good place for an aspiring cook to decide his or her preferences in cooking—baking, sauces, salads—and if everything is appealing, to gain the full complement of culinary skills as well as management training needed to be a lead cook. It is also possible to learn this work on the job, starting as a cook and moving through the stations to learn the gamut of required techniques. A cooperative supervisor may send a promising worker to a local trade/tech school for cooking and management training while continuing to pay salary.

Experience/Skills/Personality Traits

A head cook must have a full understanding of food preparation skills and a genuine appreciation for well-prepared dishes in every category. Attention to detail, consistency, a desire to produce quality food and a desire to please its recipients are all characteristics of a successful commercial cook.

Unions/Associations

In some major urban areas membership in the culinary workers union is a requirement, although membership may be obtained at the time of hiring.

There are some broad-based associations, the International Association of Culinary Professionals local guilds, that will appeal to cooks who want to upgrade their skills with master's classes and other educational programs.

Membership in the American Culinary Federation may be encouraged by the food service director, and this can lead to participating in ongoing educational opportunities, depending on the local chapter's program.

Tips for Entry

1. Locate a nearby college or trade/tech school with a culinary program and talk to the job counselor about local opportunities, including cooking at an entry level.
2. Using the yellow pages of your local phone book, call the food service department of hospitals, schools, and major hotels to ask about any job openings for beginners.
3. Take an entry-level job in an institutional kitchen and let your supervisor know that you are eager to learn about all of the stations.

COMMUNITY
AND SOCIAL SERVICE

EXECUTIVE DIRECTOR, COMMUNITY FOOD BANK

CAREER PROFILE

Duties: Solicits contributions of food and labor (volunteers) for the food bank program, provides short-term storage and arranges prompt distribution of supplies to organizations and families, hires and supervises a paid staff for office operations and food distribution, solicits funding for the program from the community and foundations, administers budgets, oversees benefit events, supervises a periodic newsletter and local publicity, produces an annual report on finance and program to the board of directors

Alternate Title(s): Food Bank Manager

Salary Range: $45,000 to $75,000 and up

Employment Prospects: Limited

Advancement Prospects: Fair

Best Geographical Location(s) for Position: Large cities with low-income population who need this support

Prerequisites:

Education or Training—A master's degree in organizational planning or in not-for-profit management can make the difference in being hired over other candidates.

Experience—Prior experience in community service organizations serving the needy; public speaking, benefit-event planning, and fund-raising will be beneficial.

Special Skills and Personality Traits—Team-building success, an innately cheerful nature during hard times and in depressing situations

CAREER LADDER

```
┌─────────────────────────────────┐
│       Board of Directors        │
└─────────────────────────────────┘

┌─────────────────────────────────┐
│   Food Bank Executive Director   │
└─────────────────────────────────┘

┌─────────────────────────────────┐
│        Deputy Director or        │
│ Food Bank Development Director   │
└─────────────────────────────────┘
```

Position Description

Food banks (and similar programs under different names) exist in cities and towns throughout the United States. They are community-sponsored programs to collect and distribute food to programs and individuals serving the homeless and the hungry of all ages, backgrounds, and ethnic origin. Incorporated under not-for-profit regulations, they are governed by a board of directors, usually representing broad community interests—banking law, accounting, business, medicine, advertising, education, and publishing. A typical mission statement would include their intention to collect and distribute nutritious foods, provide health and culinary education, and to network with the community to feed the hungry.

The job of the executive director is to keep all the above goals in constant forward motion. A paid staff will be responsible for office operations, computer hardware and software, publicity and public relations, fund-raising, and accounting. The collection and distribution staff will consist of an operations manager, warehouse managers, truck drivers, and inventory managers. Using either a pyramid arrangement or direct reporting, the executive director is responsible for the smooth operation of these various activities.

Throughout the year, the executive director solicits sources for contribution of food and labor (volunteer workers) to the program, supports civic organizations who plan and produce benefit gala events (such as Share Our Strength's annual Chef's Dinners across the United States), directs the publicity and public relations manager on placement of news releases to local periodicals and a periodic newsletter to the bank's mailing list of supporters. He or she also recruits, hires, trains, motivates, and fires staff, reports regularly to the governing board of directors, and prepares and distributes an annual report of operations. The executive director's every effort leads to more needy people within its operating area receiving food and learning how to use it most productively for the benefit of their families.

Additionally, it is the job of the executive director to participate in community events, maintaining a visible presence in the city or towns of the food bank's operations. This involves seeking speaking engagements where the director can increase community awareness of the bank, explaining what it does and how it does it, thereby recruiting individuals in the audience to support the bank's program, either personally with volunteerism, with cash contributions, or generally by passing on to colleagues and friends the message that the executive director has delivered.

As part of the nationwide network of executives working in the social services community, the director attends one or more training conferences every year. These are places to interact with counterparts from other communities and to share information about what processes are growing or waning at home, while learning about equivalent changes in other states and cities.

Salaries
Salaries for food bank executive directors are influenced by the size of the community served, the level of community support in the form of financial sponsorship, and the education, prior experience, and skills of the individual. The salary range is between $45,000 and $75,000 and up.

Employment Prospects
Usually a single food bank serves a large city or an entire county. There may be other related programs in the same vicinity. (See the position profiles for Restaurant Food Runners Dispatcher from restaurants and Prepared Meals Program Manager.)

Advancement Prospects
Advancement means moving to a larger or better-funded program elsewhere. Other community service organizations—Salvation Army, rescue missions, halfway houses,

and family service organizations—provide some of the same service and have most of the same executive needs; such jobs are comparable to directing a food bank.

Best Geographical Location(s)
These jobs are available nationwide in cities and large towns or any place with a low-income population that needs this support.

Education and Training
A master's degree in organizational planning or in not-for-profit management will result in preference in hiring and/or a higher salary in these jobs. Completion of specific certification training that directly applies to community and social service work is also beneficial. A typical educational background would consist of a B.S. degree in psychology followed by a master's in social work, planning and administration.

Experience/Skills/Personality Traits
Any prior experience, paid or volunteer, in privately managed social service programs will prove useful. Benefit-event planning, public speaking experience, and existing contacts, both social and professional, in the community will all prove effective in publicizing the agency, its benefits, and its needs.

Fund-raising skills, team building, creativity in applying old ideas to new situations, and an outgoing nature will be some of the first tests of a director. The work involved in these jobs needs a person with a caring nature, who recognizes the immense needs and is willing to use all the energy available to meet them.

Unions/Associations
The Association of Fundraising Professionals (AFP) (formerly known as National Society of Fund Raising Executives, NSFRE) is a membership organization that manages an annual conference, provides professional certification, and oversees continuing education.

Tips for Entry
1. Offer to volunteer for the local food bank in any capacity that interests you—from warehouse assistance to benefit-event planning. If the fit is comfortable, let the executive director know you would be interested in a paying job with the bank.
2. Contact the development director (fund-raising manager) of the food bank and ask about any volunteer opportunities; if the work is enjoyable, let them know you would like a paid job with the bank.

PREPARED MEALS PROGRAM MANAGER

CAREER PROFILE

Duties: Securing adequate funding, administering the budget, developing appropriate menus and ingredient and supply sources, maintaining a public-health-approved cooking facility, and scheduling staff and volunteers to cook, package, and deliver meals and companionship to the program's clients on a reliable schedule

Alternate Title(s): Program Director

Salary Range: $24,000 to $48,000

Employment Prospects: Limited

Advancement Prospects: Limited

Best Geographical Location(s) for Position: Cities and towns with medical centers and areas with mild winters that attract senior citizens

Prerequisites:

Education or Training—No specific requirements, just enthusiasm

Experience—Quantity cooking, for large groups, and previous fund-raising success are helpful

Special Skills and Personality Traits—Compassion and ability to motivate a team

CAREER LADDER

```
┌─────────────────────────────┐
│        Director of          │
│  Not-for-Profit Corporation │
└─────────────────────────────┘

┌─────────────────────────────┐
│       Prepared Meals        │
│      Program Manager        │
└─────────────────────────────┘

┌─────────────────────────────┐
│     Cooks and Delivery      │
│       Crew Manager          │
└─────────────────────────────┘
```

Position Description

Programs that deliver nutritious meals to the housebound—elderly, physically handicapped, or suffering from a life-threatening condition—are usually run by local government agencies or by nonprofit organizations, although there are some that are independent, run by one or a few individuals who have found the means without organizational funding and support services. Regardless of whether the support system exists inside or outside of the distribution unit, the program manager is responsible for seeing that adequate funding is available, administering the budget, developing appropriate menus and ingredient and supply sources, maintaining a public-health-approved cooking facility, and scheduling staff and volunteers to cook, package, and deliver meals and companionship to the program's clients on a reliable schedule.

The key to success in these programs is financial support from the community. Whether the program is guaranteed by a local government agency or a nonprofit organization, annual budgets must be projected containing all the expected and unexpected expenses, usually starting with rental of an appropriate kitchen facility and utilities service. Any shortfalls between the budget and allocated funds have to be rethought, and if essential, a sponsor or a grant to cover the budget item must be found. Independent programs and those that have incorporated as not-for-profit entities have a never-ending process of fund-raising from the public as part of their schedule.

Budgeting for a food program starts with lease negotiations to rent the space and public health approval of the kitchen where meals will be cooked and packaged. An alternative to a sole-use space is sharing a kitchen in a dinner-only restaurant; the meals program arranges to use the space in the morning and leave it clean by 11 A.M. when the first cooks come to work. Another opportunity is the use of a church kitchen. At least one (and preferably more) of the kitchen staff has to be trained and certified in safe food practice. Appropriate recipes must be gathered and tested, and menus developed. Only then can food costs and preparation time/labor costs of each recipe be figured. Food packaging, for refrigerator and freezer storage and for microwave and oven heating has to be selected and priced into the budget. Refrigerator space and storage closets may be rentable, or the program may need to find off-premises solutions. Liability insurance is a costly item in a food program budget, especially for an independent program.

These programs usually deliver meals to their clients on a limited schedule, once or twice a week to supply three to six days of meals. Cooks have to be scheduled for the days when meals are prepared; shopping and picking up donated goods takes additional time every week. The crew that packages the finished food for clients may be independent of the cooking staff and work under the supervision of the manager or someone who is concerned about the nurturing impression the client will have when it is received. Those who deliver the meals are chosen for their compassion and their respect for the individual's self-esteem. The visit from the food program may be one of the few social contacts the needy person has every week.

The manager is usually responsible for any publicity or public relations outreach into the community. This can be as simple as a quarterly newsletter to recognize the individuals who have contributed time, products, or money and to identify needs the program has for equipment, volunteers, or referrals of additional clients. It may also be necessary to hold one or more fund-raising events in the community; this encourages the community to take responsibility for the program.

Salaries

Fortunately, the person most interested in doing this work is usually doing it for the inner satisfaction of helping his or her community and making life better for the needy, because salaries are necessarily low. A not-for-profit organization with a high-powered board of directors and broad fund-raising capabilities will pay the most, up to $48,000 a year for full-time employment. Local government agencies will pay on a scale that parallels other government jobs, ranging from $24,000 and up, depending on the number of hours worked per week.

Employment Prospects

Many of these programs were set up originally by the people who hold them, and they rarely have an opening at the manager level. A community may have more than one such program, each targeting a different group of recipients. When there is a call for manager applicants, it is usually filled from inside, or from the staff of similar programs in the community. The best chance of getting the job is to be employed at a lower level and to let the manager know you want to advance.

Advancement Prospects

Advancement in these programs may not be to a higher salary, but to a larger or more ambitious program in the community, one looking for a manager with broader skills.

Best Geographical Location(s)

Cities and large towns, those with medical centers, and in southern and Pacific Coast states with warmer climates that attract the elderly are most likely locations.

Education and Training

No specific study or training is required for these jobs, but any job experience working with people and building teamwork units is useful.

Experience/Skills/Personality Traits

These jobs use the manager's unique skills to motivate staff and enlist community involvement in the organization's goals and mission statement. The manager is constantly soliciting contributions of products and services to keep costs under control. Volunteers must be recruited for meal delivery and social companionship with the clients. Patrons must be recruited to sponsor, plan, and execute benefit parties that encourage community support of the program. For all of these needs, a manager who has a deep-seated sense of compassion serves to enhance the program.

Unions/Associations

There are no membership organizations that serve people in these jobs. Locally, there may be a consortium of public service or not-for-profit programs that functions as a support group.

Tips for Entry

1. Work as a volunteer in one or more of these programs to learn if this work fits comfortably with your skills and interests.
2. Attend any benefit parties for such programs in your community and get acquainted with the staff and the manager; let them know you are interested in working for them.

RESTAURANT FOOD RUNNERS DISPATCHER

CAREER PROFILE

Duties: Establishing and maintaining communication with the social service programs that distribute food to needy individuals and setting schedules to pick up food from restaurants, cafés and gala dinners

Alternate Title(s): Program Manager

Salary Range: $18,000 for half time; $12/hour to $18/hour

Employment Prospects: Limited

Advancement Prospects: Very limited

Best Geographical Location(s) for Position: Wherever there is a sizeable and good-hearted restaurant presence

Prerequisites:
Education or Training—None needed
Experience—Any delivery work
Special Skills and Personality Traits—Generous, patient, cheerful, persuasive, and motivating

CAREER LADDER

```
┌─────────────────────────────────┐
│   Manager in Food Services Agency │
│            for Needy              │
└─────────────────────────────────┘

┌─────────────────────────────────┐
│      Food Runner's Dispatcher     │
└─────────────────────────────────┘

┌─────────────────────────────────┐
│           Food Drivers            │
└─────────────────────────────────┘
```

Position Description

The manager of a restaurant-to-rescue-mission food runner program can either be an employee of a participating restaurant or someone from the receiving end. Depending on the volume of food transported weekly, with modest financial support from restaurants or the community a separate entity may be created to pay a manager/dispatcher as well as the other minimal expenses of the program—liability insurance, telephone, and gasoline. The manager/dispatcher is responsible for establishing and maintaining communication with the social service programs that give the food to needy individuals and for setting up schedules to get usable food from restaurants and cafés as well as from gala dinners and other fund-raisers.

A key component in many communities for these programs is an established food bank, where supermarkets, grocery stores, and farms contribute usable but unsalable food to be distributed. With a food runners program, the significant difference is that the food is already cooked and ready to eat, or at the least it has been kitchen-prepped in the restaurant and is ready to cook and eat. This is food that would otherwise be thrown away.

Since the heaviest volume of restaurant donations occurs on the weekends, the dispatcher may also need to arrange for interim fresh food storage from businesses that are closed on Sunday and Monday. This can be well-ventilated warehousing for shelf-stable foods, walk-in refrigeration for cooked dishes and prepped ingredients, or merely dry storage for bulk products.

The manager has to know where the greatest needs are among the multiple local agencies providing meals for low-income seniors and families, homeless and rescue mission clients, and ill or handicapped persons who are unable to cook for themselves. The needs in any medium-to-large community are endless, but there is also a grid of social service programs that help identify the needy for a program that is designed to meet the needs.

Once the delivery destinations are programmed, the manager must maintain day-to-day contact with a key person at the contributing restaurants. It is quite feasible for a restaurant worker to deliver his or her own contribution (even pick up from other nearby restaurants) directly to the facility or agency that will use the food.

In addition to regular restaurant food, the manager works with gala benefit events, which usually have a surfeit of food and beverages to justify their high ticket prices. This bonanza of prepared food has to be preprogrammed even though the actual volume of the contribution won't be known until the day of the event. Since the restaurants usually send staff as well as their "name" chef, those people can be asked to deliver their surplus directly to the shelters where it will be welcomed.

The manager or sponsors of the program spend as much time as they can in fund-raising to cover expenses. This is done by writing proposals to established charities, such as United Way, and direct mail solicitation of a carefully compiled mailing list of supporters.

As soon as the program will warrant a deputy manager, the creation of this position will make the never-ending need for the services less stressful and less likely to cause "burnout" during the year. This goal is one that the manager should anticipate from the very start of the program.

Salaries

Too often, these jobs are seriously underpaid. Because the work of scheduling pickups and deliveries always comes first, the manager may give insufficient effort to seeking financial support from the community. At the very least, working half time, the manager should be guaranteed an annual salary of $18,000. It doesn't always happen.

Employment Prospects

This job is the genre of "find a need and fill it." If the job already exists, the manager has probably been the instigator. The possibility of becoming a deputy manager is something an eager candidate can explore; there may be the opportunity to duplicate the services in another area of the city, first confirming that the restaurant community is there and is interested.

Advancement Prospects

Advancement, once a person is established in this type of work, can come through offers to join other programs or to move upward into charity management.

Best Geographical Location(s)

There has to be a restaurant community of sufficient size to make a meaningful contribution to the poverty needs in the area. This is usually present in medium to large cities.

Education and Training

No specific education or training is required to set up a food distribution program for the needy.

Experience/Skills/Personality Traits

A big heart, infinite patience, a cheerful personality in the face of adversity, a talent for persuading contributors, and the ability to build a team and get the very best energy, reliability, and dedication from volunteers and staff are essential.

Unions/Associations

The local chapter of the United Way may have a support group for participating agencies. There are no unions for this work.

Tips for Entry

1. If your community has a food bank, talk to the director about how realistic starting this type of food collection from local restaurants would be.
2. If there is already a food runner program in your community, talk to the manager about volunteering with the goal of moving into a paid position.
3. If you have good contacts with the restaurant owners and chefs in your community, explore their interests in starting food distribution to the needy.

FARM TOUR MANAGER

CAREER PROFILE

Duties: Solicits participation from farmers and attendance from schools and recreation department field trip programs, develops a budget and a tour plan with the cooperation of the participating farmers, determines who will fund the plan, initiates publicity, signs up schools and organizations and tests the program.

Alternate Title(s): none

Salary Range: $24,000 to $60,000

Employment Prospects: Limited

Advancement Prospects: Limited

Best Geographical Location(s) for Position: Upscale urban areas where farmer's markets create interest among residents

Prerequisites:
  Education or Training—None required
  Experience—Teaching both children and adults
  Special Skills and Personality Traits—Persuasiveness to enlist farmer participation; entertaining to hold tourist attention; entrepreneurial to start program successfully

CAREER LADDER

```
┌─────────────────────────────────┐
│   Farm Owners or Tour Sponsors   │
└─────────────────────────────────┘

┌─────────────────────────────────┐
│        Farm Tour Manager         │
└─────────────────────────────────┘

┌─────────────────────────────────┐
│    Farm Guides and Teachers      │
└─────────────────────────────────┘
```

Position Description

Unless a farming family has at least one adult member to set up and manage incoming tours, this is work that will be hired; ideally it will be someone who has been a part of the farmer's market community. The farm tour manager will work with the interested farmers to learn what their goals are in opening their farm property to visitors and work with local schools and businesses to learn what groups want to provide tour takers.

Farm tours attract schoolchildren, senior citizen activities groups, and travel/study farmers from other states and regions. With weekly farmers markets becoming commonplace in many cities and towns, public awareness of fresh-picked produce and of the farming families who live nearby has mushroomed into curiosity on the part of customers to see the farms and talk to the farmers. Senior activities groups are often herded to interesting parks, museums, and historic gardens as some of the programs of their residence facility or by joining a social group sponsored by the local bank or recreation department. Many children of the last 25 to 30 years (and, in many cases, their parents as well) survive almost entirely on processed food: frozen meals, boxes of "add water, stir, and bake," and fast-food takeout. The astonishment and delight they show as they walk around the crop-rich farms is cemented when they are given a sample of fresh vegetables and fruit to take home with them. If the farm is making and selling value-added products, such as homemade preserves, they may offer them for purchase, and take-home sample bags of farm product can be priced into the tour.

Once the manager develops a pattern for the tours and identifies the potential tourists, unless the farm is willing to underwrite the costs of the program, the manager will seek community funding to cover expenses: salary, vehicles, telephone and computer costs, and liability insurance. Sponsorship may be available from the local farmers market organization or with a "seed" grant through a community foundation.

The manager's initial work is to develop a budget and a tour plan with the cooperation of the participating (one or more) farmers, determine who (farmers, sponsors, both) will fund the plan, and initiate publicity to get the word out, sign up schools and organizations (who can provide safe transportation) and begin to test the program for a limited time (several weeks or up to two months). Once tours are underway, the manager will stay in close communication with the farmers to hear their comments and suggestions for any changes.

A related program, the growing nationwide movement of Community Supported Agriculture (CSA) has created a new kind of customer who subscribes for a year at a time to weekly fresh produce from a local farm. The customer drives to the farm once a week, returning the farm basket or tub from the prior week and picking up a new basket filled with the week's harvest. The farmer may also have written an informal newsletter listing what uncommon foods (persimmons, kohlrabi, bok choy, golden Yukon potatoes) may be in the basket and include some recipes or hints on preparing them. Subscribers often bring their children or friends with them to visit the farm—an informal hour.

Salaries

Jobs such as this one, which depend on the efforts of the jobholder to find sponsors and agencies to fund the project, are quasi-entrepreneurial, and the jobholders literally have to create their own income and benefits. A realistic salary for this work, especially since it has such a strong marketing feature, would be in the range of $24,000 to $60,000 and up, depending on the number of hours worked a week, the manager's former salary history, and the willingness of the sponsors to approve the budgeted salary.

Employment Prospects

Farm tourism is a new and growing field. Most managers of these programs have initiated their own job. Within a few years, some job turnover is to be expected, and then there will be prospects for newcomers into this field of work.

Advancement Prospects

A chance to move to a larger tourism program or to one paying a higher salary would most likely require a geographical move on the part of the manager. By participating in the statewide direct market association, the manager can stay informed about all tourism programs being developed and watch for a chance to made an advancement move.

Best Geographical Location(s)

Regions or states with moderate climate that are friendly to year-round farming—eastern Washington, Oregon, Califor-

nia, Nevada, Arizona, New Mexico, and Texas—will be able to sustain a year-round tourism business. A manager who wants to take time off in the winter for, say, skiing, might consider starting this business in a state with major snow sports—Colorado, Montana, or Utah. Within any chosen state, upscale urban areas are more likely to support direct market farming (farmers markets), which is where these jobs exist.

Education and Training

There are no certificates or college degrees needed to establish and run one of these programs. Any schooling and/or reading about marketing is helpful.

Experience/Skills/Personality Traits

Employees of a successful farmers market association will have the necessary work contacts with local farmers, a history of being part of the movement, and the respect of farm families who may be interested in bringing tourism onto their land. This will be essential in the start-up phase of the project. Management experience of any sort is helpful, especially sales management. Teaching experience will provide tricks for getting the visitor's attention, making the visit interesting and entertaining, and result in the visitor being an ambassador to encourage their friends to participate. If the program includes additional staff, skill in team-building will be needed.

Unions/Associations

The North American Farmers' Direct Marketing Association holds an annual conference in January and can supply information on individual state farmers market associations, most of which also hold a yearly conference.

Tips for Entry

1. Ask for a volunteer job with your local farmers market association, helping at the weekly markets, to get acquainted with the participating farmers as an insider.
2. Find the nearest farm tourism program and write or phone asking to visit; if you are comfortable with the people and like the way their program is set up, ask for a job in order to learn how it was developed and how it works.

SPECIALTY FOOD PRODUCTS

CHEESE MAKER

CAREER PROFILE

Duties: Purchases milk product for cheese making; supervises production from milk delivery through finished product and controls product quality; trains cheese-making workers.

Alternate Title(s): Food Technologist; Dairy Product Technologist; Plant Chemist; Production Manager

Salary Range: With food technology education and degree, a starting salary of $25,000 with advancement based on experience up to $48,000

Employment Prospects: Limited

Advancement Prospects: Limited

Best Geographical Location(s) for Position: Areas with lots of dairy farms to supply milk product

Prerequisites:
   Education or Training—Food technology degree, not necessarily in a dairy-related field, or apprenticeship training
   Experience—Food production in almost any field; work with fermentation and yeasts
   Special Skills and Personality Traits—Scientific curiosity, people management and training or teaching

CAREER LADDER

```
┌─────────────────────────┐
│     Vice President,     │
│   Charge of Production  │
└─────────────────────────┘

┌─────────────────────────┐
│      Cheese Maker       │
└─────────────────────────┘

┌─────────────────────────┐
│  Cheese Maker's Assistant │
└─────────────────────────┘
```

Position Description

A cheese maker in a commercial plant is responsible for the production of cheese products to rigid standards of quality, including taste, texture, shelf life, appearance and volume.

The raw materials for a cheese product are milk—from cows, goats, buffalo, or sheep—and a fermenting agent. Cheese is a food that has survived for centuries, originating as a way to preserve milk. Its invention was accidental; nomadic tribes loaded skin pouches filled with milk on their camels or horses to travel, and the movement hastened the separation of the curds and whey, creating cheese. With the development of refrigeration, cheeses are now made by preference rather than necessity or accident.

Cheese production is a process that starts with fermentation, and continues through aging, packaging, and selling. Each step has its own time demands and industry standards, depending on the variety of cheese being produced. Dry cheeses, such as Parmesan or Asiago, must be carefully aged to protect their flavor and grating qualities while fresh cheeses, such as mozzarella, are sold within days of their production, and freshness brings a higher price.

A cheese maker uses the best-quality fresh milk that is available, either from his or her own herds or purchased from nearby dairies. The quality of the milk is dependent on the feed of the animals, the milk's storage and cleanliness, and the season of the year, so the cheese maker is constantly checking the standards of the dairy manager wherever he or she buys the milk. Milk delivery must be timed to provide sufficient flow for the cheese-making schedule.

Fermentation is a chemical process utilizing microbes and enzymes. The cheese maker constantly seeks improvement of the product, both by monitoring ongoing fermentation and by constant reading and researching for new products and equipment to use.

Aging requires temperature and humidity controls either in natural caves or under refrigeration. The design of the plant, and especially any enlargement of the premises, directly affects the cheese; the cheese maker is involved in all of these decisions. Aging of specific cheeses is government-regulated; for example, blue-veined cheeses must be aged at least 60 days, and high-quality "blues" are aged six months before they can be packaged and shipped.

Cheese making is a hands-on process and very labor intensive. The cheese maker hires, trains, fires, and promotes workers from the milk receiving stage through to the technicians handling the finished product.

Salaries

Many cheese makers own their own business, so salary or income figures are not standardized. A recently-graduated food technologist hired to manage cheese production would start at $25,000 a year and could advance to $48,000.

Employment Prospects

Although American specialty cheeses are becoming more available as demand grows, there are a limited number of producers, and jobs are limited.

Advancement Prospects

There is usually only one cheese maker to a company, so advancement may only be possible by moving higher into management within the company. Another form of advancement is to take a job with a larger or more prestigious cheese company.

Best Geographical Location(s)

Cheese making is done in dairy country, the rural areas where the special herds flourish.

Education and Training

Most cheese companies will require a cheese maker to have a college degree in food technology, although not necessarily in a dairy-related field. A cheese maker may also get training as an apprentice, working alongside a skilled craftsman who enjoys sharing his or her knowledge.

Experience/Skills/Personality Traits

Scientific curiosity is a valuable asset for making a cheese product and especially for troubleshooting the production of a living organism. Managing people requires consistency and a natural inclination for teaching. Pride in the necessary workmanship that produces a superior product is essential.

Unions/Associations

The American Cheese Society is an educationally-oriented professional association dedicated to quality, handcrafted, American-made, specialty and farmstead cheeses, and they hold an annual educational conference.

The Institute of Food Technologists publishes a monthly newsletter and a bimonthly journal, and holds an annual meeting and a food exposition.

Tips for Entry

1. Write to the American Cheese Society for the names of any cheese companies near you, and contact them about available jobs.
2. Talk to the dean of the nearest college or university that has a dairy program about opportunities in cheese production.
3. Check with your local University Extension farm adviser about cheese making in your area, even farm cheeses made and sold at a local market, where you might work in exchange for learning.

SAUSAGE AND HAM PRODUCER

CAREER PROFILE

Duties: Supervises all stages of sausage making and brining, curing, and smoking of related meat products; responsible for quality control, especially sanitation, during production and the marketing of meat products

Alternate Title(s): *Charcutier*

Salary Range: $25,000 to $48,000

Employment Prospects: Fair to moderate, both for large commercial production plants and small boutique companies

Advancement Prospects: Good

Best Geographical Location(s) for Position: Areas with a strong ethnic population having a culinary tradition of sausage dishes

Prerequisites:
  Education or Training—Meat processing education in agricultural school or culinary academy
  Experience—Any recipe development experience
  Special Skills and Personality Traits—Trained flavor palate to fine-tune seasonings; physical strength for heavy lifting and carrying

CAREER LADDER

```
┌─────────────────────────────┐
│    Charcuterie Manager      │
└─────────────────────────────┘

┌─────────────────────────────┐
│  Sausage and Ham Producer   │
└─────────────────────────────┘

┌─────────────────────────────┐
│       Meat Trainee          │
└─────────────────────────────┘
```

Position Description

In Europe, the genius who creates the flavorful variety of sausages and smoked and cured meats is called a *charcutier,* a fancy word for which there is no English equivalent. It is a branch of butchering founded on the pig that has a restrictive tradition: the work is limited exclusively to males in France, a prejudice that does not extend to the United States.

Spotless cleanliness is the essential characteristic of the sausage maker's workplace, a condition impressed during apprenticeship or schooling and enforced by government regulations. The sausage maker is totally responsible for the quality control in every aspect of food handling and production: vats are giant stainless steel caldrons; floors are made of textured concrete sloping to drains; workers are garbed in freshly-laundered whites and their hair is restrained with caps or nets. The workplace has to be maintained in pristine condition at all times for the good of the product and in anticipation of public health and U.S.D.A. inspection agents.

The romantic tradition of sausage making and cured meats goes back to Roman times. For centuries it was a preservative process to extend the useful life of some freshly-butchered meats. Hams—cured, smoked, hung—can be kept a year without spoiling. Hot dogs, bratwurst, salami, Polish sausage, Italian sausage, and headcheese all come from the same traditional sources; many now incorporate beef, veal, lamb, and turkey, but the preserving spices are still the *quatre épices* (four spices) of peppercorns, cloves, nutmeg, and either cinnamon or ginger, plus mustard seed, allspice, coriander, and herbs of thyme, marjoram, parsley, and chives.

A sausage maker must be trained in historic recipes in order to experiment with new flavors for his or her products. The scientific understanding of preservation methods extends through brining, smoking, and salting. These methods were devised long before refrigeration made them unnecessary; now they are treasured for the flavor and texture they add to the meat.

It starts with the meat, and most sausage makers are fastidious about the wholesale source of their meats. A careful marriage is built between the sausage maker and his or her supplier, but it may be subject to flirtations with other suppliers who promise to deliver a better quality meat. Meats that require less trimming, and thus less waste, are always preferred. Animal fats must be pure and white; they make up as much as 30 percent of the product.

In the large curing vats, where legs and shoulders of pork are becoming hams, and briskets of beef are being corned, the degree of saltiness is tested constantly to ensure that it is doing its curing work as well as protecting room-temperature meat from spoiling. There are devices that monitor brine intensity, but German-trained old-timers drop a raw egg into the brine; if it floats, okay; if it sinks, add salt.

As in any food processing plant, the maintenance of cleanliness consumes a good portion of time of many workers. Everything is hosed down, cleaned with antiseptics, and protected against unclean air, and the workers are as aseptic as uniforms and gloves can guarantee. The constant training and performance standards for plant workers are the sausage maker's responsibilities.

Finally, there is the job of selling and delivering the product. It may be to counters in the front of the building, or it may be by air shipment, refrigerated, to quality delicatessens across the country. Some sausage companies do the bulk of their business by mail order to retail customers. Seasonal marketing influences the balance of product that is made—more hams near Easter and New Year's, corned beef in March, sausages when summer grills are in use.

Salaries

Meat processing jobs are subject to union membership and union pay rates. If the manager has culinary training in an academy or an agricultural college, his or her salary would range from $25,000 (starting) to $48,000 (experienced).

Employment Prospects

Commercial brands of sausage are expanding the space they occupy in supermarkets, indicating that more jobs are available in production. Simultaneously, small sausage and cured meat companies are proliferating in major urban areas and even in regional pockets where mail order delivers their refrigerated product to the customers.

Advancement Prospects

With appropriate culinary training or meat product schooling, a plant worker can expect to be promoted. By working

for a specialty producer of choice sausages, pâtés, and terrines, an employee can learn the technical skills to qualify for promotion or for employment in a larger company.

Best Geographical Location(s)

Some ethnic pockets of the United States have a sausage and ham tradition from the immigration of Germans, Swiss, Austrians, Poles, and Eastern Europeans; Jewish cuisines have strong ties to veal sausage dishes. New York and Wisconsin are two productive sausage states.

Education and Training

Meat processing is taught in agricultural colleges and polytechnic schools; this education gives the student the technical background needed. *Charcuterie* is taught in culinary academies and cooking schools; this training gives the student a familiarity with aspects of flavor, texture, and variations.

Experience/Skills/Personality Traits

The single, most important characteristic for a sausage and ham maker to have is a flavor palate to judge his or her own product. Although the work is a scientific process, the success of the product in the marketplace depends on its flavor.

A sausage and ham maker must be physically strong to carry the meats, move vats, brine, smokers, and process large quantities of meat and seasonings into casings.

Unions/Associations

Depending on local area conditions, the sausage and ham maker may need to belong to the meat cutters union.

There are trade associations for those producers who are marketing their products over a large area. The sausage and ham maker may want to join a broad-based culinary association, such as a local culinary guild or the International Association of Culinary Professionals.

Tips for Entry

1. Take a class or two from a local cooking school in sausage making, pâtés, terrines, and charcuterie to learn whether or not you like the production process.
2. Visit any local sausage-making business and ask about employment to learn on the job.
3. Investigate the meat processing course at your local agricultural college, and discuss job placement opportunities for graduates.

SAVORY AND SWEET CONDIMENTS MAKER

CAREER PROFILE

Duties: Purchases and manages timely delivery of ingredients and packaging materials; hires, trains, and schedules production workers to match delivery needs based on orders; maintains equipment; ensures product quality control

Alternate Title(s): Production Manager

Salary Range: $22,000 to $35,000

Employment Prospects: Numerous

Advancement Prospects: Good to Excellent

Best Geographical Location(s) for Position: Anywhere, urban and rural, where products originate

Prerequisites:
　Education or Training—Food technology education or on-the-job training
　Experience—Supervising employees in any business; quality control
　Special Skills and Personality Traits—Concern for quality; teaching skills for worker training; natural ability to organize

CAREER LADDER

```
┌─────────────────────────────┐
│     Company President        │
└─────────────────────────────┘

┌─────────────────────────────┐
│     Condiments Maker         │
└─────────────────────────────┘

┌─────────────────────────────┐
│       Plant Worker           │
└─────────────────────────────┘
```

Position Description

Condiments, otherwise known as jams, jellies, mustards, salsas and seasonings, are commonly begun as a business that is converted from a holiday production to a cottage industry, and moves into rented space as it grows.

The entrepreneur behind the company often started with a single recipe for mulled wine spices, candied citrus peels, a new chutney made of dried fruits, salad dressing, fruit syrups, or herb-infused vinegars. By starting small and creating a market for the product in increments, a cottage-industry producer can survive the start-up financial demands as long as he or she meets the local and state public health and registration requirements for food.

The source of raw ingredients is the challenge of increasing the business output from 10 pounds of product to 1,000 pounds of product. If the ingredients are spices, the producer might be dealing directly with an importer as effectively as with a wholesaler. If the ingredients are fresh berries, the producer might be dealing with the produce market or venturing into the fields to buy directly from a grower.

With ingredients on hand, the producer determines which products to make and how much of them to produce. Batch sizes have to be standardized. A system has to be devised to create a smooth process from receiving the ingredients through preparing the product and finishing with packaging and shipping. The minimum number of employees has to be selected, hired, and trained. It may be a matter of months before the system works smoothly, with periodic adjustments and staff retraining to get it right.

Packaging presents the next challenge. The producer has to find sources for jars or boxes, decide on new product names and label designs, and choose a printing company. If the product is being marketed in supermarkets, the industry will influence package size and shape. If it is being sold through specialty-food stores, the producer may need to create and provide display racks and other materials.

Once the product is available to customers, in stores and/or by mail order, it has to be advertised to reach its audience. The producer may also select a number of trade shows to attend and display the products.

When the business is new, the producer may secure a small business loan, working with SCORE for business advice at every stage of the start-up. (SCORE, Service Corps of Retired Executives, is an organization of experienced executives who are available for individual counseling and advice. SCORE is operated by the U.S. Small Business Administration. It is usually listed in the phone book under "U.S. Government—SBA.") As the business grows, the producer develops his or her relationship with the bank, an insurance broker, advertising agency, attorney, accountant, marketing consultant, and trade association for the specialty food.

Salaries

The production line manager of a condiments company earns from $22,000 to $35,000 depending on the size of the company, the volume of product, and sales. A single-line company with 10 to 20 employees would pay the manager up to $60,000 a year.

Employment Prospects

Hundreds of these companies are started each year. Employees who start with the company at the first growth stage usually stay to become managers as the product line develops. Because these are such new companies, starting salaries are low, but an ownership interest in the company as it succeeds financially is a type of repayment for the low-wage years.

Advancement Prospects

Assuming the company succeeds in the marketplace, there is steady advancement possible as more employees are hired. A successful manager from one start-up company will be in demand by other companies and can use job hopping as a means of advancement.

Best Geographical Location(s)

Good locations for these jobs are plentiful. The companies are in cities and in farm communities in every state.

Education and Training

A food technology course will cover most plant management aspects and bring a manager up-to-speed quickly. This is also the type of work one learns on the job.

Experience/Skills/Personality Traits

A constant concern with the quality of the product and an understanding of the factors that contribute to it are essential to produce a successful line.

A manager is constantly training—new employees, long-term employees in new skills, and retraining workers who need improvement. The patience, humor, and organization required of any teacher are important to a manager. As these companies expand, product development is the key to growth. The vision to identify appropriate ideas for additional products and the skill to create new products are invaluable.

Unions/Associations

A graduate food technologist will benefit from membership in the Institute of Food Technologists.

The company may choose to join the National Association for the Specialty Food Trade, Inc.

A manager may join the Association of Food Industries, a trade association.

Any of the company's executives will be eligible for individual or company membership in the International Association of Culinary Professionals.

Tips for Entry

1. Wangle a pass to any specialty food trade show in your area and cruise the aisles to talk to the owners and managers of small food production companies. Learn whether they are planning to hire and arrange to visit their plant.
2. Check the catalog of your community college for food technology courses and make an appointment with a faculty adviser to learn about job placement for graduates and certificate holders.
3. Call the University Extension Service in your county and question both the farm adviser and the home adviser about small companies that may be experiencing growth and be looking for more workers.

PLANT OPERATIONS MANAGER

CAREER PROFILE

Duties: Responsible for every stage of production from ingredient delivery through processing, plant and equipment maintenance, supervision of workers, quality control, and packaging for shipment

Alternate Title(s): None

Salary Range: $22,000 to $120,000

Employment Prospects: Excellent

Advancement Prospects: Very good

Best Geographical Location(s) for Position: Well distributed throughout the United States, especially in urban centers with an ample work force

Prerequisites:

Education or Training—College degree in food technology or engineering; vocational certificate in heavy equipment maintenance and repair

Experience—Production supervision and human relations development in any plant or factory; food processing experience of any kind

Special Skills and Personality Traits—Systems-oriented to develop the most efficient production line design; flexible and dedicated to work whatever hours are needed

CAREER LADDER

```
┌─────────────────────────────┐
│      General Manager        │
└─────────────────────────────┘

┌─────────────────────────────┐
│   Plant Operations Manager  │
└─────────────────────────────┘

┌─────────────────────────────┐
│      Plant Supervisor       │
└─────────────────────────────┘
```

Position Description

The operations manager of a food processing plant is responsible for the smooth production of the company's product, from receiving raw ingredients at the back dock to loading cartons of finished product for shipment to customers. Between those two points, the work consists of making efficient use of every inch of the production plant, maintaining highly complex machinery to run nonstop, managing the employees who work the equipment, and implementing quality-control measures at every step of food processing.

Most food production plants run 24 hours a day at least part of the year to keep up with orders. During slack times they may cut back to 16 hours a day, running only two shifts instead of three. The production manager schedules all workers, keeping the shifts balanced between old hands and trainees, and relies on a supervisor for each shift to

keep training and cross-training in progress without slowing production.

Regardless of the product the company makes, the production plant follows a reliable pattern. The delivery point for ingredients must be spotlessly clean, dry, and able to accommodate the storage of materials until they are used. These shipments might be flour for crackers or breads, spices for seasoning mixes, fresh dairy products for cheese, or just-harvested vegetables and fruits for freezing. Every delivery is examined for quality and checked for quantity against the packing slip or invoice before it is accepted and moved onsite. Goods are stored to rotate, so new material is in the back and on-hand goods moved to the front, where they will be used first.

The production plant is an orderly design with concrete floors and drains, stainless steel processing equipment, and stacks of racks on wheels or roller-operated tracks to move the product from one stage to another—from mixing to batching to baking or from sorting and grading to boxing. Smaller food businesses seek used equipment, especially when a second-hand oven or proofing box may cost several thousand dollars compared to tens of thousands of dollars when new.

A primary skill of the plant manager is the mechanical knack of keeping everything up and running steadily. If one machine or one work station breaks the pattern, everything is thrown off and production halts. Production costs sky-rocket during downtime, while workers stand around earning wages. The production manager's job is to get things fixed and on-line with the least amount of time lost. He or she has to know how to fix simple breakdowns, when to call the repair service, how to get a needed part to the plant without delay, and how to improvise systems to keep production moving without jeopardizing quality.

Labor is the greatest portion of product cost. Finding and training workers is an ongoing process in every production plant. The work is highly detailed and requires specific skills, but it is boring and holds no challenge from day to day. If two workers who like each other are stationed together, their work may take on a social quality, but the manager has to ensure they don't let their attention wander from the work. In some parts of the country where there are large populations of immigrants who don't speak or understand English, the production manager has to know a second language to run the plant.

While other company employees are at work in efficient offices elsewhere in the plant—devising sales promotions, seeking new customers and keeping old customers happy, poring over financial statements to guard the company's profitability—the plant production manager is the hardworking key to their success. He or she is the boss of the production operation, providing the highest-quality merchandise on time and cost-effectively.

Salaries
Starting salaries for plant production managers with suitable education and training range between $22,000 and $30,000 annually, and experienced managers in larger companies earn up to $120,000. The work is often far more than 40 hours a week; benefits and bonuses for exceptional performance add value to the annual salary.

Employment Prospects
There are exceptionally good opportunities for trained and experienced managers at every range from start-up companies to established multiproduct plants. This is also a job area that does not shrink during recessionary times.

Advancement Prospects
It is possible for a plant worker to advance to management with additional training in equipment maintenance and employee supervision, both of which can be acquired at local community colleges. A plant worker who demonstrates an interest in advancement can develop management skills by stepping up in the pyramid from a worker to a unit supervisor, then shift supervisor, then assistant to the plant manager.

Best Geographical Locations(s)
Food-processing plants are dispersed throughout the country, but clustered in regions where their ingredients are available nearby and in cities where the necessary work force is available.

Education and Training
A plant manager needs a college degree in engineering or food technology with additional studies in management, human relations, and heavy equipment maintenance, or the equivalent job training.

Experience/Skills/Personality Traits
Any food-processing experience is valuable, as is management experience in a non-food production company.

A manager needs team building skills to maintain a smoothly operating work force, the teaching techniques to encourage workers to learn new skills, and the perception to identify those who can be promoted from within to move up the management ladder. The manager is on call for every emergency, even those that happen at night, so developing reliable supervisors is vital.

Unions/Associations
Even if the plant workers are unionized, management employees are generally exempted from membership.

The Institute of Food Technologists is a professional association of food scientists, engineers, product development managers, and quality control specialists. It holds an annual meeting, publishes a newsletter and a journal, and is affiliated with food technology organizations worldwide.

Tips for Entry
1. If you have a knack for equipment maintenance and repair, apply for any food-processing job in your area, make your special skills known, and work for advancement.
2. Study the second language that is spoken in your area and take any management seminars available, especially if they relate to food processing. You are likely to meet food-processing managers among fellow students and can learn of possible jobs firsthand.
3. Ask your local library for food technology publications and check for classified ads for management opportunities.

CONSUMER SERVICES DIRECTOR

CAREER PROFILE

Duties: Coordinates with the company marketing director to exchange information on consumer concerns, preferences, and questions; hires, trains, and supervises staff to interact with consumers; develops questionnaires and systems for collecting and processing information

Alternate Title(s): None

Salary Range: $28,000 to $75,000

Employment Prospects: Limited

Advancement Prospects: Good

Best Geographical Location(s) for Position: Scattered throughout the United States

Prerequisites:

Education or Training—A college degree with either a communications and home economics major or combined major of both
Experience—Information processing; teaching and training; public speaking
Special Skills and Personality Traits—Curiosity and organization

CAREER LADDER

```
┌─────────────────────────────┐
│     Marketing Manager       │
└─────────────────────────────┘

┌─────────────────────────────┐
│ Consumer Services Director  │
└─────────────────────────────┘

┌─────────────────────────────┐
│     Consumer Liaison        │
└─────────────────────────────┘
```

Position Description

In large food product corporations, the consumer services department is in daily contact with consumers, and its concern is with public awareness of the company's products. The company's system may consist of a toll-free number printed on every package, pamphlet, and advertisement of the company's product. Consumers who call are connected to dozens of advisers trained in every aspect of the product who can convert a homemaker's simple question into a response to the current company survey. Even smaller companies have some system to evaluate consumer interest.

The director of this department works closely with the marketing director to learn the public's reaction to new ads and new products. By feeding this information on a weekly, monthly, or quarterly basis to upper management, the company can respond to trends and seasons.

The director hires and trains consumer liaisons to know the answers to common questions about the products and to probe further with survey questions to learn consumer desires. If the advertising push of the month is a single product prepared in various ways, with full-color photographs of a variety of recipes, the survey may focus on where the callers saw the ad, what part of the country they live in, which recipes they plan to use, and what preferences they have for other products made by the company.

This essential heartbeat of customer data is usually located in a maze of office cubicles fitted with telephones and computer monitors and staffed with home economists, nutritionists, cooking specialists, and company-trained communicators. The selection and training of this staff is a primary job of the consumer services director.

The director consults with the marketing staff to learn what advertising will be released in the near term—one month, three months, or six months later—as this will stimulate calls from consumers. Based on anticipated market stimuli, the consumer services director develops questionnaires to gather new information from callers about geographic trends and preferences. When the new questionnaire has been approved by marketing and other executive departments, the director can proceed to train the telephone staff on it.

In this information and electronic age, most consumers will reach for the telephone (particularly if it is to call an 800 number), but fax machines and traditional letter writing provide additional consumer input. When the hot line isn't ringing with incoming calls, the telephone staff responds promptly to these other questions.

Periodically, the director submits reports to management on all the data gathered by his or her department. Weekly and biweekly reports typically contain pure statistics of the number of calls, their origination (state, city, population), and who they were from (male or female, age, education, income). Monthly and quarterly reports contain a review of the current questionnaire responses and types of initial questions generated by package and advertising information.

Annually, the director is responsible for his or her department's budgets. Labor costs, specific costs, and capital equipment purchases have to be predetermined, and the director is on-the-line to meet those numbers. The annual performance review is based as much on financial accomplishments as on other negotiated goals and objectives.

Salaries
Depending on the size of the department the director is managing—number of staff, size of annual budget—the director's annual salary will range from $28,000 for a small, multiproduct company, to $75,000 and upward for a conglomerate corporation.

Employment Prospects
The number of such jobs is limited, and most of them are held by career professionals with degrees in home economics and/or communications. A creative freelance individual can provide this service to local, start-up companies and develop a business of gathering, analyzing, and providing similar information to the company owners on a contract basis.

Advancement Prospects
Career advancement is most likely by moving to a larger company. To move up the career ladder, additional marketing skills are essential and can be acquired by taking marketing courses at a local college.

Best Geographical Location(s)
Corporate product headquarters are usually located in large urban areas, not necessarily where their product is produced, and are well scattered throughout the country.

Education and Training
A bachelor's degree with a combined major of home economics and communications is the logical education path for corporate consumer services management. By starting with a new company, it is possible to create such a position and learn as the company and the job grow.

Experience/Skills/Personality Traits
This job requires a wide range of people skills: an interest in people and a genuine pleasure in being with those from all backgrounds and interests. The consumer services director is the voice of the company to the customer. How that voice comes across is essentially how the company is perceived in the marketplace.

An abiding curiosity—"I wonder what people think about _____"—is an essential component of the researcher. This needs to be accompanied by organizational skill to shape useful reports from the data for others in the company to use.

Unions/Associations
Two home economist associations have strong ties to consumer service managers: American Association of Family and Consumer Sciences and an independent branch of AAFCS, Home Economists in Business (HEIB). HEIB accepts membership from college graduates without a degree in home economics if they are employed in a food-related field.

Tips for Entry
1. Take any available staff job in a large corporation's consumer services department to see if the work appeals to you.
2. Check your local phone book for customer-service consulting firms who conduct consumer surveys for food companies and apply for a research position.
3. If you already have a good foundation of food-related skills, take any communications courses at your local community college; the department will be aware of job opportunities in the area.

STATE AGRICULTURE MARKETING ADVISER

CAREER PROFILE

Duties: Assists local growers to develop value-added products from their crops; provides information about government regulations, packaging, marketing; assists at trade shows

Alternate Title(s): Agricultural Consultant; Agricultural Adviser

Salary Range: $20,000 to $75,000

Employment Prospects: Limited

Advancement Prospects: Fair

Best Geographical Location(s) for Position: Not every state government provides this service; make inquiries at the Department of Agriculture in your state capital

Prerequisites:

Education or Training—A college degree in marketing, communications, agriculture or home economics provides a solid background, but it is not essential

Experience—Any food-related marketing experience

Special Skills and Personality Traits—An insatiable appetite for information about food product development; organizational skills to develop, maintain, and disperse data; interest in promoting agriculture-related businesses

CAREER LADDER

```
┌─────────────────────────────────┐
│   State Agriculture Director     │
└─────────────────────────────────┘

┌─────────────────────────────────┐
│ State Agriculture Marketing Adviser │
└─────────────────────────────────┘

┌─────────────────────────────────┐
│   State Marketing Assistant      │
└─────────────────────────────────┘
```

Position Description

State agriculture departments encourage farmers and growers to expand their activities into "value added" products—making apple butter, cider vinegar, dried apple wreaths, or apple juice from surplus or damaged apples, for example—because it creates additional income for growers and also increases state tax revenues. More products means more sales, and more income to the farmer, to the processor, and to the state treasury.

To promote these activities, many states offer assistance in start-up and marketing to the farmer or the cottage-industry food processor to create a successful and profitable business. Assistance often begins with a call to the agriculture department from a grower asking what to do to sell the farm's popular jam, nut brittle, sweet wine, or whatever.

The state marketing adviser is a resource who provides a wealth of assistance. First, he or she can tell you the name and phone number of the proper office for licensing a product. Depending on the workload the next few weeks—trade shows around the country, state budgets and reports that are due, state advertising spreads being prepared for trade magazines—the marketer will probably pay a visit to the novice food processor soon after the call to see the product, taste it, assess the producer's business acumen, and let him or her know what assistance is available.

The state marketer is strictly an adviser; to give professional services to the companies would constitute a conflict of interest with private businesses who do the same work for income. An example of this is helping the processor write press releases to food publications. The state marketer will supply three or four sample releases from other companies to give an idea of how it is done; the private consultant would write the releases and develop a press package for a fee.

At major trade shows, some states take a block of space or multiple booths to promote the Bounty of Oregon or the Flavor of New Mexico. They resell space to the newer companies on the scene, usually those the marketer has been working with in their first year of existence. By now the young company is in start-up production, has brochures and sales sheets, and enough product to give away for tasting at the show. The state marketer is there to help newcomers set up their booths, relieve them during the show times so they can cruise to see competing products, and provide encouragement.

Depending on the available state department budget, a state marketer travels widely throughout the country, introducing customers in other areas to the products of his or her home state. While visiting major trade shows, the marketer calls on local newspaper and magazine food editors (and other local taste mavens) with handouts, such as news releases, samples, and brochures. He or she also cruises the boutique grocery stores in the area, looking for possible customers for home products. Upon returning, the marketer calls the companies and makes suggestions, giving them the names of people and stores to contact.

About half of a marketer's time is spent on the road, both for trade shows and for visiting, and the rest is in the office. There are hundreds of regional trade shows to be tracked, requiring a master calendar. There are hundreds of monthly, weekly, and daily agriculture publications to scan and pass on to others in the department, or articles to clip and send to clients who are still in a start-up mode. At trade shows and in the mail the marketer amasses a load of information about packagers, graphics artists, label designers, test marketers, and other private consultants who want business from new companies. A computer database of state companies has to be maintained by the marketer.

Salaries

Salaries for full-time state employees, depending on the scope of the job description, range widely from $20,000 to $75,000 a year.

Employment Prospects

There are a half dozen or more employees in an average state agricultural marketing section; some start in clerical positions and move into technical jobs. Similar jobs are available at regional product associations—for hazelnuts, chilies, almonds, lemons, beef, dairy—that do much the same work for their special food groups.

Advancement Prospects

State employees are advanced by grade level and salary range or by applying and being hired for a new job category, all based on performance evaluations and testing. In private industry—product associations—advancement depends on promotion and budget availability.

Best Geographical Location(s)

State jobs are normally in either the state capital or in the major business city. For example, Oregon's agricultural marketing section moved several years ago from the state capital to a commercial center in Portland. Product association jobs are generally in the heart of the product's production area or near the legislature.

Education and Training

Marketing and communications courses are available in community colleges and universities. Nutrition, dietetics, and home economics are good majors for advancement in these jobs.

Experience/Skills/Personality Traits

A state agricultural office entry-level job will not require extensive work experience unless there are many applicants for the job. It is possible to start as an administrative assistant (clerical support job) and work into a marketing assignment, but salary in this case would be in the lower range.

The best attributes for this work are an ability to put yourself in another's shoes without trying to steal the shoes; the goal is to provide business development materials without an attempt to tell the company what to do and how to do it.

Pack-rat tendencies in gathering peripheral data for redistribution are useful. A phenomenal memory helps to re-find or retrieve an appropriate magazine article, the name of a food writer met at a trade show, and the location of unique shops ideal for an unusual product.

Unions/Associations

There are trade associations that provide useful marketing services for established companies; among them are the Association of Food Industries and the National Association for the Specialty Food Trade. These groups produce annual trade shows that buyers attend.

The International Association of Culinary Professionals welcomes food product marketers as members.

Tips for Entry

1. Wangle a pass to any food industry trade show in your area and cruise the aisles to get a sense of the range of products and the type of people involved in the businesses. You may meet a state marketing specialist and get a chance to discuss job opportunities.
2. Take an entry-level job in the agricultural department of your state government and make your interests to learn marketing and communications assignments known.

WINERIES

WINEMAKER

CAREER PROFILE

Duties: Responsible for the style and quality of wine. Starting at harvest, the winemaker tests the grapes in the vineyard and decides when to pick each grape variety, supervises crush, controls stages of fermentation and aging, and determines the schedule for bottling and release of wines. In many wineries the winemaker also travels and makes appearances at winemaker events to promote the winery and trade shows to promote sales.

Alternate Title(s): None

Salary Range: $20,000 to $68,000, depending on winery size

Employment Prospects: Limited

Advancement Prospects: Limited

Best Geographical Location(s) for Position: Areas with an established wine industry, such as California, Oregon, Washington, New York, and emerging areas such as Texas, Oklahoma, Virginia, Rhode Island, Missouri, and New Mexico

Prerequisites:

Education or Training—A university degree in enology or training with a wine master

Experience—Hands-on winemaking experience, as an assistant winemaker or home winemaker

Special Skills and Personality Traits—Mechanical aptitude; good palate and sense of smell; organized sense to control multilevel scheduling, good people manager to supervise workers

CAREER LADDER

```
┌─────────────────────────────┐
│        Wine Master          │
└─────────────────────────────┘

┌─────────────────────────────┐
│         Winemaker           │
└─────────────────────────────┘

┌─────────────────────────────┐
│     Assistant Winemaker     │
└─────────────────────────────┘
```

Position Description

The winemaker has the ultimate responsibility for the production of quality wines in a winery. This extends to selecting the grapes (either from their own vineyards or by purchasing grapes or juice); supervising the crush; storing the juice and managing fermentation and aging over a period of several months (for white wines) or several years (for red wines); making the critical decisions at specific periods in the life of the wine; and sequencing the moves between large stainless steel vats, wooden casks, oak barrels, and eventually into bottles. In doing all this, the winemaker is in charge of all the winery staff that participates in the winemaking process.

The process of selling wine has become tied to personalities, and the winemaker is expected to meet major clients either in the winery or the vineyard, or by traveling to discuss the nuances and personalities of his or her wine at trade shows. Locally, in the wine region, winemaker dinners are sponsored by top-quality restaurants; the chef plans a special menu to highlight the wines, and the winemaker attends to meet guests who have paid a premium for this privilege.

A year in the life of a winemaker starts at the harvest, in late summer. The crush, when grapes are brought into the winery and processed, extends over five to eight weeks as sections of the vineyard ripen and tests for sugar, pH, and acid confirm that each grape variety is at its optimum stage for picking. For example, pinot noir grapes may be picked first, various white wine grapes next, and cabernet sauvignon grapes at the end. For the next two to three months, the wine is developing in tanks and barrels, and the winemaker is attentive to the process, topping up barrels to keep oxidation from weakening the flavor. Some wineries bottle a young, fresh, red wine in the style of French Beaujolais in November and fruity whites (white zinfandel and Johannesberg riesling) from November to January. By winter, work in the winery has slowed, and the winemaker oversees maintenance of the crush equipment, getting it ready for the next year. In the spring, the new wines have to be clarified, refined, and filtered; these are very precise processes, and the winemaker has his or her hands on each step of the process. The last five to six months of the winery year are spent bottling the new white wines from the current harvest and the new reds from the earlier year.

Sales trips to areas where the winery has established markets, or is trying to break into new markets, fill any extra time for the winemaker until harvest begins.

In very small boutique wineries the winemaker may manage the vineyards as well as the winery, and on the other end of wine production he or she may also be production master, cellar master, or any other of the two or three jobs that would be under the winemaker in a large production facility.

Salaries

Winemaker salaries are strongly influenced by the size (thousand gallons of production) of the winery and by geography (Pacific Coast or Eastern United States). In the largest wineries on the Pacific Coast, salaries range between $40,000 and $68,000, and in the smaller wineries in the Eastern United States, between $20,000 to $35,000 a year.

Employment Prospects

There is rarely more than one winemaker in a winery, making the opportunities for such jobs very limited. With new wineries starting in every part of the United States, the number of jobs is increasing.

Advancement Prospects

Winemakers, unless they are also owners of the winery, seem to play job musical chairs, moving to larger or more important wineries as their reputations and experience increase.

Best Geographical Location(s)

Areas with an established wine production are primarily California, Oregon, Washington, and New York. New wine districts are emerging throughout the United States.

Education and Training

A degree in enology from one of the major university programs is the most accepted credential; some winemakers have moved from vineyard management with a degree in pomology into the winery, but that is becoming rarer.

Training with a wine master is another way to learn winemaking, but in practice this is usually combined with university extension classes for the scientific background that is needed.

Experience/Skills/Personality Traits

Winemaking is a science and a craft. Hands-on experience is essential. A winemaker must also know styles of wine, understand classic wine varietals, and develop a reliable palate and sense of smell for sampling wines at every stage in their development.

The winemaker needs to be a skilled mechanic and electrician to keep the machinery functioning (especially during times of heavy use), and have an innate sense of organization to manage the logistics of wine sequencing and production.

Unions/Associations

The American Society for Enology and Viticulture requires professional members to have a bachelor's degree and five years of working experience; however, there are also categories of membership for associates, students, and affiliates.

Tips for Entry

1. Locate home winemakers and offer to help in return for training.
2. Consult the *Wines & Vines* annual directory for wineries nearby, and talk to local winemakers about any opportunity to assist in the winery production.
3. Some of the major enology schools hold weekend seminars to teach interested consumers more about wine production; local winemakers may be part of the program and available to tell about any possible jobs in their own winery or neighboring ones.

WINERY CELLAR MASTER

CAREER PROFILE

Duties: Reports to winemaker with full responsibility for production equipment, plant operation, and workers

Alternate Title(s): Production Manager

Salary Range: $18,000 to $38,000 for full-time employment

Employment Prospects: Good

Advancement Prospects: Limited

Best Geographical Location(s) for Position: Wine production areas of California, Oregon, Washington, Texas, Oklahoma, Missouri, and New York

Prerequisites:

Education or Training—High school diploma and good grasp of math, science, reading and writing English. A college degree is helpful, but not necessary. Vocational training with factory equipment provides an advantage.

Experience—Plant operations work in any food production company or any work in a winery will provide familiarity with the process and the equipment

Special Skills and Personality Traits—Attention to detail; physical strength; quickness to respond to quickly changing conditions

CAREER LADDER

General Manager

Cellar Master

Operations Manager

Position Description

The cellar master is in charge of the winery, and the winemaker is in charge of the wine. It is up to the winemaker to decide which responsibilities he or she wants to delegate to the cellar master and which to retain with the winemaking assignment.

Starting before the harvest, the cellar master must see that all available fermentation vats and barrels are in tip-top shape, clean, and ready for new wine. Weeks are spent hosing out all the winemaking vessels, checking for necessary repairs, and maintaining the highest sanitation standards.

As soon as the grapes are delivered and the crush begins, the cellar master has to be on hand to supervise and assist with transporting the grapes, pumping the free-run juice and the *must* to their destinations. Since the harvest and crush demand up to 20-hour works days, the cellar master must see that the optimum number of skilled workers are available for every step, that the winery is maintained as an injury-free workplace, and that every piece of equipment is functioning properly.

While the wine is developing over the next two to three months, the winemaker makes daily checks on the vats and barrels, deciding when to "top up" to protect against too much air in contact with the wine. The cellar master sees that every detail of the winemaker's decisions is carried out either personally or by the winery crew. At the same time, the crush equipment that was used has to be cleaned, checked, repaired, and stored for the next year. Any worn parts have to be replaced and every joint has to be checked for weakness before the machinery is stored.

As the wine develops, the winemaker makes decisions that influence the final product, such as the blending of two or more varietals, whether and how to filter, and the specific methods for clarifying and refining the wines. Once again, the cellar master is responsible for the work.

By winter, some wines are ready for bottling—the white zinfandel and Johannesburg riesling mature quickly and fresh red wines of the Beaujolais type are ready even earlier, in mid-November. Depending on the available space in the winery, there may be a permanent bottling setup or the equipment may have to be assembled every time it is needed. The cellar master assembles the appropriate channels (hoses, piping) to transfer wine from barrels into tanks to the bottling line. Bottles are sanitized, the corking equipment is checked and stocked, and the cellar master must have the correct varietal labels ready to go on every bottle as it is filled. Bottling work is done under the direct supervision of the winemaker, and it consumes up to six months of the winemaking year.

Salaries

Cellar masters' incomes range between $18,000 and $38,000 a year depending on experience, training, and skill. Cellar masters' salaries are relatively uniform regardless of the volume of wine produced or the area of the country, but there may be significant differences in the number of hours worked, and that can decrease the cellar master's annual income.

Employment Prospects

Jobs are strictly limited by the number of wineries. Areas with a newly emerging wine industry may have start-up jobs to fill. Wineries with cellar masters who have held the job for decades are more likely to be training their replacement as an assistant cellar master.

Advancement Prospects

Promotion to one of the technical (winemaker) or marketing (sales manager) positions at the winery is rare; an administrative promotion is in the realm of possibility, but the cellar master is already at the center of administrative management for production.

Best Geographical Location(s)

Winemaking regions are limited, although more are emerging. Keeping up with wine news and classified ads is the best source of information about jobs.

Education and Training

A good general education with emphasis on math, science, and communication (both writing and speaking) is the cornerstone for success in a jack-of-all-trades job such as cellar master. Vocational training with factory equipment provides the hands-on knowledge to keep intricate equipment working properly.

On-the-job training supplies the specific knowledge of wine production, working under the direction of the winemaker.

Experience/Skills/Personality Traits

Plant operations work in any food production company will be useful in a winery, and any work in a winery will provide some familiarity with the equipment and the process.

To keep everything in top running order, especially under the pressures of the incoming crush and the outgoing bottling stages, the cellar master needs an aptitude for working with machinery. Managing the temporary and part-time work force that handles peak production periods calls for leadership to encourage the best teamwork from the crew.

To be a high-performance worker under harvest-time stress, alternating with a thorough attention to detail during maintenance periods, requires traits that aren't always balanced in one individual, such as flexibility and precision, thoroughness and quickness. The cellar master must be able to draw on the specific skills needed for each part of the job.

Unions/Associations

The wine producing industry is not unionized. The membership organizations that attract winemakers and vintners may be of interest to production managers. Acquaintance with one's peers in nearby wineries comes about by professional calls.

Tips for Entry

1. Wineries hire temporary employees at peak production season to assist with the crush. An energetic performance and a willingness to learn quickly will be noticed by supervisors and lead to additional work.
2. Visiting and touring wineries to learn the nuances of differences in their production methods is one way to meet and talk with the winery crew and a good way to learn about job openings.

WINERY CHEMIST

Duties: Responsible for testing grapes before harvest, juice during press and crushing, and wine during fermentation and aging to provide the winemaker with data that assists in production decisions

Alternate Title(s): None

Salary Range: $15,000 to $35,000, if employed full time

Employment Prospects: Limited

Advancement Prospects: Limited

Best Geographical Location(s) for Position: Pacific Coast states with growing wine industry, and any other area where wine is made

Prerequisites:
    Education or Training—A sufficient knowledge of principles of chemistry to conduct testing
    Experience—Any chemistry testing job in the food industry
    Special Skills and Personality Traits—Dedicated to scientific method and conscientious about record keeping

```
┌─────────────────────────┐
│       Winemaker         │
└─────────────────────────┘

┌─────────────────────────┐
│     Winery Chemist      │
└─────────────────────────┘

┌─────────────────────────┐
│     Winery Helper       │
└─────────────────────────┘
```

Position Description

The chemist in a winery supplies the winemaker with scientific data to make the appropriate decisions about when to pick grapes; how to handle the crushed grapes or juice at harvest; how the wine is developing during fermentation and aging; what measurable characteristics will influence blending the wine; and the wine's readiness for bottling and release.

As the grapes are ripening in the vineyard, sample clusters are tested for 1) sugar as brix, 2) total acid, and 3) pH measuring both acidity and alkalinity. As the decision to harvest comes closer, sugar should be rising, acid should be dropping and pH levels increasing. In a large winery with vast vineyards, this data is plotted on graphs by date to monitor the very best time to pick each block of grapes for the best flavor and other desirable characteristics. Testing allows the winemaker to hit target ranges of the three indicators depending on what type of wine will be made from the grapes. (In addition to noting the chemistry reports, the winemaker walks the vineyard to judge the visual appearance of the grapevines and the taste of the fruit.) If grapes

are left on the vines too long, the resulting wine can have unwanted prune and raisin flavors.

While the harvest is in progress and grapes are arriving steadily at the winery, the chemist takes samples of juice from each vineyard unit of grapes. Again, the chemist tests for sugar, acid and pH. As the wine ferments in casks and vats, it is tested periodically for residual sugar. White zinfandel, for example, should have 1.5 percent residual sugar, and when that reading is reached the winemaker stops sugar depletion. As a wine tests closer to its ideal sugar, the chemist does titration testing and tests every tank three times a day.

Before the wine is bottled, it is tested for both cold and heat stability. Because wine is sometimes improperly stored after leaving the winery, with insufficient care about temperature and humidity factors, ensuring stability before it is released is an important protection for the consumer. To test for cold stability, a sample is frozen and then thawed and watched for unstable potassium bitartrate visible in the solution. To test for heat stability, the wine is subjected to 140-degree temperatures for eight to 48 hours and watched for development of an unstable protein in the wine that looks like an amorphous, gray, fluffy cloud. If the wine needs to be treated, the cellar master conducts the necessary bentonite tests.

Other chemical tests the winemaker needs are for malolactic bacteria and the finished wine analysis for percentage of alcohol. Only the last test is required by government regulations because it affects the taxation basis of the wine. Table wines must be between 11 percent and 14 percent alcohol; if they exceed that range, the tax collected is higher. Both residual sugar and total alcohol are usually printed on the wine label; the sugar data is shown for the consumer.

Salaries

In wine production in California, Oregon, and Washington, a chemist will earn between $24,000 and $35,000 a year if employed full-time; salaries in the rest of the United States are lower, in the range of $15,000 to $22,000.

Employment Prospects

Wineries producing 40,000 gallons of wine a year employ about eight full-time workers for this production, and smaller wineries employ anywhere from two to six workers, ranging from the winemaker to laborers. In some wineries, the winemaker doubles as chemist, or the cellar master might be responsible for testing. There are a limited number of jobs for full-time winery chemists, mostly in larger production wineries.

Advancement Prospects

If the winery chemist has an enology (winemaking) education, he or she may aspire to assistant winemaker, but such opportunities are limited.

Best Geographical Location(s)

Winery jobs are more numerous in California, Oregon, and Washington, but also in New York, Rhode Island, Missouri, Texas, and other states with emerging wine industries.

Education and Training

A winery chemist must have a good scientific background and knowledge of chemistry testing, although a degree in chemistry is not essential. Training in the specific testing needed for wine production can be gained in a college with an enology program or on the job in a winery.

Experience/Skills/Personality Traits

Any chemistry testing work in the food industry is excellent experience. A chemist must be scientific in his or her methods and extremely accurate and conscientious about record keeping.

Unions/Associations

The American Society for Enology and Viticulture accepts memberships from students and affiliates, and professional members must have a bachelor's degree and five years of working experience.

Tips for Entry

1. If any of the schools in your area have either an enology or viticulture program, contact the departments counseling office about any available entry-level jobs.
2. Visit, phone, or write to all the wineries in your area asking about job opportunities. A job in the tasting room might lead to a job in the winery laboratory. *Wines & Vines,* an annual directory, lists more than 1,200 bonded wineries in the United States—although many are large-production home winemakers.
3. Talk to the counselors in your local colleges and universities about jobs in chemistry testing in any area of the food industry. A period of several months or a year doing similar work will be a good recommendation for a job in a winery.

WINERY PUBLICIST

CAREER PROFILE

Duties: Responsible for all publicity and public relations programs on behalf of the winery, including advertising, TV, radio, newspaper and magazine contacts; provides for the entertaining at the winery and on the road; represents the winery in trade and commercial associations

Alternate Title(s): None

Salary Range: $20,000 to $40,000+

Employment Prospects: Fair but limited

Advancement Prospects: Good

Best Geographical Location(s) for Position: Jobs are found almost exclusively in major wine-producing areas

Prerequisites:
   Education or Training—A college degree in communications or marketing; promotional work for any business is helpful
   Experience—Writing, either ad copy or journalism; computer skills for word processing and desktop publishing; public speaking, wine knowledge
   Special Skills and Personality Traits—Aspects of teaching are valuable for communications; enthusiasm about the product is essential

CAREER LADDER

```
┌─────────────────────────────┐
│     Marketing Director      │
└─────────────────────────────┘

┌─────────────────────────────┐
│         Publicist           │
└─────────────────────────────┘

┌─────────────────────────────┐
│     Assistant Publicist     │
└─────────────────────────────┘
```

Position Description

The publicist for a winery is a party host one day and a technical writer the next, a product designer and retail buyer for the tasting room at times and a public speaker at other times. Every opportunity to promote the name and the products of the winery must be seized for whatever beneficial effects can be gained.

Working closely with the winemaker, the publicist will work on all the winery's printed materials such as brochures, advertising copy, press releases, newsletters, and wine label designs. The computer application of desktop publishing means most of these jobs can be done by the publicist without hiring graphics-design consultants, and copy is provided camera-ready to the printer.

All special events held at the winery and most off-site parties are the responsibility of the publicist. This starts with the decisions about what to publicize (a new varietal release, the harvest, or special events for local conventions), whom to invite, and the type of party to be given (i.e., an inexpensive reception or a sit-down dinner). Every aspect of planning the event must be overseen by the publicist: scheduling the date and the necessary staff, choosing the guests to be invited, designing the invitation, planning and ordering decorations, hiring the caterer and choosing the menu, ordering party rental equipment, hiring musicians, managing the budget, checking the inventory of wines and accessories, and serving as host or hostess during the event.

An essential activity of the publicist is participation in industry associations, and communications with the local government and regulatory agencies. Major wine-producing regions have vintner's associations that function to enforce ethical business practices and to enhance the regions' public image. It is valuable for the publicist to be active in the local chamber of commerce and arrange participation of the winery in local tourism events.

Some wineries conduct a major mail-order business through a membership wine club; catalogs and sale announcements are planned, designed, and distributed by the publicist, working with the sales manager. The production of winery-related items such as sweatshirts with the winery logo, bottle openers with the winery name, wine-cooler carriers, and gift baskets are often the work of the publicist.

Salaries

The winery publicist earns a salary in the neighborhood of $20,000 to $40,000 a year at a small winery, and up to $60,000 or more in a large (over 100,000 cases annually) operation, including sales commissions on wines and accessories purchased in the tasting room and annual bonus. These estimates are based on an hourly wage around $10.00. Benefits will vary depending on the management philosophy of the owners and the size of the winery.

Employment Prospects

Except in extremely high-volume wineries, there is only one full-time publicist. The extent of the job responsibilities depends on the size and production volume of the company, and even then the next move is more commonly to an advertising and public relations firm.

Advancement Prospects

If the company is growing—increasing wine production and expanding vineyard holdings—the publicist's job will expand and require an increasing level of skill and success. Another means of advancement is by changing jobs to work for a larger company.

Best Geographical Location(s)

Winery jobs are available only in wine regions, though some corporations that own wineries and other unrelated companies may center their publicity operations at corporate headquarters instead of the production facility. As more winemaking regions develop in the United States, jobs will become more widespread.

Education and Training

Advertising and communication skills are taught in community and state colleges; some offer degrees in tourism, as well. These provide a basic knowledge essential for such a job, but additionally a publicist must have excellent computer skills, writing experience, and the specific knowledge of the lore and technology of the winery. Being a community representative requires training in public speaking, as well.

Experience/Skills/Personality Traits

Any advertising and public relations experience will help a winery publicist get started.

Communicating information about a product is a form of teaching, and these instructional skills will serve a publicist whether the work at hand is writing press releases, making press kits, producing consumer newsletters, or interacting with industry and government groups.

Enthusiasm about the product, imagination in creating special events, and the knack for building teamworking skills among the winery sales staff will all enhance the publicist's work.

Unions/Associations

Local advertising clubs may allow company publicists as members; these groups provide an excellent network of peers.

Industry associations consist of any local vintner's organization, local wine and food societies, and local business groups such as chambers of commerce.

Tips for Entry

1. Contact nearby wineries to suggest an internship working with the publicist; while pursuing a degree in communications or a related field, internships may count as college credits subject to the approval of the department.
2. Take a tasting room job in a small winery and take advantage of any opportunity to assist the publicist in any of his or her work; discuss the possibility of promotion from the tasting room to assistant publicist.

WINERY SALES MANAGER

CAREER PROFILE

Duties: Develops marketing program for the winery and, after approval by the management team, implements the program; hires and trains sales staff; oversees entertainment program at the winery and on the road; represents the winery at trade tastings

Alternate Title(s): Marketing Director

Salary Range: Combined yearly income of $20,000+ with commissions and bonus payments could aggregate as high as $75,000+

Employment Prospects: Moderate to limited

Advancement Prospects: Good

Best Geographical Location(s) for Position: A home base in a winemaking region, but extensive travel is involved

Prerequisites:
   Education or Training—Good general education with emphasis on communications and marketing skills
   Experience—All sales experience is valuable and especially sales in any part of the food and wine industries
   Special Skills and Personality Traits—Good record-keeping skills; conscientious about required paperwork; outgoing and fond of people

CAREER LADDER

```
┌─────────────────────────────┐
│      General Manager        │
└─────────────────────────────┘

┌─────────────────────────────┐
│       Sales Manager         │
└─────────────────────────────┘

┌─────────────────────────────┐
│       Sales Assistant       │
└─────────────────────────────┘
```

Position Description

The sales manager is the primary marketing director for the winery. Responsibility starts with the development of a marketing policy, to determine the type of consumer to be targeted and how widely the company's products should be distributed, among other considerations. Once this plan has been reviewed by the general manager and the winemaker for their input about production schedules and volume projections, the sales manager is accountable for achieving the written goals and objectives.

The sales manager usually has the authority to hire all sales employees, and, in consultation with the general manager and/or the winemaker, negotiates contracts with distributors who handle the winery's products across the country. The determination of territories for both winery sales employees and the distributors also belongs to the sales manager, subject to approval by the general manager.

The sales manager sets up all entertaining for sales accounts, whether the potential customers come to the winery for tastings or whether the manager goes to them. In the wine region this may consist of a tour of the winery, an opportunity to meet the winemaker and discuss varietal styles and characteristics, and a catered lunch or dinner, perhaps set in the bucolic beauty of the vineyard. Outside the wine region, the winemaker might travel with the sales manager to meet with large-scale clients such as a major grocery chain, the chefs' association in a major urban area, or a dominant retail wine company. Away from home, entertaining consists of employing local chefs to showcase the winery's products by pairing them with special menus.

The sales manager also takes the winery's product to trade tastings, especially to judged tastings that present awards. Having a gold medal winner is a major marketing asset. The winemaker will also attend these shows to meet and talk with industry experts and wine writers who are invaluable for spreading the word about a wine they like.

In a smaller winery, the sales manager may also be in charge of winery operations, particularly the inventory, transportation and shipping, and warehousing of the product.

Salaries

A sales manager is usually paid on a salary-plus-commission basis. The sales base and the percentage of commission are dependent on the volume of wine produced. Beginning sales personnel start at about $20,000 a year, and the larger the salary, the smaller the percentage of commission, ranging between 15 percent and 40 percent.

Employment Prospects

Sales opportunities are generally plentiful in every industry, and winery sales jobs are no exception. A tasting room manager with a good sales record might move up to a better, on-the-road sales assignment. A sales representative who is acquainted with the local restaurant community can easily make the jump from food or equipment to wine based on his or her valuable contacts.

Advancement Prospects

A sales manager can aspire to running the winery as general manager. Another route to advancement is moving to a larger winery or even a same-sized winery with a better sales base.

Best Geographical Location(s)

The sales manager belongs out on the road, not in the winery, but home base needs to be near the winery for training, entertaining, and paperwork time. There are more jobs in California, Oregon, Washington, and New York because of the density of wineries there.

Education and Training

Sales skills are generally acquired on the job. Marketing techniques in principle may be taught in colleges, but the successful sales manager acquires the necessary skills and techniques through making sales.

Experience/Skills/Personality Traits

Any and all sales experience is worthwhile, especially any experience that familiarizes the salesperson with fine food and beverage customers.

Sales skills hang on three aspects: knowledge of the customer, knowledge of the product, and a learned ability to achieve closure of the sale.

Being faithful to the paperwork that goes with sales may be dull, but it is essential for successful management. A sense of order, the instinct to follow up with a specific customer for a special discount, and a sincere interest in the customer's pleasure with the product can increase sales markedly.

Unions/Associations

There are no unions or associations that specifically influence a winery sales program, but maintaining relationships with the fine food and beverage organizations within the sales territory and donating wines for benefits and tastings will contribute to sales.

Tips for Entry

1. Inquire about the possibility of an internship working directly with the sales manager while pursuing a marketing program in college; subject to the approval of the department, college credit may be gained for the time invested.
2. Working in a specialty wine shop allows the time to learn about local wines and to watch the sales skills of representatives from specific wineries as they sell to the shop. By building relationships with these agents, you may learn of openings for sales jobs.

WINERY BUYERS CLUB DIRECTOR

CAREER PROFILE

Duties: Managing the winery's buyers club, participating in the selection of wines to offer and degree of discount, designing mailers to be sent to members, logging all orders received, supervising shipments to members, reporting sales to the winemaker and the vintner, planning the next periodic club offering

Alternate Title(s): Mail Order Sales Manager

Salary Range: $30,000 to $80,000

Employment Prospects: Fair to good

Advancement Prospects: Limited

Best Geographical Location(s) for Position: Any wine region in the United States

Prerequisites:
   Education or Training—Sales and marketing major in college or self-directed study
   Experience—Broad knowledge of area wines and especially an employer's wines
   Special Skills and Personality Traits—Detail-oriented, persuasive use of language, energetic and enthusiastic

CAREER LADDER

```
┌─────────────────────────────┐
│   Winery General Manager    │
│    or Director of Sales     │
└─────────────────────────────┘


┌─────────────────────────────┐
│  Wine Buyers Club Director   │
└─────────────────────────────┘


┌─────────────────────────────┐
│    Tasting Room Servers      │
└─────────────────────────────┘
```

Position Description

A winery buyers club provides its members with moderately discounted wine prices, small production wines not for sale in stores, the opportunity to receive advance shipment of new vintages, and occasional special offers. Membership may commit the buyers to a minimum purchase, usually four to six times a year. These programs are especially popular with tasting room customers who live out of the wine region area or out of state; while touring the area they learn of wines that really appeal to them and which they know they won't be able to purchase at home. Smaller wineries that have a prestigious reputation but don't produce a large enough volume of wine to be available in wine stores around the country use this means to increase their customer base. (There are legislative limitations in certain states that do not allow wine to be shipped to individuals. With these exceptions, the winery tasting room staff is eager to explain how the wine club program works and to encourage visitors to sign up.)

Once a winery decides to establish a wine club, in the first months or year this can be managed by the Tasting Room Manager because the volume of shipments is small. The example set by other wine buyers clubs can easily be followed since clubs have become almost commonplace in wine regions. The advantage to the winery is in capturing a tourist or even a visitor from a nearby city as a regular customer. The advantage to the buyer is not having to visit the winery in order to buy its wines. There is no charge for membership, merely the expectation of sales with every mailer sent to the club members.

When the program is up and running, the club director follows a standard procedure for managing the club. The vintner and the winemaker decide which of the recently released (or about to be released) wines to offer and at what discount, which wines already for sale should be included, possibly one or more that are not selling briskly through their distributor or at the winery. The club director takes this information and designs a mailer to club members, arranges for printing, and produces the mailing labels to send out the notice as soon as it comes back from the printer. As orders are received with credit card authorization or checks, the director logs all sales using a standard procedure that will also produce shipping labels with coded information about what each carton should contain. Warehouse workers convert the coded labels into filled cartons and arrange for shipping. The club director prepares a sales report to the vintner and the winemaker on the volume of business that the mailer generated, and then it's time to start planning the next club offering.

The design capabilities of the computer software program used by the winery combined with the copywriting skills of the club director are the tools to produce a persuasive mailer. With each shipment, the vintner, winemaker, and director analyze the sales records and use them to fine-tune their next offering. Buyers want to know that they are getting the best bottling or special exclusive varietals from the winery at the best price. The director is responsible for ensuring that the winery is consistently reliable in offering and delivering something special. This may involve hard negotiations with the winemaker to release some limited bottling through the club.

When the sales management of the winery takes to the road in the months after harvest has been completed, they are presenting their wines to major sales markets as well as to boutique wine stores and popular restaurants. Where winemaker dinners are set up in eastern or mid-western cities, someone makes sure that wine club membership flyers are taken along and distributed to potential customers.

Salaries

Salaries for these jobs are based on sales and a standard commission. In the start-up period, there may be a base salary with a draw related to earned commissions. Earnings can range from $30,000 to $80,000 and up if the volume of work and the level of sales is high enough. If the work is not full time, the director may also work as a tasting room server and that work will carry an hourly wage.

Employment Prospects

In all wine regions, there are sales positions for experienced marketers. If the winery doesn't already have a wine club director, this is something that can be explored by a new employee with a willingness to set up the program.

Advancement Prospects

A successful wine club director can move to a larger winery where the greater volume of sales will mean higher commission income for the director.

Best Geographical Location(s)

The greatest density of wineries is on the Pacific coast in California, Oregon, and Washington, but there are wine regions in many parts of the United States including New England, Rhode Island, the midwest, and Texas. This job, unless it is affected by legislative restrictions on shipping wine, can be found wherever there are wineries.

Education and Training

This is basically sales work and any courses in sales and marketing will be helpful. It also requires knowledge of desktop publishing and other computer skills; classes in improving these skills are available at community colleges.

Experience/Skills/Personality Traits

Being detail-oriented is very important for sales work and also for mail order businesses. The best experience the club director can bring to this job is knowledge of wines and varietal characteristics, plus the tasting profile of the wines being sold. This is essential both for writing the club's flyer and for fielding telephone queries from wine club members who have questions before they place their order.

Unions/Associations

No unions are required in this business. The winery will be a member of the local vintner's association, and volunteering in any of their events can help you build a bond with wine club directors from nearby wineries. A network of colleagues is always valuable.

Tips for Entry

1. Visit wineries near your home and ask them about their wine club, take the literature, and compare styles. Then follow up with the ones that seem the best, asking if they are hiring.
2. Take a tasting room server job in a winery as a way to get comfortable with wine, to learn if this winery is a place where you will be comfortable working, and keep asking for more responsibility if you want to get promoted in this job.

WINERY TASTING ROOM MANAGER

CAREER PROFILE

Duties: Manages all staff, displays, and merchandise for direct sales at the winery; trains tour guides and tasting hostesses and hosts; assists sales manager with on-site entertaining and tourism events

Alternate Title(s): Hospitality Manager

Salary Range: $12,000 to $20,000+, plus sales commissions

Employment Prospects: Limited

Advancement Prospects: Good

Best Geographical Location(s) for Position: Limited to wine-producing regions

Prerequisites:

Education or Training—Knowledge about wine production and specifically well-informed about the employer's winery

Experience—Any wine sales work is helpful, as well as experience in training and motivating staff

Special Skills and Personality Traits—An outgoing and friendly manner is essential for the primary host or hostess for the winery

CAREER LADDER

```
┌─────────────────────────────────┐
│       On-site Sales Manager      │
└─────────────────────────────────┘

┌─────────────────────────────────┐
│       Tasting Room Manager       │
└─────────────────────────────────┘

┌─────────────────────────────────┐
│       Tour Guide and Pourer      │
└─────────────────────────────────┘
```

Position Description

The tasting room in a winery operation is a direct sales outlet. Many tourists visit as many wineries as they can in a region, tasting the newly released vintages, and buying bottles or cases for personal consumption. The success of the tasting room manager is measured by sales made to these daily visitors.

The tasting room manager is the host or hostess of the winery; the tasting room is basically a retail store. Every aspect of visitor facilities is the responsibility of the manager, from the friendliness and knowledgeability of the staff, the effectiveness of the displays to attract attention, the cleanliness of the wine glasses and restrooms, and everyone's sales ability to turn a taster into a buyer.

The manager hires and fires the tasting room staff, trains and grades their work performance, sets salaries, and assigns work and schedules. Depending on the size and wine production volume of the winery, the tasting room staff may have dozens of full- or part-time employees, or it may have only the manager and one or two on-call, part-

time helpers. A well-established boutique winery, with an annual production of less than 25,000 cases, will probably have only three to four part-time workers.

The winery may also stage special events—such as dinners, receptions, or new vintage release parties—for a nominal cost to attract regular customers and guests. The tasting room staff will work at these extra times, as well. Special events are usually planned along with the winery publicist, but the tasting room staff is essential to their success because these people are trained to discuss the winery's varietals and production process.

Salaries

The tasting room manager earns a salary of $12,000 a year at a small winery and up to $20,000 in a large (over 100,000 cases annually) operation, which is augmented by sales commission on wines and accessories purchased in the tasting room. These estimates are based on an hourly pay of $7.00 to $12.00. Benefits will also vary, depending on the management philosophy of the owners and the size of the winery.

Employment Prospects

There are only as many tasting room managers as there are wineries in a given area. A person with an avid interest in wines and winery operations and a knack for sales and marketing will be given a chance if an opening exists.

Advancement Prospects

Success as a tasting room manager is a step toward sales management and winery publicity jobs as they open. Another form of advancement is to move to a larger winery with an opportunity to work more hours, make a higher volume of commissionable sales, and manage a larger staff.

Best Geographical Location(s)

The only geographic locations for tasting room managers are in winemaking regions. Almost all of California, parts of Oregon and Washington, upstate New York and Long Island are the primary areas; emerging wine industries in other states will spawn a future employment market for winery staff.

Education and Training

The tasting room manager must be fully knowledgeable about the winery's production methods, the styles of the available wines, and the history of the winery in order to entertain and inform visitors and to train the tasting room staff for the same duties. A general knowledge of wine lore is valuable. This background is obtained by reading wine literature and by on-the-job training.

Experience/Skills/Personality Traits

Experience in any wine sales work or, in fact, in any direct consumer sales is advantageous for tasting room management.

The ability to successfully manage a staff relies heavily on people skills; the abilities to motivate, train, and build employee loyalty are essential. The talent for sales consists of winning customer confidence, radiating credibility, and having skills in closure to make a sale.

The tasting room is the hospitality center of the winery, and its manager must set the style of friendliness and cordiality toward visitors.

Unions/Associations

Local wine and food organizations provide networking with peers and allow meeting knowledgeable consumers who can be attracted to visit the winery and purchase the product.

Tips for Entry

1. If you already live in or near a major wine-producing region, visit the local winery tasting rooms to get an idea of the different styles of hospitality and talk to tasting room staff about job possibilities.
2. If you don't live near a wine region, plan a trip by first learning as much as you can about the wineries of the area you want to visit.
3. Visit any local specialty wine shops to learn about American wines from the owner or sales staff.

GOURMET FOODS
AND GROCERIES

FARMERS MARKET MANAGER

CAREER PROFILE

Duties: Responsible for negotiations with local government for use of public property as a marketplace; enlists local growers to sell at weekly street market; advertises the market to attract customers; ensures quality control of all products; settles disputes with adjoining businesses, participating growers, or customers to maintain a genial environment

Alternate Title(s): Green Market Manager

Salary Range: Managers earn about $50 per market day; in an active urban/agricultural community, annual salary ranges from $40,000 to $75,000

Employment Prospects: Limited

Advancement Prospects: Rare

Best Geographical Location(s) for Position: Nationwide in small towns as well as cities close to agricultural areas

Prerequisites:
  Education or Training—Good general education with a high school diploma; no special credentials needed
  Experience—Any sales and marketing experience, preferably with food
  Special Skills and Personality Traits—Negotiating and promotional skills, and a love of quality produce

CAREER LADDER

```
┌────────────────────────────────────────┐
│      Regional Farmers Market Director    │
└────────────────────────────────────────┘

┌────────────────────────────────────────┐
│        Farmers Market Manager            │
└────────────────────────────────────────┘

┌────────────────────────────────────────┐
│            Marketing Intern              │
└────────────────────────────────────────┘
```

Position Description

The manager of open-air markets of fruits, vegetables, and flowers, whether in a large city or a small town, has the obligation to find farmers who will bring quality produce to the market to sell it directly to consumers and who will pay a percentage of their market sales to the direct market (nonprofit) association. (Certified Organic Farmers, a group with chapters across the country, is a primary source of sellers.) New truck farmers coming into the business need to be located, inspected, and encouraged to bring their product.

The manager must be able to lure enough quality-conscious customers to the market—using flyers and weekly paper ads, public service radio announcements, and word of mouth—to make the farmers' custom harvests and trips to market financially profitable.

Farmers markets have restrictions on who can sell their goods there, and the manager is responsible for enforcing

them. The first step in this process is usually a visit to the farm to confirm that the individual is actually growing what he or she wants to sell (and not buying the produce from a broker or jobber). Farmers markets work closely with Certified Organic Farmers chapters because the assurance the food has been grown without herbicides and pesticides is one that draws customers. Buyers look for the organic certificate at stalls.

The manager needs to locate a generous variety of produce for the market. A successful market will offer a choice of berries, apples, citrus, grapes, bananas, tomatoes, lettuces, mushrooms, potatoes, asparagus, artichokes, summer squashes, herbs, root vegetables, winter squashes, cut flowers, plants, dried flowers and exotics, dates, raisins, nuts, eggs—in short, if it can be farmed in the area, it should be represented at the market. The manager's job is to maintain the widest variety of products, encouraging the farmers to extend their growing and selling seasons if possible. The more products the market displays, the more customers will come to buy, making the venture profitable.

These markets are usually held in a city-owned parking lot or on a downtown city street, often with traffic banned for the one or two blocks of the market. The manager sets up the arrival and placement system for the trucks, and assures that everyone is in place at market time and stays until its close. The contract with the local government is the responsibility of the manager; it is usually renegotiated annually, and sometimes it involves relocation of the market because of land use changes.

Some cities have several markets a week—on Saturday morning, Tuesday evening, and Thursday evening. Some markets allow food vendors, such as barbecue grills selling oysters on the half shell and local sausages; this concession is at the discretion of the local governing body, county board of supervisors, city council, and heavily influenced by testimony from the local public health officer. Some markets allow churches or schools to hold their bake sales at the produce market.

Any consumer complaints have to be given attention, thoroughly investigated, and followed up to remove or solve the problem. A complaint may arise over the quality of product from a particular farmer, the unsafe walking conditions at the market, or the insufficient parking space for customers, or a farmer may have a disagreement with a neighboring truck, or want a more prominent selling place at the market.

In addition to market hours, a manager spends time on bookkeeping, studying and meeting local and state regulations, and locating and signing up additional farmers to participate.

Salaries

The market has to generate sufficient income to pay all operating expenses including office rent, telephone, manager's salary, and advertising or promotion costs. The market association receives 5 percent of the gross sales from sellers, and may have an annual budget as high as $150,000 for operations. In a small city with three to six markets a week, the manager earns an annual income of between $15,000 to $65,000 if the markets are open year-round. Managers of a single market, one day a week, earn between $10 and $15 an hour. Most farmers markets are spontaneously generated in the locality, either by the Main Street business owners, by community churches, or as a cooperative venture by the local farmers.

Employment Prospects

Except in major urban areas where there are as many as a dozen farmers markets a week overseen by one manager, this is not full-time work. Turnover in these jobs is rare; new jobs are usually created by opportunities to open new markets.

Advancement Prospects

Because these jobs are in short supply, advancement is rare. A successful farmers market manager can go on to jobs in the Certified Organic Farmers association, in the state agriculture department's marketing division, or in managing the produce department of a commercial natural foods store. Produce specialists who are familiar with high-quality product are in demand at upscale grocery stores in the produce department and at produce brokers in the wholesale market.

Best Geographical Location(s)

These jobs are found nationwide, in small towns as well as cities. In some areas, because of hard winters, they are seasonal (summer only) jobs.

Education and Training

A manager needs a good general education, including writing and math, but broad knowledge is more essential than a high school diploma, and no special credentials are required.

Experience/Skills/Personality Traits

Patience, diplomacy, negotiating skills, salesmanship, and a love of fresh produce are essential characteristics for a market manager.

Unions/Associations

The National Direct Marketing Association provides educational and business operations support. Most states have an association which sponsor annual conferences.

Tips for Entry

1. Offer to assist the local farmers market manager to see whether this is work you like.
2. If there isn't a market in your area, visit one in a nearby town and talk to the manager about what it takes to start one.

SPECIALTY FOOD STORE BUYER/MANAGER

CAREER PROFILE

Duties: Orders and maintains inventory of specialty food products, domestic and/or imported; hires, trains, and schedules all sales staff; maintains and develops customer base; if appropriate, encourages and manages mail-order business

Alternate Title(s): Gourmet Foods Specialist; Ethnic Foods Merchandiser

Salary Range: $22,000 to $60,000

Employment Prospects: Limited

Advancement Prospects: Good

Best Geographical Location(s) for Position: Communities with a strong ethnic population from Asia, Europe, Central America, or the Middle East, and wherever specialty foods are made and sold

Prerequisites:

    Education or Training—Business management course from a community college or higher institution

    Experience—Sales experience; culinary skills to demonstrate uses of off-beat products

    Special Skills and Personality Traits—Fascination with new foods and ingredients; friendly with customers; teaching instincts

CAREER LADDER

```
┌─────────────────────────────────────┐
│    Store Owner or General Manager    │
└─────────────────────────────────────┘

┌─────────────────────────────────────┐
│  Specialty Food Store Buyer/Manager  │
└─────────────────────────────────────┘

┌─────────────────────────────────────┐
│      Sales Clerk, Stock Handler      │
└─────────────────────────────────────┘
```

Position Description

The buyer/manager for a specialty food store is dealing with products not found in the major supermarkets, products the food-smart customer will go out of the way to locate and purchase. These specialty, or boutique, stores are proliferating as the general consumer becomes more knowledgeable about ethnic cuisines and high-quality ingredients.

A dedicated cook who is shopping for a dinner party or just picking up standard ingredients for his or her well-stocked pantry will drive many miles and make dozens of stops to satisfy a shopping list, which may include olive oil, balsamic vinegar, coffee, *panko, dashi,* chocolate, stone-ground flours, Niçoise olives, green lentils, flageolets, grape leaves, pomegranate syrup, Barolo wine, Arborio rice, basmati rice, garam masala, marrons glacés, mascarpone, triple cream brie, *boudin blanc,* tasso, preserved lemons, tamarind, *biscotti,* nopal, chayote, oysters, gravlax, organic honey, dried cherries, and fresh chervil. Considering the vast number of ingredients that have found their way onto supermarket shelves in the past decades, it is impressive that so many more ingredients are in sufficient demand to warrant specialty shops. Many of the above ingredients—the shelf-stable and shippable ones—are also available from mail-order catalogs and Internet shopping services, but in cities with a strong ethnic presence there are still plenty of city shops that cater to customers seeking Italian, Middle Eastern, Greek, kosher, French and Asian foods, and coffee, flour mills, sausage, baked goods, organic produce, chocolate, cheese, dried fruits and nuts, wine, and seafood.

Ethnic neighborhoods spawn the shops catering to recent immigrants and first-generation residents, but the ingredients are also sought-after by adventurous home cooks. The buyer/manager of such a store has two groups to please: the neighborhood (who may speak a native language instead of English) and the food mavens (who speak culinary slang). As a shopkeeper seeking the highest volume of sales in specialty food products, the challenge is to relate equally well to both groups of customers.

Buying commodities for specialty food stores requires working with distributors who represent small, start-up companies and importers. Trade shows are a vital resource for finding quality ingredients and connecting with their sellers. Managing a specialty store often means hiring sales clerks who are fluent in both English and the language of the neighborhood. This can be French, German, Russian, Chinese, Japanese, Arabic, Spanish, Italian, Greek, Hebrew, Thai, Vietnamese, or Hindi. When the customer is basically a culinarian in search of rare ingredients for an obscure dish, he or she is usually looking for some cooking advice as well. For these culinary customers, product-tasting tables are an effective way to stimulate extra sales.

Some of these specialty stores are also mail-order and Internet e-commerce sources for fine ingredients. This applies equally to non-ethnic shops; stores that carry fresh and smoked sausages, pâtés, European chocolate, flour mills; makers of spice mixtures; cheese makers; wine brokers; and processors of jams, honeys, pickles, chutneys, and varied condiments. With this additional source of sales, the store buyer/manager has the motivation and financial ability to seek a broader sampling of food stuffs. Some mail-order solicitations are merely typed lists of brands and jar sizes along with a price list; for a very trusted purveyor, these lists are enough to satisfy customers who already know the seller. Other managers distribute an annotated price list, with a few sentences describing each product, so the mailing can inform a larger market. The next step is to include photographs and, finally, in a full burst of marketing skills, a glossy paper magazine appears with food styling, graphic designs, and product layouts to tempt an armchair customer to try some extra items.

The essential challenge for a specialty food store buyer/manager is maintaining quality control. Product quality can change as quickly as one shipment to the next, and the buyer has to be alert to catch this.

Salaries

Workers in specialty food stores can earn anywhere from minimum wage to $12.00 to $18.00 an hour plus commission or profit sharing. The volume of business isn't the only variable that affects salaries in these stores, but it is significant. Annual income for a buyer/manager may be as low as $18,000 a year up to $60,000 a year plus benefits and bonuses.

Employment Prospects

These jobs exist throughout the country in significant numbers, but turnover is rare, meaning that job prospects are also minimal.

Advancement Prospects

Often the owner of a specialty shop is both the buyer and the manager; starting as an assistant or a clerk is a way to enter the field and to acquire detailed knowledge about the specialty products. As the business grows, there may be openings for a dedicated buyer or manager.

Best Geographical Location(s)

Communities with dense ethnic populations from Europe, Asia, or Central and South America have the largest numbers of ethnic grocery stores. Single-ingredient producers (flour mills, spice brokers, sausage and pâté makers) are scattered randomly wherever an entrepreneur has chosen to start a business.

Education and Training

To be promoted to management or to start a specialty food business, community college courses in business management are valuable. With a deep interest in the cuisine of a specific area, a manager who has traveled in the country where the products originate has an advantage for judging product quality. By visiting the suppliers, a buyer learns how to check for quality and sanitation controls and acquires a trove of stories about the uses of the products, an entertaining and informative feature that lends credibility as a seller.

Experience/Skills/Personality Traits

Any sales experience, culinary skills with the products, and management practice in any retail company will have direct application. Interest in new flavors and ingredients is essential. A congenial manner with strangers, to make customers feel at home in an aromatic environment that may be new to them, is beneficial.

Unions/Associations

If the business sells ethnic food specialties and ingredients, there may be a community cultural association—German club, Mexican-American affiliation, Chinese benevolent society—and entering its ranks could be a source of new products, additional customers, and an opportunity to learn more about the culture.

Tips for Entry

1. Wangle a pass to any of the major food trade shows to cruise the aisles looking for specialty food products that appeal to you personally and ask the sales representatives where their products are sold in your area.

2. Approach the shop owners of any specialty food business that appeals to you (and for which you have a good culinary background) for a training job, with the understanding that you are interested in buying or managing.

3. Check the program of any nearby cooking school for specialty classes in an ethnic cuisine or particular food, such as sausage or chocolate. Sign up for the class to learn more and talk to the teacher about related food shops.

SUPERMARKET MANAGER

CAREER PROFILE

Duties: Responsible for running the store: orders all supplies and stock; hires, trains, and disciplines employees; helps with checking and bagging of customer purchases; ensures safety and sanitation in the workplace; plans display and sales promotions; develops and maintains public relations

Alternate Title(s): Store Manager

Salary Range: $50,000 to $120,000, including performance bonuses

Employment Prospects: Plentiful, but one has to start at entry level—bagging

Advancement Prospects: Unlimited; encouraged by management

Best Geographical Location(s) for Position: Everywhere in the United States

Prerequisites:
Education or Training—High school education augmented by on-the-job training for all promotions
Experience—Working up through every department in the store is required to be a manager
Special Skills and Personality Traits—Even-tempered, outgoing, friendly; concerned for staff and their advancement; good communication skills

CAREER LADDER

```
┌─────────────────────────────┐
│     District Supervisor     │
└─────────────────────────────┘

┌─────────────────────────────┐
│    Supermarket Manager      │
└─────────────────────────────┘

┌─────────────────────────────┐
│      Assistant Manager      │
└─────────────────────────────┘
```

Position Description

A supermarket manager is responsible for every aspect of running the store: ordering all supplies and inventory; overseeing stocking of shelves; hiring, training, and disciplining all employees; overseeing checking and bagging of customers' purchases; ensuring sanitation and safety in the workplace; planning displays and sales promotions in the store; developing and maintaining good customer and neighborhood relations.

Starting with the merchandise, the corporate management of a supermarket chain supplies the approved list of grocery and nonfood items from which the store manager may order. Computers have streamlined and automated the buying process, providing the manager with weekly and monthly reports that consolidate the purchasing and checkout records and track what items are selling and selling out and those not moving at all.

An exotic item prized by a few customers, such as sesame seed paste or braised red cabbage, may be stocked for a period of months to see if it sells, but unless the sales volume reaches an acceptable, profitable level it is ruthlessly purged from the list to make room for more salable merchandise (and the customer must hunt for another supplier).

Even the most wonderful and popular local products must be approved by the corporate buyer, and the vendor has to supply proof of adequate product liability insurance before the local store or the entire chain will purchase and sell it. This standard has to be followed whether the product is a mixed *mesclun* blend of baby lettuces from a local farmer or award-winning bottled barbecue sauce from the best rib joint in the state.

Computer printouts give the manager prompt reports of labor costs to assist in the constant challenge of having enough employees, but not too many, to serve the erratic daily flow of customers. Staffing is an incessant test of experience and guesswork, influenced by discrimination regulations and minimum hours guaranteed by work contracts to checkers, courtesy clerks, baggers, and stockers.

The store manager has the authority to hire and fire; recruiting from another store in the chain is an accepted practice. The point where every food clerk's career starts is as a probationary courtesy clerk. This probationary period gives the manager a look at the potential employee's work ethic, attendance habits, and ability to take direction. It's not a foolproof precaution: Human nature induces some people to show off when they know they are being judged, and then, once the test is over, their abilities abruptly relax. The manager has to exercise perception and experience with people to sift through and find the good, reliable workers.

Training employees at every level is ongoing—almost incessant—both in the store and at regional corporate headquarters. To be promoted from bagger to checker requires between three and six months of training. The next step an employee takes is up the first rung of the managing ladder; the store manager's ability to produce future managers and executives for the company is the necessary proof of the manager's own potential for further promotion.

Firing is an unpleasant but necessary responsibility of the manager. It has to be done on-the-spot at any evidence of theft; eating a doughnut out of a storeroom package is one example of theft. If an employee is being held in jail for any criminal action—like drunk driving or public brawling—when he or she is scheduled to be working, it means immediate termination. Insubordination is a cause for firing. The manager really doesn't have any leeway in acting on causes such as these; even if the doughnut was eaten thoughtlessly by a promising bagger on impulse, the manager has to take the same disciplinary action, or the system breaks down. Most firings take place early in an employee's tenure, at the lowest levels.

The computer terminal in the manager's office is the communications link with corporate headquarters. Instant electronic information about products, safety warnings, regulations, company policies, and display and promotion tips scroll effortlessly from data points throughout the company. There are also trade magazines, newsletters, and customer correspondence to keep a manager reading for over an hour a day.

Customer complaints take many forms, but they are often hostile. Impatience is the common cause of customer dissatisfaction; the same person who will wait three hours in line for tickets to a rock concert bridles at being delayed 10 minutes at rush hour even though every checkout stand is open. A vital area of employee training is teaching methods to defuse customer anger.

The store employees get to know regular customers and often enjoy the brief conversations that update them on the kids' prizes at school and adult promotions at work. There are always a few lonely customers who shop several times a day for the social contact the market gives them.

The supermarket manager's satisfaction comes from watching store sales increase and seeing employees forge themselves into an effective team of customer-conscious diplomats.

Salaries

Pay scales for managers vary among the large companies and on the region of the country, but the general range is between $50,000 and $120,000, including performance bonuses. At the top of the range, this may involve working six- and seven-day weeks under demanding pressures from the corporate office.

Supermarket employees receive benefits including medical and life insurance and paid vacation and sick leave; companies often provide time for college courses and pay a portion of tuition to help an ambitious employee advance.

Employment Prospects

These jobs are numerous, especially considering there are two more levels of assistant manager at every branch store of the supermarket chain.

Advancement Prospects

The path from courtesy clerk to manager takes between four and 10 years of steady promotion with the company. Most important is that promotion is available to every incoming employee, depending solely on his or her dedication, ambition, and energy.

A college student who starts with the company while studying for a degree in communications, computer science, psychology, sales and marketing, or business management and moves through the prescribed steps of bagger, stocker, and checker has the opportunity to transfer after graduation into the advertising department, the computer field, human relations office, or real estate management services.

Every corporate executive has done a stint in the warehouse, at the shelves, and in checkout to better understand every aspect of this complex business.

Best Geographical Location(s)

Supermarkets are everywhere in the United States, merely more numerous in major urban areas.

Education and Training

A high school diploma or GED certificate is sufficient for advancement to managing a store. Entry-level employees are often still in high school when they start their careers with the company.

Company training is required at every stage of store work, and the store manager is responsible for providing approved training to the staff.

Experience/Skills/Personality Traits

Experience within the supermarket chain is required for promotion to management. An employee who has worked for another chain will still go through the steps, starting from courtesy clerk, but it will be a fast track to management.

Management requires an even temperament, level-headed judgment, and an outgoing personality. Excellent communication skills with customers, employees, and bosses are essential. It is still the rule that the customer is always right.

Unions/Associations

Managers are ineligible for union membership, but until that level, all retail clerks are required to join the United Food Clerk Workers union. The union is the benefactor who ensures job security and insurance benefits for workers.

Tips for Entry

1. Start as a courtesy clerk in a neighborhood supermarket as early as possible.
2. Take the time to shop at different markets in your area and talk to the checkers and managers about career opportunities; this will help you pick the company that best matches your own interests.

RESTAURANT SUPPLY BUYER

CAREER PROFILE

Duties: Responsible for selecting products and equipment to be sold through mail order or by district salespersons; investigates all product manufacturers; negotiates volume orders; trains company sales force in the benefits of product; attends trade shows to learn about new and improved products

Alternate Title(s): Merchandise Manager

Salary Range: $30,000 to $75,000+

Employment Prospects: Good

Advancement Prospects: Good

Best Geographical Location(s) for Position: All major metropolitan areas, especially where there is a large restaurant presence

Prerequisites:

Education or Training—No special education as a prerequisite, but courses in marketing, quality control, and food production are beneficial. On-the-job training is customary in major sales companies

Experience—Any buying experience is valuable

Special Skills and Personality Traits—Inquisitive nature; taking pleasure in the detail work of research

CAREER LADDER

```
┌─────────────────────────────┐
│     Restaurant Supply       │
│    Purchasing Manager       │
└─────────────────────────────┘

┌─────────────────────────────┐
│   Restaurant Supply Buyer   │
└─────────────────────────────┘

┌─────────────────────────────┐
│    Purchasing Assistant     │
└─────────────────────────────┘
```

Position Description

The buyers who select products and equipment for a restaurant supply company are responsible for the quality reputation of the business. They decide whose products to list in their catalog and stock in their warehouse, train their salespersons about the product line, and stand by the reputations of these companies with their customers.

A buyer's telephone never stops ringing, with calls from suppliers who want to show him or her their newest product and update information about their standard line of goods in hopes of improving their sales to the restaurant supply company. To deal with product representatives, the buyer has been trained and has built his or her own experience in quality control, production systems, government rules and regulations, and price/volume ratios. The buyer has to learn volume discounts and marketing programs for both the manufacturer and distributors. It is not unusual for a buyer to tour the production plant of a major supplier, just to see personally that all of the

precautions that lead to a reliable and consistent product are in place. As simple a requirement as cleanliness, if it is not up to the highest standard, would prompt a buyer to discontinue selling the company's merchandise.

It is the buyer's job to train salespersons in the details and nuances of the product line. The buyer must also listen to these employees to stay in front of the competition, as the sales staff knows what new products and trends chefs are chasing.

Seasonal products, processed fruits and vegetables, may vary in quality from one year to another. With huge volumes to purchase, the buyer has to be the first to be told when new crops are being shipped. The supplier will set up a tasting to prove that this year's product is as delicious and as consistent as last year's; otherwise, the order won't be repeated.

Trade shows are an important source of information about new products. Many state agricultural agencies encourage their growers to develop value-added products, such as turning berries into dessert sauces and nuts into candies; new products are exposed to the buying public at hundreds of trade shows around the country. The biggest show is the semiannual National Association for the Specialty Food Trade; before being allowed to have booth space, a company must have been in business more than one year. Buyers for all types of food businesses cruise these shows looking for the next food trend.

The buyer reads financial newspapers to keep informed about the management of all major food companies he or she buys from. Mergers, spinoffs, factory moves to another state or another country, employee layoffs—all of these changes affect the manner of manufacturing and processing, and the quality of the product.

Salaries

Depending on background, experience, and years with the company, the buyer's salary will range from $30,000 to $75,000. Buyers are salaried employees of the restaurant supply company, and are usually eligible for profit sharing or bonuses.

Employment Prospects

Large, nationwide restaurant supply companies employ dozens of buyers in their purchasing departments; even a small local or regional company will have several buyers.

Advancement Prospects

By starting out in purchasing, a talented and perceptive buyer can expect to be promoted within his or her own company. While employed at a local company, a buyer might be recruited to join the purchasing staff of a larger regional company.

Best Geographical Location(s)

Wherever there are restaurants there are supply companies serving those businesses. There are more jobs available wherever there are dense restaurant communities—in large cities, resort areas, and affluent communities.

Education and Training

A good general education with courses in marketing, quality control, and food production is the best background. A buyer will receive a lot of training on the job. Any experience in purchasing restaurant supplies will benefit a buyer. The more the buyer knows about the restaurant business, the faster he or she will understand the company's policies and systems of purchasing.

Experience/Skills/Personality Traits

A buyer has to understand the basics of marketing in order to make the most advantageous deals with suppliers. An inquisitive nature is essential to seek out new companies making exceptional products. Researching a company or a source for a unique product can be time-consuming and dull to one person and fascinating to another; it is the latter individual who will do well in purchasing. With experience, the buyer will develop an investigative system to discover new products and to supply the insider knowledge the company's salespersons will devour.

Unions/Associations

There is a variety of trade associations in the food industry, including the Association of Food Industries and the National Association for the Specialty Food Trade. These groups produce annual trade shows that buyers attend.

Tips for Entry

1. Learn about food, quality, and ingredients by whatever means is available; the more you know, the more valuable you will be as an employee.
2. Track down and talk to one or more of the restaurant supply buyers in your geographic location for advice on where a job might be available. Aim for the very best company with the most extensive training program.
3. Scan the classified section of your nearest big-city newspaper for jobs in food purchasing; there may be an opening to work with a veteran buyer.

RESTAURANT SUPPLY SALESPERSON

CAREER PROFILE

Duties: Calls regularly on chef-customers in local restaurants to sell them staples and exotic ingredients; attends company briefings and presentations to stay well informed about the line

Alternate Title(s): Supplier

Salary Range: $28,000 to $350,000, based on commissions

Employment Prospects: Excellent

Advancement Prospects: Very good

Best Geographical Location(s) for Position: Any metropolitan area with a strong restaurant presence

Prerequisites:

Education or Training—A good general education with courses in sales and marketing, and as much knowledge as possible about the restaurant business to be able to understand the customer's concerns

Experience—Any sales experience is beneficial; restaurant experience is especially valuable

Special Skills and Personality Traits—An upbeat personality is essential to successfully make cold calls to customers

CAREER LADDER

```
┌─────────────────────────┐
│   Restaurant Supply     │
│   District Manager      │
└─────────────────────────┘

┌─────────────────────────┐
│   Restaurant Supply     │
│   Salesperson           │
└─────────────────────────┘

┌─────────────────────────┐
│   Restaurant Supply Trainee   │
└─────────────────────────┘
```

Position Description

Restaurant supply salespeople deal daily with chefs in restaurant kitchens and with purchasing managers in hotel, hospital, and school offices. They have to develop and maintain a good relationship with customers, because success is based on repeat business and reorders.

The salesperson has to know more than just the supply company's list of merchandise; he or she must know as much as possible about running a restaurant in order to communicate effectively with the customer.

The supply company holds mandatory sales meetings at least monthly to introduce new products, to meet product representatives, and to connect with fellow salespersons. There may be as many as 50 product representatives displaying their goods at the sales meeting, hoping to make the company's list and place their product in the company's warehouse. It is important to know what the company is carrying as it is to know what it isn't carrying and why. It may be that an entire crop in the last season, such as pears, was

of inferior quality, so the company has declined to offer any canned goods containing pears. The salesperson needs to know this information to effectively serve the chef or buyer.

A salesperson with an average customer load of about 50 business accounts will visit or call every one of them at least once a month, but some of them twice a week. The chef's advantage in ordering from a restaurant supply company is prompt delivery; next-day service in most cases. For small restaurants, where most of the available space is invested in the dining room, thus making the storage area minuscule, inventory is not deep and supplies are ordered as they are used or needed.

Salespeople work for a commission on their sales, not a guaranteed salary. Their income depends on their customers doing well and paying their bills promptly. A restaurant supply person has to be astute at noticing when the account is slow to pay bills or in arrears. Then it's time for some intervention, and the salesperson will bring up the matter of non-payment and may suggest the chef go on a COD basis and pay off the outstanding account at a certain rate per week. The salesperson, along with the credit manager, acts as a friend and a helper through these tough times, and doesn't cut off a customer just because payment is slow.

Experienced salespersons are especially valuable to the company for training new employees. Some companies have a formal mentor program, pairing a neophyte with an old hand and rewarding both, possibly with a commendation for the newcomer and extra vacation credits for the veteran.

Salaries

At the entry level, during training, salespersons are paid a meager salary while working extensive hours to learn every segment of the company's business—the warehouse, credit department, purchasing, and deliveries. As one becomes a food service specialist and moves into a sales territory, salary shifts to being a commission payment as a percentage of sales. With five to ten years of work experience and carefully gained associations in the local restaurant scene, a dedicated salesperson can achieve an annual income of between $28,000 and $300,000, working an average of 10 to 14 hours a day, five or more days a week.

Employment Prospects

There are several national restaurant supply companies and thousands of small regional companies. The telephone book's yellow pages list them under "Restaurant Supply."

Advancement Prospects

In every type of work, the pyramid narrows as it nears the management level. In a large city, the district sales manager might oversee dozens of salespersons; in a small town or affluent community, the district supports a half-dozen salespersons with one manager.

Best Geographical Location(s)

Wherever there are restaurants there are supply companies serving the business. There are more jobs available where there are dense restaurant communities—in large cities, resort areas, and affluent communities.

Education and Training

An excellent source of training for sales is a period as the purchasing manager of a restaurant complex, such as a major hotel. Another desirable background for salespersons is restaurant kitchen experience; the best understanding of what a chef needs comes from having been in the kitchen as the chef or manager. Chefs, however, don't always make good salespersons.

Experience/Skills/Personality Traits

Restaurant experience—cooking, managing, and/or purchasing—gives a restaurant supply salesperson an advantage because it means he or she understands the business.

A personality that is not easily discouraged is indispensable for sales work. Coming in the back door of the kitchen with an order pad in hand always benefits from a bit of fun, a good story, or just gossip about the local restaurant scene. A salesperson's experience and good judgment tells him or her when to stop talking and let the customer decide what to buy. Knowledge of the restaurant business also helps in knowing if the timing of the call is correct.

Unions/Associations

There are no unions that serve wholesale/retail salespersons, and associations that might attract their membership are broad-based culinary groups that develop a network of chefs, teachers, writers, and retailers.

Tips for Entry

1. Track down and talk to one or more of the restaurant supply salespersons in your geographic location for advice on where a job might be available. Aim for the very best company with the most extensive training program.
2. A short course from a vocational trade school covering ordering (vending) and inventory control, will provide credentials and training to be a purchasing supervisor in an institutional food environment such as a hospital, major hotel, large country club, or resort.
3. Learn about food, quality, and ingredients by whatever means is available; the more you know, the more valuable you will be as an employee.

COOKWARE
AND EQUIPMENT

COOKWARE STORE BUYER

CAREER PROFILE

CAREER LADDER

Duties: Selects and orders all equipment sold in the cookware store; meets sales representatives in the store; attends trade shows; manages inventory; meets deadlines for seasonal promotions

Alternate Title(s): Purchasing Manager

Salary Range: $40,000 to $75,000, plus benefits and incentive bonuses

Employment Prospects: Very good

Advancement Prospects: Very good

Best Geographical Location(s) for Position: From large cities to small towns; every community with a main shopping district or mall

Prerequisites:

Education or Training—A good general education with courses in business management or art design will be beneficial

Experience—Any retail selling experience provides an understanding of retail customers and what they want

Special Skills and Personality Traits—Familiarity with computers and financial reports; energy, efficiency, and ability to remain calm

```
┌─────────────────────────────┐
│     Purchasing Manager      │
└─────────────────────────────┘

┌─────────────────────────────┐
│           Buyer             │
└─────────────────────────────┘

┌─────────────────────────────┐
│       Assistant Buyer       │
└─────────────────────────────┘
```

Position Description

The buyer for a retail cookware store selects every item that is ordered, received, and sold in the store. This consists of housewares (kitchen appliances and tools), homewares (linens, glassware, and tableware), and food (cooking and entertaining ingredients and preparations).

The buyer's first concern is style, a many-sided figure composed of trends that drive the wholesale market, classics in every category from mixers to bakeware to table mats, and the image the store traditionally tries to present. The buyer's analysis of a single item covers its visual appeal, quality, product price, style, look, and whether it is sellable, seasonal, or promotional.

The buyer goes to major trade shows of housewares and giftwares several times a year to view new products and to learn from company representatives when certain promotions (meaning discounts) are planned. The rest of the time, he or she is constantly approached in the buyer's office by product distributors hawking their wares.

The hardest part of a buyer's job is managing time for preparing paperwork, checking computer inventory reports, and standing back to view the entirety of what has been purchased, when it is coming in, and how it all goes together for the store's promotions.

The buyer's year starts with the International Housewares Show in Chicago in January, a gigantic trade display featuring prototypes of new equipment and wares that will make it into the marketplace if enough orders are placed to make its production worthwhile.

February is traditionally the time for clearance sales and cleanup of all the store's merchandise (especially the last of Christmas leftovers), and getting ready for March, featuring bridal fairs as a sales promotion and moving a new look into the store with new merchandise. Bridal registry is an important sales aspect for both kitchen and dining room equipment. By April the store is heralding summer, with lots of plastic serving items to use at picnics, barbecues, and poolside. In April, if the store carries gourmet foods (such as *bis-*

cotti, dried pastas, vinegars and oils, dessert sauces, coffee), the buyer goes to one of the major food shows, the National Association for the Specialty Food Trade (NASFT).

By May the store launches into garden accessories for outdoor entertaining and merchandise aimed at Mother's Day gift buyers. In June the store must have appropriate merchandise on hand for graduations, Father's Day, and weddings. If the store is in a resort or tourist area, these visitors are in front of the buyer's mind because they will come shopping for mementos of the trip for themselves and for additional gifts for friends and family back home. In July the buyer has to be prepared for continuing tourists, but there is another escape to the Giftwares Show.

At about this time, the buyer has finished Christmas plans for the store. Every promotion and special look for the holidays has to be in the ordering stage, because everyone ships on September 15—including orders from January's Chicago show along with gift show merchandise. The seasonal change sweeps out the plastic merchandise of summer and displays a solid supply of appliances and serious entertaining tableware. Regardless of how large or small the buyer's shop is, warehousing is his or her concern in September and October, while the store metamorphoses from supplies for informal garden parties to elegant candlelight entertaining.

Throughout the year, distributors of houseware and homeware equipment come calling on the buyer; sometimes as often as every six weeks the same faces are sitting across the desk with their catalogs, price lists, and discount and promotion offers.

The buyer may have severe limitations on how much inventory he or she can have on order and in stock, depending on the affluence of the business or owner. This is called "open to buy," and it refers to the dollars available to control inventory. A store with a small purse will be limited in the depth of merchandise that can be ordered, and the buyer has to be ready to reorder frequently.

Salaries

Buyers are salaried employees of the store, receiving insurance benefits and paid vacation days. Since their success is judged on the store's gross sales and profits, most buyers earn an annual bonus on top of a limited base salary. The salary ranges from $40,000 to $75,000, depending on the size or the number of stores, and the bonus ranges from 10 percent to 100 percent of salary.

Employment Prospects

There may be only a few to a few dozen stores in a city that employ buyers; small stores often combine the owner, manager, and buyer in one person. But there are thousands of stores across the country. To see the number of buyers who are hunting to stock their stores, wangle a guest pass to either the Chicago housewares or the summer giftwares show and look at the hordes of customers cruising the aisles on the buyers' sides of the booths.

Advancement Prospects

A successful buyer who wants to broaden his or her job may aspire to be store manager and buyer, a major responsibility if the store is large and does volume business. If the buyer's store is one of a conglomerate under one ownership, advancement may take the jump of becoming purchasing manager, in charge of the buyers of all the units. A talented and successful buyer is always sought after by other companies, willing to hire him or her away for a higher salary, bigger bonus plan, and/or more benefits.

Best Geographical Location(s)

Such jobs are scattered across the country based on population densities—there are just so many buyers for so many stores serving so many customers.

Education and Training

A college degree in art and design or in business management, or—better yet—both, will serve a buyer extremely well. Any retail experience, because it teaches the buyer what customers want, will be an asset. Many buyers have jumped across the desk from jobs as distributors and company sales representatives to buyers; this jump allows them to live and work in the same place, with less traveling (just the trade shows) and more time at home.

Experience/Skills/Personality Traits

A successful buyer is usually known for his or her passionate attitude toward the merchandise, and excitement in discovering a new product or a better source for a standard item. The work is always fast-paced, meaning the buyer has to have a high level of energy, efficiency, and the calmness to remain unflappable when problems arise.

Unions/Associations

There are no unions serving management-level employees in sales work, and no trade associations that seek their membership. In a very family-oriented community, the buyer is most likely to belong to the groups that attract his or her affluent customers, such as the American Institute of Wine and Food and the Chaîne de Rôtisseurs.

Tips for Entry

1. Working retail in a houseware or homeware store is a chance to become acquainted with merchandise and with the buyer.
2. A guest pass to the NASFT show (held twice a year, once on the East Coast and once on the West), one of the large giftwares shows, or the International Housewares Show in Chicago provides a great chance to meet buyers and store owners in the aisles and learn about possible openings from the staff of the product booths.

COOKWARE STORE MANAGER

CAREER PROFILE

Duties: Responsible for the store's financial success; oversees merchandise displays; plans advertising and promotions; hires and fires; trains and schedules all sales and stock workers

Alternate Title(s): Housewares Department Manager; Cookware Supervisor

Salary Range: $40,000 to $80,000+, including sales commissions or bonuses

Employment Prospects: Fair

Advancement Prospects: Good

Best Geographical Location(s) for Position: In metropolitan areas and affluent communities

Prerequisites:

Education or Training—Business management/retailing courses; cooking classes

Experience—Any retail experience; extensive culinary knowledge and entertaining style

Special Skills and Personality Traits—Enjoy people and have a sincere desire to help them; motivational with store employees

CAREER LADDER

```
┌─────────────────────────────┐
│    Cookware Store Owner      │
└─────────────────────────────┘

┌─────────────────────────────┐
│   Cookware Store Manager     │
└─────────────────────────────┘

┌─────────────────────────────┐
│    Cookware Store Clerk      │
└─────────────────────────────┘
```

Position Description

The manager of a specialty cookware store is responsible for the financial success of the business, a goal that involves overseeing the display of merchandise, placing regular advertising and arranging special promotions, hiring/firing employees, training and scheduling the staff of clerks and stock workers, and if the store has a buyer (a full-time staff person who hunts out, selects, and purchases the stock), the manager probably supervises him or her.

Everyday operations are the major concern of the manager, from the moment of unlocking the doors, activating the cash register system, greeting the employees as they come on the floor to their own departments, and opening the store to customers. As the day continues, the manager spends intermittent time on the sales floor as needed, and keeps up with the constant office work of checking inventory; reviewing weekly and seasonal receipts reports; attending to inevitable human relations activities to provide a safe and satisfying workplace for employees;

keeping payables and receivables current; projecting seasonal promotions and coordinating newspaper, radio, and local TV advertising; interviewing job applicants; and counseling and reviewing employees' performances to maximize sales.

The high points of the sales year in cookware are May and June for Mother's Day, Father's Day, and weddings, and the Christmas holidays (starting as early as October for well-organized shoppers). At those times, the staff will be expanded to the maximum with clerks and stock workers to keep up with seasonal demands.

Early-in-the-year clearance sales generate a high volume, with marginal profits, to clear the floor for new arrivals of appliances, equipment, linens, and tableware. After the flurry of June, more clearance sales take place to make room for summer specials, such as poolside and barbecue accessories.

A manager with an artistic flair will take responsibility for all the stock arrangements on the floor and in the windows, keeping a careful eye on what is creating sales or pulling impulse shoppers into the store. Otherwise, one of the staff is given this responsibility, and the manager oversees his or her work and judges it by the success it has in generating sales.

Staff training, especially in new equipment, is done by the manager. During interviews and hiring, the manager looks for employees who know and love food, cook well themselves, and can communicate their delight in a particular slicer or strainer, extol the wonders of the newest espresso machine, and demystify the skill needed to perform wonders on a *mandoline*. Even so, when a special demonstration is advertised—perhaps for a cutlery line or an appliance manufacturer or bread machines, ice cream makers, or juicers—all salespeople need to be pretrained in the nuances of the equipment so they can answer customer questions.

The success of the manager is ultimately judged by the profitability of the store. The manager has to be attentive to reports generated by the accounting department, making relentless comparisons of monthly and weekly sales against the reports of the prior year, always seeking an increase in the volume of business and the percentage of profit over operating costs. Success in this one aspect translates directly into sales commissions or annual bonuses to increase the manager's annual income.

Salaries
Depending on the size of the business, a manager could earn between $40,000 and $80,000 in annual salary, including sales commissions and/or bonuses.

Employment Prospects
Many cookware stores are owner-managed small operations. In larger cities or affluent communities, a more extensive store featuring all kinds of lifestyle equipment, including cookware, is likely to employ a manager. Chain stores, such as Williams-Sonoma, Crate & Barrel, or Pottery Barn, have managers who report to district supervisors in charge of a region.

Advancement Prospects
Small, individual stores offer little opportunity for advancement. Branch operations have opportunities for both vertical and horizontal promotions.

Best Geographical Location(s)
These stores are well-scattered throughout the United States, but most numerous in metropolitan areas, cities with a large professional population, and affluent communities.

Education and Training
Business management programs are given in community colleges and universities; retailing is usually a business school course. Courses in design and display, human relations, accounting, sales and marketing are all valuable for a store manager.

Cooking classes in techniques that concentrate on the proper use of classic tools are a good source of culinary knowledge, and will help in assisting customers to select merchandise they will be happy to use.

Experience/Skills/Personality Traits
Any retail experience is valuable, but personal enjoyment of cooking and entertaining is essential.

Culinary skills and knowledge, awareness of entertainment styles, technical aptitude with complex cooking equipment, and up-to-date knowledge of food trends are vital.

Enjoying people and having an instinct for helping them is the key to success in retail work. An equivalent interest in the employees affects their performance on the job and contributes to a profitable operation.

Unions/Associations
In some major urban areas, retail clerks' unions are influential.

The International Association of Culinary Professionals accepts membership from retailers, especially if there is a cooking school as part of the store. Regional culinary associations usually seek the local cookware emporium owners and managers as members.

Tips for Entry
1. Check the yellow pages of your local telephone book for cookware stores and call for job opportunities.
2. Ask the manager of your closest cookware store if there is any opportunity for demonstration work for appliance promotions, or if they hire seasonal employees for busy times. Any opportunity to show your willingness and success at sales will put you in place for a permanent job.
3. Pursue business management courses at your local college and meet with the job placement counselor to seek out openings in any nearby cookware stores.

MAIL-ORDER CATALOG DESIGNER

CAREER PROFILE

Duties: Responsible for production of all mail-order catalogs; works with buyers, designers, photographers, copywriters, and printers

Alternate Title(s): Editor; Catalog Production Manager

Salary Range: $36,000 to $75,000

Employment Prospects: Very good as the opportunities for new catalogs increase

Advancement Prospects: Limited

Best Geographical Location(s) for Position: All over the country, wherever food products are made or marketed

Prerequisites:

Education or Training—A good general education with courses in advertising and communications; computer skills including desktop publishing; art and graphics training

Experience—Any experience in print production is useful

Special Skills and Personality Traits—Highly organized; leadership and teamwork skills

CAREER LADDER

```
┌─────────────────────────────┐
│     Mail-Order Manager       │
└─────────────────────────────┘

┌─────────────────────────────┐
│      Catalog Designer        │
└─────────────────────────────┘

┌─────────────────────────────┐
│      Graphic Designer        │
└─────────────────────────────┘
```

Position Description

The advent of on-line shopping through the Internet and retail web pages has not eliminated the paper version of catalogs, received in the mailbox and browsed in relaxed moments with a beverage alongside. (See Web Site Catalog Designer.)

The catalog designer for a mail-order company is responsible for the production and distribution of periodic catalogs of merchandise. Many mail-order companies issue a completely new book every three months and then send a reminder catalog with the pages somewhat rearranged and with a different cover. Two or even three catalogs may be in the process of production at the same time. Food and cooking equipment catalogs are closely tied to festive, homecoming holidays: New Year's, Valentine's Day, Easter, graduations and weddings, Fourth of July, family reunion picnics, Labor Day, Halloween, Thanksgiving, and Christmas.

The catalog director works with the mail-order manager to identify all the items to be advertised. Each item is photographed, and copy is written to describe its merits, list its features, and give the ordering number and price. Pages are laid out to cluster several related items and encourage cus-

tomers to buy a few more items: perhaps the decision between cake pans of two different sizes is to buy both of them, or the herb-painted salad plates really need the place mats and napkins to show them off, and we might as well order the expensive olive oil and balsamic vinegar, too. Every idea that will stimulate sales is considered during the layout stage.

The catalog director works closely with the photographer and the copy editor until the layout is final. The type is set and production pages are reviewed with the mail-order manager before printing. Computers and user-friendly desktop publishing software have transformed catalog production; catalog directors need to be familiar with software features or work with a design consultant for that part of the work.

Merchandise buyers for the company have to confirm delivery dates of any new items; warehouse managers must confirm that inventory is on hand for every listed item as well.

As soon as the galleys are released to the printer, the catalog director is fully absorbed by the demands of the next catalog, already in progress.

Salaries

If catalog design is a full-time, salaried job, a designer can expect to earn between $36,000 and $75,000. A lot depends on whether the print catalog designer is also involved in the website catalog production. Much of this work may be freelance, as a designer can work for several food companies developing small brochures and catalogs, charging an hourly rate between $20 and $45.

Employment Prospects

Employment is limited by the number of mail-order companies in the fields of cookware equipment and quality ingredients. This is increasing, seemingly by the month, as food product lines expand into mail-order sales to increase their production volume.

Advancement Prospects

Promotion depends on the size of the company, and whether it produces catalogs for more than one line of merchandise with separate design directors. Other advances would be to move to a company with a larger mail-order program or to move out on your own to put out a totally new type of catalog.

Best Geographical Location(s)

Mail-order catalog businesses are all over the country—in major urban areas where distinctive food products are locally produced or imported and where printers and mail services are at hand for production and distribution, but also in rural areas where value-added products increasingly result as farmers and growers look for additional crop income.

Education and Training

Basic advertising and communication skills are taught in community and state colleges. These provide a basic knowledge essential for this job, but additionally a catalog designer must have excellent hands-on computer skills, writing experience, knowledge of the uses and lore of the merchandise, and magazine publishing background. Art schools have many courses that train the student's eye for layout and perspective; this work is very much art related, and the practitioner needs a good foundation in color values, relationships, and design.

Experience/Skills/Personality Traits

Any experience in print production—brochures, sales fliers, advertisements—is useful as hands-on practice. A strong interest in art studies is valuable.

Production work such as this requires a highly organized individual to bring all the pieces to closure within a tight deadline. Teamwork is essential to elicit all input items from buyers, photographers, copywriters, and graphics specialists.

Unions/Associations

Advertising clubs provide members with a sounding board for ideas and referrals to skilled freelance consultants. Membership in regional culinary groups provides a network of knowledgeable food professionals.

Tips for Entry

1. Phone or write to receive as many cookware and food product catalogs as you can to learn which ones appeal most to you; write to those companies about job opportunities.
2. Contact your state agricultural marketing board for information about new products being developed that might use a part-time employee to assist with marketing.
3. Attend food trade shows and talk to the booth staff of any product that seems right for mail-order marketing about the chance of a job.

KITCHEN DESIGNER

CAREER PROFILE

Duties: Works with homeowners to redesign or remodel existing kitchens, or design kitchens for new construction; acquires broad knowledge of available appliances and accessories, cabinets, flooring, windows, lighting, and every detail of kitchen installation

Alternate Title(s): Kitchen Planner

Salary Range: $30,000 to over $100,000

Employment Prospects: Good

Advancement Prospects: Limited

Best Geographical Location(s) for Position: Wealthy but older communities where large homes are well maintained and regularly remodeled to bring them up to date

Prerequisites:

Education or Training—A good general education with an emphasis on art and design; training and practice in drafting plans; any business training with contracts, bookkeeping, and data collection

Experience—Working for any kitchen design showroom; working in retail for any kitchen-related construction business, such as cabinets or appliances

Special Skills and Personality Traits—Love of shopping and a trained memory for size, color, design, and manufacturers; persuasiveness to guide both clients and subcontractors; an even temperament on the job site

CAREER LADDER

```
┌─────────────────────────────┐
│   Kitchen and Bath          │
│   Showroom Manager          │
└─────────────────────────────┘

┌─────────────────────────────┐
│   Kitchen Designer          │
└─────────────────────────────┘

┌─────────────────────────────┐
│   Drafting Assistant        │
└─────────────────────────────┘
```

Position Description

A kitchen designer has to know in detail what kitchen components—appliances, cabinets, windows and floors—are available, both wholesale and retail, and must keep up with the new products constantly being developed and brought onto the market. It is this vast store of information and sources that the client is counting on when he or she hires a kitchen designer.

Kitchen designers work on many kinds of projects: new residential developments, home remodels, apartment conversions to condominiums, and some commercial work for caterers and restaurants. Often the job starts with a phone call from a potential client followed by a meeting at the site of the project. This tests the designer's skill to listen to the client describe the way he or she wants to live and how central the kitchen area is to his or her lifestyle. The designer

must perceive from this what the client will most comfortably enjoy in the finished design.

The designer leafs through product brochures with the clients to assess their needs, taste, and priorities and also to determine what size budget the client realistically has for this kitchen. Once the basic investigation is done, the designer measures and lays out a kitchen plan, suggesting a variety of equipment to meet the client's taste, and meets again with the client to formalize all the decisions. Choosing major appliances—the stove, ovens, hoods and fans, refrigerators, freezers, sinks and faucets—may require a trip to the nearest major city with design showrooms where the designer and client together can see equipment on-line and learn about the advantages and disadvantages of each item.

Once the equipment has been chosen, the designer draws plans to scale for all components of the finished kitchen and prepares a detailed budget for the client—listing all the equipment to be purchased, the cost of installation, and the designer's estimated fee—and draws up a contract. There are several ways designers charge for their time and services: hourly rates for design time with all purchases at cost, a percentage of the entire cost of construction, or some combination of the two.

Every designer has a Rolodex with a goldmine of names and numbers of trusted workers and craftspeople including electricians, plumbers, carpenters, dry wall and plaster workers, and painters. Designers' reputations stand or fall on the quality of work done by the people they hire. Rounding up reliable subcontractors is a never-ending process. The designer is always looking at the work of colleagues, whether by attending open houses or by asking questions at professional meetings of designer associations.

Keeping up with information about available appliances takes constant reading of trade magazine ads, visits to nearby or big city design showrooms, and travel to major trade shows in the United States and Europe.

A niche market has developed for those who design for the disabled, either visually or physically handicapped. (A valuable resource for accessible design information is Easy Access Research in Ft. Collins, Colo.)

Satisfied clients are the ideal advertisement for a kitchen designer. They talk to friends about designing their dream kitchen, which designer they used, if there were any accidents, delays, or disappointments, and if it was all worth it. So every job must be the designer's best.

Salaries

Kitchen designers work on a commission sales basis in a showroom, on a flat fee for quoted services, on an hourly rate, or on a time-and-materials basis. The amount a designer can earn is limited by the geographic area and the number of kitchen design jobs available there. Earnings can range annually from $40,000 to well over $100,000. A kitchen designer on the staff of a housing tract development firm will be paid in the range of $30,000 to $60,000.

Employment Prospects

Most of this work is in retail showrooms and, to a lesser extent, as freelance design work. Designers who are available in showrooms for kitchen installations usually work without a salary and earn commissions on sales. Major residential development companies sometimes have a salaried kitchen specialist on staff.

Advancement Prospects

Advancement is a matter of public reputation and gaining status as a "big name" designer known for exceptional kitchens. Certain clients in a geographic area can make a designer's reputation and offer the opportunity to incorporate the highest-priced appliances available with elegant installations of floors, windows, and cabinets.

Best Geographical Location(s)

This work is spread across the country, and an area that is booming with population growth will have more new design work, especially in custom-built homes. Remodeling work in established, high-income communities is a huge segment of kitchen design.

Education and Training

A college degree in art and design is excellent background for a kitchen specialist. Community colleges and adult education programs often offer design classes. The National Kitchen and Bath Association offers a certified kitchen designer certificate. Because most designers work for themselves on commissions, time and materials, and percentage fees, a background in small business management is valuable.

Experience/Skills/Personality Traits

A designer needs a steel-trap memory for products and subcontractors, the persuasive ability to talk a client into choices that reflect their own lifestyle, the willingness to work within the client's budget even if it means compromising quality in some ways, the ability to get along with all sorts of people (especially subcontractors doing the construction work), and a love to shop.

Unions/Associations

The National Kitchen and Bath Association provides information and educational material for members, holds an annual trade show, and conducts a certification program for designers. Many designers practice other related interior design consulting and are members of the American Society of Interior Designers and the International Interior Design Association.

Tips for Entry

1. Take high school or college drafting classes and look for work in a kitchen design showroom.
2. Ask any local kitchen designers for a job as a gofer, doing research through catalogs and trade publications and picking up samples for clients.
3. Work for a cabinetmaker, floor supplier, lighting showroom, or any of the wholesale or retail businesses related to kitchens.

PUBLICITY,
PUBLIC RELATIONS,
AND MARKETING

HOTEL OR RESTAURANT PUBLICIST/PR DIRECTOR

CAREER PROFILE

Duties: Managing news and general interest stories about the property in local and regional publications with the aim of attracting customers, building a network among the press, developing contacts with influential people in all segments of the community, establishing a publicity calendar for the coming months in consultation with the general manager, producing an outreach newsletter and writing all publicity copy that is released to the press

Alternate Title(s): Press Contact

Salary Range: $40,000 to $160,000 and up

Employment Prospects: Limited

Advancement Prospects: Fair

Best Geographical Location(s) for Position: Major tourist cities and popular resort areas

Prerequisites:
   Education or Training—B.A. degree in communications
   Experience—Any journalism work for developing writing skills
   Special Skills and Personality Traits—Clear understanding of protecting confidentiality; social skills in assembling a community network

CAREER LADDER

```
┌─────────────────────────────────┐
│        General Manager           │
└─────────────────────────────────┘

┌─────────────────────────────────┐
│     Hotel or Restaurant          │
│     Publicist/PR Director        │
└─────────────────────────────────┘

┌─────────────────────────────────┐
│      Publicist's Assistant       │
└─────────────────────────────────┘
```

Position Description

A full-time publicist or public relations (PR) director for an upscale hotel property or chain or for a high-end restaurant is responsible for placing news and general interest stories about the property in local and regional publications with the aim of attracting customers. The business philosophy is that when local residents read interesting stories about the property in their local newspaper, tabloids, or magazines they will be interested to see (and eat) for themselves at the property. The reverse of the coin is that publicists have to do everything they can to block the printing of any adverse stories. An unexpected, sudden death among the guests is "bad press" and should not be publicized; even though it is probably simple coincidence and not food poisoning that caused the death when and where it did, the publicist uses all of his or her resources to hush up the news.

The publicist works diligently to build a network among the press and in the publicity area that serves the property. Social editors, restaurant reviewers, and public interest columnists are all kept informed of happenings, invited to special events, and hosted at one-on-one lunches just to keep them interested in the hotel so they can slip a paragraph about it into anything they are writing if it has a connection. Just as important, the publicist develops contacts with all segments of the community, starting with chamber of commerce "mixers." The publicist is not just a party goer, but is "working the room" to meet community leaders, gathering business cards while chatting about what hobbies and recreation hold their interest, and jotting this on the back of the card for later follow-up. The property will carefully consider popular benefit events to host on their premises. The publicist develops an annual calendar of these, learns whether they are always held at the same site or whether they might host the next one.

As this information is gathered and begins to make sense, the publicist reviews it with the general manager (G.M.) to develop a program for the coming months. Each event is considered and rated by the G.M.'s interest; the publicist uses this to put out feelers toward having the event moved to their location. Significant individuals in the areas that the publicist has met and cemented a contact with are also reviewed with the G.M. to rank the ones they will invite to lunches, small dinners, and special events. Even if it doesn't result in articles and other print publicity, these people talk up places they like around town, contributing to the buzz. Buzz is valuable in its own way.

If the hotel or restaurant property distributes a newsletter, heralding the special events of the coming season, including photos taken at recent gala events for the public and bragging about anything that seems appropriate, it is the publicist's job to write and produce this, using desktop publishing skills. Press releases, when they are appropriate, are the work of the publicist, all subject to the review and approval of the general manager of the property.

Finally, the publicist is one of the keystone employees of the property, and his or her relations with fellow employees, not only in the executive offices but throughout the property, make him or her part of the eyes and ears the G.M. needs in order to stay on top of potentially difficult situations such as disgruntled staffers who unwittingly make a bad impression on guests.

Salaries

Salary for these jobs ranges broadly depending on the work experience of the candidate and level of skill. The size of the property, the cost of lodging and meals, and the social style of the community also significantly influence how much the owners want to invest in publicity and public relations costs. The range can be as broad as from $40,000 to $160,000 and up.

Employment Prospects

High-end hotel companies—Ritz-Carlton, Four Seasons—and individual properties that are members of elite associations—Relais & Châteaux, Historic Inns—are most likely to have a full-time publicist.

Advancement Prospects

Hotel chains offer frequent opportunities for advancement by moving from one property to another, with the ultimate assignment being at the flagship property, which is usually corporate headquarters as well.

Alternatively, in a city or resort area with a number of top properties, most of the hospitality publicists will be acquainted with each other and news of a job opening will travel fast.

Best Geographical Location(s)

Major tourist cities and popular resort areas are most likely to have publicists working to improve the position of top hotels, both locally with residents and nationally with travelers.

Education and Training

A college or university B.A. degree in communications will teach copywriting and journalistic skills. For training, the best path is to be promoted to positions of higher responsibility while moving from smaller properties to larger ones; this provides hands-on work in a variety of styles and from entry level to the top.

Experience/Skills/Personality Traits

A publicist needs to observe the utmost confidentiality about the business and its clients, while simultaneously spreading as much news and name recognition as possible in the community.

Accurate writing and communication skills are essential. No casually selected adjective should ever be chosen for a press release or a print advertisement; misunderstanding by the reader can lead to greater job jeopardy than being rude to a customer.

Unions/Associations

A local ad club will supply contacts with a broad range of colleagues for networking. A local press club or media association, if they exist, will be a good source of key contacts within the community.

Tips for Entry

1. If the nearest community college has a communications department, contact the school counseling department about job opportunities.
2. Look for one-day or weekend seminars that provide public relations or publicity skill development and sign up. Expect to meet at least a few PR people or company publicists who can give you the scoop on jobs.

HOTEL OR RESORT SALES MANAGER

CAREER PROFILE

Duties: Active marketing to attract guests to the property to stay and to dine in the property's restaurants, making sales "cold calls," wining and dining local business leaders, and following up over time to create new business, developing contacts through chambers of commerce and local service organizations, attracting organizations and businesses to hold holiday and award banquets

Alternate Title(s): None

Salary Range: $35,000 to $80,000 and up

Employment Prospects: Limited

Advancement Prospects: Fair

Best Geographical Location(s) for Position: Resort areas and major tourist destinations

Prerequisites:
   Education or Training—None
   Experience—All sales experience is helpful
   Special Skills and Personality Traits—Thorough knowledge of culinary and hospitality features of the property; persuasive, friendly, and detail-oriented

CAREER LADDER

```
┌─────────────────────────────┐
│     Director of Sales        │
└─────────────────────────────┘

┌─────────────────────────────┐
│    Hotel Sales Manager       │
└─────────────────────────────┘

┌─────────────────────────────┐
│  Assistant or Support Staff  │
└─────────────────────────────┘
```

Position Description

The sales manager for a hotel or inn is an active marketer who works to attract guests to the property as overnight guests, to dine in the property's restaurants, and seeks groups to hold lunch and dinner events in the banquet rooms. This is done by making "cold calls" (making a sales call to a company or a person you have never met) to selected business offices (chosen for their likelihood to be interested in the call) to learn who makes their local travel and entertaining arrangements, talking to that person as a form of introduction, and making an appointment to meet in order to further discuss mutual business.

"Cold call" sales contacts are rarely very successful in quantity; on average a sales manager will be satisfied to get as few as 10 percent who are willing to take the call. Once that hurdle has been passed, the salesperson continues the process by supplying information about the property (lodging specifications, description of dining facilities and sample menus, and other printed material that is designed to encourage new customers), and if the call seems promising,

the potential customer will be invited to visit the hotel, join the salesperson for lunch in the highest quality dining area, and be shown around the property.

The sales manager rarely expects to set up any firm business at this point. The process is one of building a relationship. A reasonable estimate is that this effort represents 80 percent of the effort to create a new customer. From this point on, the sales manager will follow up with occasional mailings, announcements of special events at the property, and phone calls just to keep in touch.

In most cities and large towns there is a local Chamber of Commerce and sometimes a business and industry subsection of the chamber. The sales manager attends Chamber "mixers" to meet representatives from larger local companies. To develop more contacts, membership in local and national service organizations—Rotary International, Downtown Organization—is encouraged by the hotel. They see it as a way to contribute to the community and make contact with potential customers at the same time.

If the sales manager has a professional interest in culinary activities, he or she will likely join the American Institute of Wine and Food, Women for WineSense, and any local culinary guild or society. Becoming active in these organizations allows the salesperson to suggest the property for organizations' events—wine tastings, holiday dinners—thus generating business for the property and also creating more customers when the group is pleased with the special event.

Salaries

The sales director works to meet sales goals set for monthly performance that are negotiated with his or her immediate boss and agreed upon at the start of each fiscal year. Meeting or exceeding these goals guarantees a higher commission or bonus; not meeting the goals means only the base salary will be paid. The salary range is usually between $35,000 and $80,000.

Employment Prospects

Sales positions in top hotels are highly sought after by proven salespersons who know the community, already have a business network to draw on, and who are confident that the style of the property matched with their own skills will enable them to reach the top of the salary range.

Advancement Prospects

A salesperson at a lower rung in the individual hotel or a hotel chain can aspire to a higher position or to being transferred to another location with greater sales potential.

Best Geographical Location(s)

Prime locations include resort areas, coastal, desert, and mountain communities with high-end lodging properties and major cities that draw high-income visitors who prefer to stay at more expensive hotels and eat at restaurants with celebrity chefs.

Education and Training

There is no specific educational course for sales work, but marketing courses and seminars will always help a beginner get a head start and demonstrate confidence as he or she enters this field. Developing a network of colleagues in similar work builds an excellent support system.

Experience/Skills/Personality Traits

Hotel catering managers are often promoted to sales positions. After several years of working with the hotel's kitchens and satisfying customers who are very fussy about their private events, an aspiring employee has an advantage for sales performance.

Unions/Associations

These jobs rarely require joining a union, even in large cities where culinary unions are very strong. This especially applies to New York City and other major metropolitan areas.

Tips for Entry

1. The chain hotel companies are more likely to hire inexperienced or, at least less experienced, salespersons; they will pair them with an experienced one for training for the first few months.
2. On a job application, list every possible example of sales experience, including cookie sales for the Scouts and raffle tickets for the P.T.A.

DESTINATION MANAGEMENT COMPANY ACCOUNT MANAGER

CAREER PROFILE

Duties: Serving an out-of-town client in bringing a conference or business meeting to a local hotel property, supplying meals, transportation, catering, and special entertainment needs, developing a budget for client approval, booking all services, staying in close contact with clients during their stay, reviewing and forwarding invoices for payment, and following up with clients to determine level of satisfaction about the visit

Alternate Title(s): None

Salary Range: $60,000 to $100,000

Employment Prospects: Limited

Advancement Prospects: Fair

Best Geographical Location(s) for Position: Major tourist and resort areas with high-end hotels and restaurants

Prerequisites:
Education or Training—Hospitality industry vocational training
Experience—Hotel sales positions
Special Skills and Personality Traits—Skill at pleasing very critical customers, creative, flexible, gracious, friendly

CAREER LADDER

```
┌─────────────────────────────────────┐
│          Director of Sales           │
└─────────────────────────────────────┘

┌─────────────────────────────────────┐
│      Destination Management          │
│    Company Account Manager           │
└─────────────────────────────────────┘

┌─────────────────────────────────────┐
│   Operations/Arrangements Manager    │
└─────────────────────────────────────┘
```

Position Description

The account manager at a destination management company (DMC) works with an out-of-town client who is bringing a conference, business meeting, or an (incentive) award winner to stay at an upscale local hotel or resort, dine at local restaurants, and enjoy the unique facilities of the area. Usually the client has already booked the lodging, and it is their planner who brings in the DMC for all other arrangements. The company account manager's primary interactions are with (1) the client and (2) the company's operations manager, who will supply specific recommendations for outside companies who contract for meals, transportation, catering, and special entertainment needs of the client.

Destination management companies are located in cities and towns that have a strong tourist appeal: resorts, beaches, mountains, wine regions, and art and culture centers. The companies serve as booking agencies and on-site service for groups who are sent to the location for either business or entertainment purposes by their employer or as an award for outstanding performance. The DMC may also specialize in theme events and team building programs for their clients. The comfort and pleasure of the traveler, before, during, and after the visit, is the principal concern of the manager.

As soon as the sale of services is booked (either by the sales manager or by the account manager) work begins in detail on the account, by telephone and email with the client. The types of meals are defined and caterers or restaurants are booked, any necessary transportation (luxury buses for a group or limousines for a few) is scheduled, and outside staffing is hired. At the time of the event, the account manager meets the awarded individual or the conferencing group on arrival and welcomes them to the area. During the visit, the account manager is at their beck and call to ensure that every aspect of the program is of the highest quality and smoothly executed. Following the departure, the account manager reviews and approves all billing, forwards a detailed invoice to the client, and follows up by phone with the client to determine satisfaction for the services performed.

The account manager is responsible for cost controls and strict financial accounting to meet the originally contracted price. A major qualification for being hired is knowledge of the area and an existing network with local culinary and hospitality businesses. Once in the job, a manager will be judged by client satisfaction, skills as a team player, being a self-manager and self-motivator, the flexibility to solve unexpected problems, and a positive attitude.

Salaries

Because these jobs involve making sales and providing client satisfaction in an expensive market, salaries are generous, ranging from $60,000 to $100,000.

Employment Prospects

The number of destination management companies is small. This is a high end of the hospitality business that focuses on personal service, and since the client base is small, there are few companies doing the work. Prior experience as catering sales manager for a very upscale hotel or chain may lead to one of these jobs.

Advancement Prospects

Advancement is mostly in the form of salary increases. If the company is growing by hiring more managers and increasing capital equipment, this will lead to business volume growth as well as growth as a tourist destination; the best managers on the staff will be promoted to the highest rung on the company's internal ladder.

If there is more than one such company in a geographic area, top managers are always subject to being recruited.

Best Geographical Location(s)

These companies only flourish in areas that are major tourist destinations and where upscale lodgings and recreation opportunities exist. Golf, wineries, gourmet chefs, exclusive spas, and natural beauty are the environment that spawn upscale hotels, restaurants, and recreation—the draw that provides a client for destination planners.

Education and Training

A good grounding in the hospitality industry and experience in catering to affluent clients are the basic skills for a destination manager. Self-education can best be obtained by traveling as a visitor to competing locations: ski resorts, southern climates, and sophisticated cities with expensive accommodations.

Experience/Skills/Personality Traits

A dedication to please the client, the creativity to imagine extra touches that will make the visit memorable, a personal fascination with the art and culture of the area in order to introduce it to the visitor as an insider, and the innate graciousness of an outstanding host or hostess are indispensible assets.

Unions/Associations

Meeting Planners International is a professional membership association of sales and management people who do this type of work.

Since the culinary aspect of the work is crucial to the satisfaction of the client, membership in groups such as the American Institute of Wine and Food and the American Center for Wine, Food and the Arts will be useful for self-education.

Tips for Entry

1. Locate a destination planning company in your area, talk to them about any openings and follow up periodically with the contact.
2. Locate one or more destination planning companies in places you would consider living and visit there to talk to someone in the company about any future hiring plans they have.
3. If your area has one or more destination planning companies, while working for an upscale hotel or restaurant you can encourage the planners to use your current company. The business relationship might lead to an offer of employment.

COOKING SCHOOLS, VOCATIONAL TRAINING, AND ACADEMIES

COOKING SCHOOL DIRECTOR

CAREER PROFILE

Duties: Plans class schedule; hires cooking teachers; writes and distributes program brochure; controls income and costs; hires, trains, and supervises staff

Alternate Title(s): Cooking School Manager

Salary Range: $25,000 to $60,000

Employment Prospects: Limited

Advancement Prospects: Limited

Best Geographical Location(s) for Position: Major urban areas that are food meccas with lots of fine restaurants and food sources

Prerequisites:

    Education or Training—At least a high school diploma or general education diploma (GED); business classes on the college level; extensive knowledge of cooking

    Experience—A year or more of teaching cooking is an advantage

    Special Skills and Personality Traits—The caring and nurturing character of a teacher and an instinct for consistent quality

CAREER LADDER

```
┌─────────────────────────────┐
│      Cooking School         │
│ Executive Director or Owner │
└─────────────────────────────┘

┌─────────────────────────────┐
│   Cooking School Director   │
└─────────────────────────────┘

┌─────────────────────────────┐
│  Cooking Teacher and Staff  │
└─────────────────────────────┘
```

Position Description

The director of a cooking school decides the schedule of classes to be given; hires and assigns teachers to individual classes or series; designs and produces the program mailer (with the assistance of a graphic designer, if the budget allows); arranges publicity; establishes class budgets; oversees all class registrations to rebudget or cancel those that are undersubscribed; sets up all arrangements for classes including equipment assembly, ingredient shopping, and recipe and handouts printing; teaches certain classes; schedules class assistants; reviews class goals and objectives with teachers following the classes; reimburses all expenses and pays teachers; and maintains the facility and equipment.

Some cooking schools present as demanding a program as ten classes a week, daytime and evening schedules, in an up-to-date, fully equipped facility, and some as few as two dozen classes a year all taught by the same person in his or her home kitchen. A typical school is one that has a comfortable facility with arenas for demonstrations with a view-enhancing overhead mirror, and hands-on, full-participation classes. Classes are taught both by local teachers who have developed series classes (such as bread, desserts, pastry, fish, basics, party food) and have a loyal following of students, and by traveling teachers who are usually cookbook authors touring with their latest book or testing recipes for the next one. If classrooms are sufficiently large, classes are usually budgeted for up to 50 students in demonstrations thanks to the development of TV technology for on-site monitors, and for 15 to 20 students in hands-on classes; class fees range from $40 to $85 for a three-hour class.

Some schools are adjuncts of upscale grocery stores, cookware stores, restaurants, and resorts. The classes are expected to lure customers to the primary business, and profit from the school is not crucial, but covering costs is essential.

The student is predominately interested in home cooking, sometimes referred to euphemistically as recreational cooking, but there is a growing student base of adults who are investigating professional food careers for themselves. These students look for advanced classes and hands-on work in specialty cooking techniques.

The director uses a well-developed knowledge of the student base for the school and a trained sense of new food trends that will be popular class subjects to draft a tentative program for the following three months. With time allowed for contracting with teachers, program design, and printing and mailing to be in the hands of students a month before the first class listed, the fall schedule for October through December has to be started about July 1; as the summer heat is ripening tomatoes and peaches, the school director is contemplating roast goose and steamed puddings for Christmas.

Local teachers have an ongoing relationship with the school, and they have usually talked to the director about new classes they want to develop. Authors of newly released cookbooks travel and teach to promote their books. Often these tours are booked by the publisher's marketing department. The school director has to establish and maintain connection with these publicists to get advance notice when a book is coming out and when the author will be traveling. Traveling teachers plan a loop of travel to save on air fares and exhaustion, so the director stays in contact with directors of other schools in nearby states to learn who is coming out this year. The director is usually a skilled cooking teacher, as well, and may regularly teach some of the series or the latest class on the hot, new food fad.

At the same time that schedule planning is taking place, the current season of classes is underway. Classes are confirmed to the teacher a week before the date, stating the number of students expected.

In certain downtimes, such as holidays and sometimes in the summer, the director can turn his or her focus to reviewing the past year and doing long-term planning for new programs, analyzing financial statements to catch costs that can be curbed or to capture available money for new equipment purchases.

Salaries

The director of a cooking school is usually the owner; if it is an ambitious, full-time program the owner might hire a director to be in charge of the day-to-day operations. Salaries depend on the income the school gets from classes, and range from $25,000 to $60,000 but with even lower numbers in the first year.

Employment Prospects

Employment opportunities as a cooking school director are limited. There are from 300 to 500 privately-owned cooking schools and culinary arts schools across the country, but most of these are small and managed by the owner.

Advancement Prospects

If the school is part of a larger institution like a university or a supermarket, the director can move to a higher administrative level. The successful manager of an independent cooking school can advance by building up the school or by seeking a similar job in a larger program.

Best Geographical Location(s)

Cooking schools are popular everywhere in the country, but they are more numerous in major urban areas that are high-end food cities with a plethora of restaurants, state-of-the-art grocery stores, and many specialty food sources. They are particularly numerous in the East Coast and West Coast states.

Education and Training

There is no specific degree or credential that is uniformly required for running a cooking school. In fact, most cooking school directors started out teaching cooking on their own. A college education is not essential, but at least an A.A. degree is recommended for gaining business skills and for managing both staff and contract teachers. The International Association of Culinary Professionals gives annual examinations to certify "culinary professionals"; that achievement has gained a high degree of respect.

Experience/Skills/Personality Traits

To run a cooking school program, a director is best served by having top teaching skills and broad management skills. Even if the director does not teach in the program, the experience is helpful for mentoring other teachers to best showcase their skills and for relating to the students' needs and questions.

The director uses both the caring and nurturing character of a teacher to ensure that students learn both what they need to know and what they want to know. An instinct for quality, consistency, and meticulousness encourages the best from teachers.

A thorough knowledge of ingredient qualities, traditional combinations of foods, some food chemistry (especially for baking), food terminology, and a moderate knowledge of food history are essential in the beginning, and the director should diligently pursue more general food knowledge over time.

Unions/Associations

The International Association of Culinary Professional (IACP) is the primary organization for cooking school programs. It holds annual meetings, publishes a bimonthly newsletter, and provides a certification program for teachers. The James Beard Foundation has a program centered at the James Beard House in New York City that maintains a year-round program of chef's dinners, cooking demonstrations, and food-related programs for the general public. Their publications are an excellent source of rising stars who can be solicited to teach.

Local culinary associations and guilds hold monthly meetings and educational programs, providing a valuable network for professionals associated with cooking programs.

Tips for Entry

1. Take any assistant job in a cooking school and show a readiness to assist the school director and learn the business.

2. Take a variety of classes at different cooking schools to study the various styles of management. Get acquainted with the cooking school owners and ask about job opportunities.

COOKING TEACHER

CAREER PROFILE

Duties: Plans class(es), writes recipes, demonstrates cooking techniques, and teaches essential ingredient information to adult students for home cooking and entertaining

Alternate Title(s): Demonstrator/Instructor

Salary Range: $75 to $750 per class for locally based teachers

Employment Prospects: Fair

Advancement Prospects: Good

Best Geographical Location(s) for Position: Cities and suburban areas with strong restaurant presences, which inspire interest in specialty cooking

Prerequisites:
    Education or Training—Cooking skills, either self-taught or professionally trained, and teaching skills
    Experience—Varies, depending on the requirements of the school and the uniqueness of the teacher's specialty
    Special Skills and Personality Traits—Enjoys being with people; able to tolerate less experienced cooks; generous in sharing knowledge

CAREER LADDER

```
┌─────────────────────────────┐
│   Cooking School Director   │
└─────────────────────────────┘

┌─────────────────────────────┐
│      Cooking Teacher        │
└─────────────────────────────┘

┌─────────────────────────────┐
│    Classroom Assistant      │
└─────────────────────────────┘
```

Position Description

A cooking teacher's work starts with class planning: selecting the recipes to be demonstrated, rewriting the recipes to match the way they will be taught, and sometimes even running through the entire class, alone or with a few helpful friends, as a rehearsal to plan the timing of each recipe, to note particular points to be emphasized, and to note appropriate anecdotes to amuse the students. (Effective teaching relies on a bit of entertainment to capture and hold a student's attention.)

Whether it is a menu class (soup to shortcake) or a specialty class (yeast breads or ice creams), the students expect a variety of recipes (five, six, or more) and ideas for variations on most of them. The cooking teacher selects recipes that teach specific techniques (boning, sauté, emulsions) that are essential for all cooks to know. Because every step of the recipe will be performed in the class, the recipe can be written in a concise manner, but it must be absolutely correct in the measurements, quality of ingredients, and timing.

The cooking teacher usually does the ingredient shopping and assembles the necessary tools for preparation, bringing many of them from home if the classroom is not

fully equipped. The day of the class, the teacher arrives an hour or more before the students to prepare (clean, cut, measure) and arrange the ingredients, with each recipe having its own tray or counter area. Often the school provides an assistant to help the teacher in preparation, during the class, and for cleanup. When the students arrive, the teacher has to be ready to hand out recipes and start the demonstration. The cooking teacher plans tastings (of a specific ingredient or a stage of a sauce) during the cooking to give every student a palate memory of key stages in the recipe that will help when they repeat it at home.

Whether the students are beginners or advanced they will have many questions, and skillful teachers encourage students to speak out for everyone's benefit. Sometimes a show-off student tries to talk too much, and teachers need to gracefully maintain control without criticizing or embarrassing a student. Every teacher has made cooking mistakes while perfecting his or her own skills, and recounting these mistakes entertains and teaches at the same time. Well into the cooking class, the scene may resemble total chaos, with several recipes underway in various stages of cooking and cooling; the cooking teacher has to clarify what students are observing so they understand how it all relates to putting a meal on the table.

Some classes are planned with tastings throughout the two to three hours of class time; others offer a meal of the demonstrated dishes when everything is ready. This tasting period is an essential test for the teacher, and it often generates a fresh flow of questions, especially about substitute ingredients and variations on the recipe. A teacher's wide-ranging knowledge about food and cooking can spill comfortably in this more relaxed exchange with students; it often inspires ideas for additional classes the teacher can offer.

Salaries

Teaching fees are closely related to the price a school can charge for the class, the popularity of the subject matter—which translates into the number of students who will sign up for it—and, to a lesser extent, the cost of cooking ingredients. Bread-making and winter soups classes have a very low ingredient cost combined with a consistently high popularity level, even though they do not cost much. Teaching fee for a small demo would be about $75 based on the number of hours of planning, preparation, teaching, and cleanup. ("Name" chefs ask [and get] up to $1,500 per class.)

Employment Prospects

Wherever cooking classes are popular, there are jobs for cooking teachers. A good cook who specializes in one category of cooking, such as breads, desserts, sausages, sauces, or who is an expert on ethnic foods, such as Central American, Middle Eastern, or Asian, has a fine chance of being hired without extensive teaching experience.

The employer may be the owner of a small school for adults who want to improve their cooking skills for family and entertaining, or the adult education program of a community college that offers a wide range of classes for primary skills and health purposes as well as introductory classes in popular restaurant cuisines (Thai, Hawaiian, Tex-Mex, and Italian); the students may be highly educated and well-traveled adults who are very informed about food, or they may be relative beginners in the kitchen who have never had to cook for themselves or others.

In recent years the number of cooking schools on both coasts, Atlantic and Pacific, have grown substantially, aided in part by healthy economic conditions.

Advancement Prospects

There is rarely any hierarchy or any higher position for a cooking teacher in a small to medium-sized cooking school. If the economy is improving and salaries in all fields are going up, it is likely a cooking teacher can raise his or her fee for classes at the start of the school year.

Popular cooking teachers attract their following by word of mouth; friends and coworkers tell each other about classes they attend. Students will request that the school offer additional classes from a well-liked teacher. Owners of small, private cooking schools pass on information to each other about a new teacher, especially if the two schools aren't close enough to be competing for the same students. Local teachers can become traveling teachers over a wide area, even nationwide, especially if they have a cookbook to promote or become known for food magazine articles about their cooking skills and classes.

Best Geographical Location(s)

Cities with an active restaurant scene stimulate home cooks to learn more demanding techniques and exotic cuisines, thereby spawning cooking school programs and opportunities for cooking teachers. Rapidly growing communities with housing booms that attract young families and first-time home-buyers stimulate all manner of culinary activity, including cooking classes.

There are growing opportunities for cooking teachers in France, Italy, Spain, Australia, and the Far East. Some of these require the teacher to speak the local language. Many of these are for classes in North American cuisine.

Education and Training

The main requirement of a cooking teacher is being well versed in basic cooking skills and techniques. Some teachers have acquired this knowledge from culinary training, cooking school classes, reading, and restaurant or catering jobs.

Experience/Skills/Personality Traits

The knack of teaching hinges on the teacher's strong desire to transfer knowledge, to share, and to confirm that the student has grasped the skills being taught. The appreciation of good food, seeking new tastes and presentation skills by reading and restaurant going, and interest and curiosity about trends in food benefit the teacher's background knowledge. Patience with beginners is essential.

Unions/Associations

Most cooking teachers are contract employees; unless they are full-time teachers in a public school system, they are not eligible for teachers union membership.

The International Association of Culinary Professionals (IACP) was started as the Association of Cooking Teachers, and it provides examination and certification of cooking teachers. Local culinary associations and guilds, where they exist, are the best place for brainstorming with colleagues, and they always seek cooking teachers and cooking school staff for their membership.

Tips for Entry

1. Locate the available cooking classes in your area through the telephone book, newspaper food editor, food magazine listings, and adult education programs. Take a few classes to sense what is popular in your area and to get acquainted with other teachers and school managers.

2. Plan and practice a sample class that you can use to audition for a school manager. Prepare your résumé listing all the travel and cultural influences that make you an expert. Assemble a package to present to a school manager consisting of the sample class, résumé, and a tasting of one of your recipes.

3. Offer to assist at cooking classes; working for a popular teacher can give you lots of pointers and give the school manager an indication of your dedication.

4. If you are an expert in an exotic cuisine, your friends may want to learn from you. Consider teaching a few classes in your own home to get started and hone your teaching skills.

COOKING TEACHER'S ASSISTANT

CAREER PROFILE

Duties: Prepares and cleans up the teaching area for classes; preps all recipes for the teacher; and assists as needed during the class; helps serve demonstrated food at tastings

Alternate Title(s): Classroom Assistant; Classroom Aide

Salary Range: Minimum wage to $10 an hour

Employment Prospects: Limited

Advancement Prospects: Good

Best Geographical Location(s) for Position: Suburban areas and cities with a variety of cooking-class programs.

Prerequisites:

Education or Training—Basic knowledge of cooking techniques, especially knife work, pastry bag, blending and pureeing skills; knowledge of standard cooking equipment

Experience—Attendance at one or more cooking classes to know what is expected

Special Skills and Personality Traits—Ability to take instruction and follow directions precisely

CAREER LADDER

```
┌─────────────────────────────────┐
│        Cooking Teacher          │
└─────────────────────────────────┘

┌─────────────────────────────────┐
│   Cooking Teacher's Assistant   │
└─────────────────────────────────┘

┌─────────────────────────────────┐
│      Prep/Cleanup Worker        │
└─────────────────────────────────┘
```

Position Description

The essential person who makes a cooking class move smoothly is the classroom assistant. It is extraordinarily difficult for a cooking teacher to do prep work, such as mincing and measuring, while talking about the recipe and its essential techniques to the group of students.

The classroom assistant has to be able to follow instructions precisely. Even if the assistant is a very accomplished cook and believes there is a quicker or easier way to do something, the assistant will follow the teacher's directions.

Before the class, the assistant checks that all the necessary equipment is available and that the working counters are all clean and ready for the demonstration. Some teachers ask the assistant to do the ingredient shopping for the class; that implies a high level of trust in the assistant. As soon as the teacher arrives, the assistant helps unload all the equipment and ingredients and set up trays (or whatever system the teacher prefers) for each recipe to be demonstrated.

The assistant has to know when to ask questions and not assume that steps are done in a particular way. The time to ask these questions is before the class, when the assistant

and the teacher review the recipes step by step. During the class, the assistant helps the teacher keep the demonstration area wiped clean, removes each piece of equipment for washing as soon as it has been used, and brings up each tray of measured ingredients and tools just before the teacher needs it. At the completion of each demonstrated recipe or at the end of the class, depending on the cooking teacher's preference, the assistant serves tastings to the students.

After the class, the assistant finishes all the cleanup, usually with the help of the teacher. In effect, the assistant has had a private, full-participation class from the teacher. Any extra questions the assistant has about the recipes and the techniques involved can be asked while they clean up and pack the teacher's equipment. This is an opportunity for the assistant to ask if the teacher has any other work he or she could do, such as testing cookbook or food article recipes or working on other classes.

Salaries

Many schools do not pay class assistants; they work as volunteers hoping to get a leg on the ladder to become teachers for the school by proving themselves. When they are paid, it is at minimum wage because these jobs are highly sought after by students who want the opportunity to get acquainted with a particular cooking teacher or with the school manager. If the assistant also does clerical work for the school, the salary can range between $10 and $12 an hour, depending on the level of responsibility.

Employment Prospects

Cooking schools usually line up between two to six assistants for a teaching season, depending on the number of classes they offer. Community colleges expect the teacher to supply his or her own assistant if one is needed. Cooking schools employ a variety of helpers, but often this means giving a free class to regular students who volunteer to assist teachers. Some cooking teachers have their own assistants who work for them in a variety of jobs, and they specify that they will provide their own staff for a class.

Advancement Prospects

Classroom assistants often aspire to be cooking teachers, and after an introductory period of working for other teachers they are able to present their own cooking class prospectus very successfully to one or more cooking school managers. This work is a good stepping stone to learn more about cooking, make contacts, and develop good work skills.

Best Geographical Location(s)

Wherever there are cooking classes—cooking schools, home-based classes, cookware store demonstrations—there are opportunities for assistants, but more often than not it is unpaid.

Education and Training

Entry-level knowledge of cooking techniques is the only requirement to get started. The more an assistant knows about cooking, the more valuable he or she is to a cooking teacher. The work that a classroom assistant does with direction from the cooking teacher is excellent training for a variety of other food-related jobs.

Experience/Skills/Personality Traits

The ability to follow directions is the most important characteristic in assisting teachers who must imprint their own style on the classes they teach. A willingness to ask questions when directions are not fully understood is essential. The assistant needs to be fast, clean, and have good knife skills.

Unions/Associations

Local culinary associations seek members from anyone who earns income in the food industry, and classroom assistants usually qualify. This is an excellent local network for finding additional work.

Tips for Entry

1. Locate the available cooking classes in your area through the telephone book, newspaper food editor, food magazine listings, and adult education programs. Take a class or two to watch different styles of assisting and to get acquainted with local teachers and school managers.
2. Offer to assist (free of charge) at cooking classes; working for a popular teacher can give you lots of pointers and give the school manager an indication of your dedication.
3. Contact any local or traveling teachers by phone or mail, offering your skills as an assistant. Just the heartfelt assurance that you love to cook and want to learn more will often incline a teacher to hire you.

TRAVELING COOKING TEACHER

CAREER PROFILE

Duties: Plans and markets a series or group of signature cooking classes to upscale cooking schools; writes recipes, demonstrates cooking techniques and teaches essential ingredient information to adult students for home cooking and entertaining

Alternate Title(s): None

Salary Range: $300 to $1,800 per three-hour class

Employment Prospects: Limited

Advancement Prospects: Good

Best Geographical Location(s) for Position: Cities and suburban areas with strong restaurant presences, which inspire interest in specialty cooking

Prerequisites:

Education or Training—Specialty cooking skills, either self-taught or trained; teaching skills

Experience—Dependent on the requirements of the school and the uniqueness of the specialty

Special Skills and Personality Traits—Credibility as an expert; enjoy being with people; ability to tolerate less experienced cooks; generous in sharing knowledge

CAREER LADDER

```
┌─────────────────────────────────┐
│      Cooking School Director     │
└─────────────────────────────────┘

┌─────────────────────────────────┐
│     Traveling Cooking Teacher    │
└─────────────────────────────────┘

┌─────────────────────────────────┐
│         Class Assistant          │
└─────────────────────────────────┘
```

Position Description

A traveling cooking teacher plans his or her schedule a year or more in advance by booking engagements with a group of cooking schools around the country. The teacher develops a season of classes, writes a prospectus of recipes and techniques to be taught, and markets this to cooking schools. The classes may be based on a newly published cookbook by the teacher, or result from research or travels the teacher has made to explore an ethnic cuisine or a demanding specialty (perhaps for the next cookbook). Repeat students look forward to new material from their favorite teachers. The schedule is best set up as a tour, to take advantage of air fares and to minimize travel fatigue.

As soon as the classes are scheduled, the teacher develops and tests all the promised recipes, writes and proofreads the class handouts (there may be cultural, travel, ingredient, or other educational materials the teacher will present in addition to the recipes), and has the student packages printed for advance mailings to each cooking school.

Depending on the prestige of the school and the popularity of the teacher, this advance packet may also contain a biography, a press release, and a photo for the school to use in local newspapers to advertise the teacher.

In addition to the recipes, the teacher sends each school a complete equipment list and detailed shopping list. Many teachers insist on doing their own shopping and allow time for that by arriving the day before the class. If the teacher needs his or her own special equipment or ingredients, they are shipped ahead whenever possible.

Traveling teachers often book two classes a day, morning and evening, at the smaller schools, and a week-long series at larger schools. The class day starts with recipe prep an hour or two before the students arrive. Usually the school provides an assistant, or the school owner pitches in. Once the students arrive and the recipes are handed out, everything possible is arranged for the teacher and put into place on the demonstration counter as it is needed. The teacher decides whether to space tastings throughout the demonstration or to time the recipes to provide a meal at the end.

In some cities the cooking school director will arrange for local publicity, such as an interview with the newspaper food editor or an appearance on the local TV channel or radio station. This can be sandwiched between two classes, or it may require an extra day on the travel schedule; if it also promotes the teacher's cookbooks, it is well worth the extra travel time and expense.

Salaries

Traveling cooking teachers are contract employees, freelancers who negotiate their own fees and compensation with each individual school where they teach.

Fees paid to traveling teachers vary widely, depending on how much the school can charge for the classes. A cookbook author or television personality will draw the maximum number of students for each session and command top dollar for the class. Such teachers charge $1,000 to $1,800 per class plus travel expenses (air fare, hotel, and meals). A beginning teacher on the travel circuit charges from $300 up, plus expenses. The school also reimburses or pays for class ingredients and the printing of handouts (recipes).

Employment Prospects

There are more than 300 private cooking schools in the United States, Europe, and Asia, with concentrations in major cities and urban areas. Cooking school owners are always looking for new talent to attract additional students to their schools and to encourage regular students to attend more classes.

Traveling teachers usually start by teaching in their home area. Word of mouth travels fast among cooking school managers, and they are always generous to help a good teacher get more bookings.

Advancement Prospects

As a teacher becomes better known, he or she can usually ask for higher fees. Publishing cookbooks, writing food articles for major magazines, and making food show appearances are all ways for a traveling teacher to improve his or her popularity with students. These extra activities that contribute to their reputation also pay good fees to food professionals, and they enhance the marketability of the teacher.

Best Geographical Location(s)

Traveling teachers can live almost anywhere, commuting to the areas where they teach. There is some advantage to living in an area with a strong restaurant presence or near a college offering cooking courses.

Education and Training

Traveling cooking teachers need the same basic knowledge and training of any cooking teacher, but in addition they

must have a specialty or expertise that draws a crowd of students to pay extra for their classes. Growing up or living in an exotic country with a unique culinary tradition, such as Morocco, Brazil, or Thailand, is a passport to teaching and writing about that cuisine. Extensive training and work experience with specialty techniques such as breads, pastries, chocolate, spa food, and vegetarian lifestyles are currently very marketable.

Experience/Skills/Personality Traits

This specialty knowledge must still be matched with outstanding teaching characteristics: the enjoyment of shared knowledge, genuine interest in students and their accomplishments at both the beginning and advanced level, and infinite patience with beginners. Flexibility is important; when a difficulty arises it is essential.

Unions/Associations

The International Association of Culinary Professionals (IACP) was started as the Association of Cooking Teachers, and it provides examination and certification of cooking teachers. This organization provides an excellent opportunity for cooking teachers to get acquainted with their colleagues around the country and to meet cooking school owners and directors at the annual meeting every spring.

Tips for Entry

1. Join IACP and attend the annual conference held every spring (usually in March or April) to meet cooking school owners and managers and other traveling teachers. By joining the "Schools" section, take part in the monthly teleconferencing to learn from the other participants and to ask your own questions for career development.
2. Start by teaching in one or more cooking schools near your home. Whenever visiting students from another city turn up in one of the classes, find out what cooking schools are doing in their area and let them serve as advance publicists for you with the out-of-town school. Follow up with a prospectus and a press package mailed to the referenced school.
3. Accept any opportunity to present a cooking demonstration at charity events, such as a Taste of the Town or a local food festival such as the Garlic Festival or Sweet Corn Festival. The tried and true food fans will see you there, and possibly even the local cooking school manager.
4. Whenever you travel to another city check to see if there are cooking schools listed in the yellow pages, drop in to introduce yourself, leave a brochure with the manager, and follow up when you begin to book your classes for the next season.

FOOD SERVICE MANAGEMENT TEACHER

CAREER PROFILE

Duties: Teaches basic kitchen skills needed for restaurant and institutional cooking, including management of inventory, production costs, menu pricing, and facility maintenance

Alternate Title(s): Instructor; Professor; Chef

Salary Range: $35,000 to $60,000

Employment Prospects: Wide-ranging throughout the United States in hundreds of vocational and professional programs

Advancement Prospects: Very good

Best Geographical Location(s) for Position: See the list of states where most of the schools are clustered, but there are community college programs in every state.

Prerequisites:
Education or Training—College degree (bachelor's or master's), culinary academy certification, or impressive work experience as an alternative, depending on the college's requirements
Experience—Professional cooking and management
Special Skills and Personality Traits—Communication skills, both oral and written; teaching skills, including patience, perception, flexibility, and the ability to plan and organize curriculum segments

CAREER LADDER

```
┌─────────────────────────────────┐
│   Vocational School Director     │
└─────────────────────────────────┘

┌─────────────────────────────────┐
│         Food Service            │
│      Management Teacher         │
└─────────────────────────────────┘

┌─────────────────────────────────┐
│    Foods Teaching Assistant     │
└─────────────────────────────────┘
```

Position Description

Vocational training in the United States is usually given as post-secondary (after high school) programs, on the community college level. Teaching in one of these programs means training students for productive jobs in cafes, bakeries, restaurants, and hotel dining and banquet rooms, including off-premises catering. Beginning students range from those with absolutely no cooking experience (or even sensitivity and curiosity), to those who may have as much as 10 years' experience working in camps, churches, or schools. The aim is to improve their skills and job potential.

From the first day, students are taught that it's important to keep their word, that they show up sober, alert, on time, ready to work, in uniform, and with a curious mind. The program teaches a work ethic that is as important to success as knife skills and sauce knowledge. Vocational teaching requires hands-on participation, and uses a lab format that, as early as two weeks into the term, becomes commercial cooking for the school cafe or dining room.

Working under the supervision of the program director, the teacher uses a preapproved, coordinated class lesson plan and selects recipes that practice essential techniques, such as eggs Benedict to teach hollandaise sauce and egg poaching. The range of skills the instructor covers in two semesters might be short-order cooking, sandwich making, soup making, deli salad making, the mother sauces, stocks and soups, compound butters, vegetables, potato, rice, legume cookery, meats, poultry, fish and shellfish, baking, fruit desserts including tarts, ice creams, and sorbets. Students learn French cooking terms as a part of culinary theory. To balance their growing culinary skills with management, students are involved in the essential responsibilities of purchasing, inventory maintenance, and menu pricing, and they often learn computer programs that consolidate these separate but related topics. In the front of the house—the dining room—they learn cashiering, personnel supervision, cost controls, and customer relations. In the classroom, they learn to analyze property for restaurants, design interiors and commercial kitchens, evaluate heavy-duty equipment, design menus, and understand financial statements. Ethics, nutrition, meat analysis, marketing, innkeeping, and other textbook subjects are covered in the classroom.

Salaries

Salary figures for these positions are surveyed and published annually by CHRIE, (the Council on Hotel, Restaurant and Institutional Education) and an interested professional can call them for this information.

Employment Prospects

About two-thirds of the vocational/professional culinary programs are located in cities of less than 500,000 people or in rural areas. Most of them are public institutions. The largest proportion of four-year schools are located in New York, Pennsylvania, Florida, Indiana, Massachusetts, Michigan, and Nevada; two-year schools are abundant in New York, California, Massachusetts, Maryland, New Jersey, Texas, Illinois, and Ohio.

Advancement Prospects

Advancement is both internal, with promotions up the staff ladder based on accomplishments, seniority, and education, and external, by applying for higher-level assignments in another school.

Best Geographical Location(s)

There are community colleges with vocational food service programs in every part of the country. The size of the program affects the number of instructor positions; densely populated geographic locations offer greater opportunity.

Education and Training

Most academic positions require at least a college degree, and some require graduate degrees. Vocational programs often substitute work experience for educational requirements; for example, two years as executive chef in a hotel dining or other white tablecloth restaurant is considered equivalent to an advanced degree.

Some vocational programs prefer to hire instructors who have been trained in similar programs or culinary academies. Others value on-the-job training as a chef or restaurant manager.

Experience/Skills/Personality Traits

Practical work experience in restaurants, both in cooking and management, is valuable in teaching students to succeed in a restaurant career. Having worked for a major, urban catering company would also be an asset.

Cooking instructors need to be familiar with all aspects of the program they teach, covering cooking techniques, mastery of equipment, and cooking theory (such as principles of emulsions as they apply to sauce making), plus safety, sanitation, employment law, and business or restaurant accounting (especially labor cost and food cost controls).

Teachers need a special sense of when students are foundering because they've missed some primary knowledge and when they are bored by repetitive tasks that they have long since mastered. The ultimate test of teaching skill is successful students.

Teachers need flexibility to allow students to experiment, generosity in sharing knowledge, and a high level of organization to plan learning blocks and cover an extensive curriculum.

Unions/Associations

The leading professional association is the Council on Hotel, Restaurant, and Institutional Education (CHRIE), which extends individual membership to educators in universities, colleges, certificate programs, and high schools, as well as retired educators, graduate students, industry professionals, and association, business, and government executives. It also has institutional memberships and corporate/organization memberships, thereby providing an expanded network and resources at annual meetings.

Additional organizations that offer benefits to culinary educators are the American Culinary Federation, the National Restaurant Association, the International Association of Culinary Professionals, regional culinary organizations, and professional associations for bakers, home economists, food technologists, and others.

Tips for Entry

1. Vocational programs often hire part-time teachers to cover a specialty, such as baking or garnishing and presentation. If you have such a skill, put together a portfolio with photographs and letters of recommendation to discuss with the program director.
2. High schools that have a vocational program are usually very limited, serving a faculty lunchroom or assisting in the school cafeteria. Teachers in these programs are primarily managers who are training students to prepare and serve a limited menu, and it is hands-on teaching experience.

VOCATIONAL SCHOOL DIRECTOR

CAREER PROFILE

Duties: Responsible for all administrative needs of the program including hiring, training, and supervising teaching staff; budget preparation and control; equipment selection, purchase, and maintenance; plant maintenance; quality control; student success and satisfaction; and sometimes teaching

Alternate Title(s): Program Coordinator

Salary Range: $38,000 to $50,000

Employment Prospects: Good and improving

Advancement Prospects: Limited

Best Geographical Location(s) for Position: See the appendix list of states where most vocational schools are clustered. There are community college culinary programs in every state

Prerequisites:

Education or Training—College degree, teacher training (especially for administration), culinary academy certification, or an impressive work résumé as an alternative, depending on the school's requirements

Experience—Professional cooking and management, teaching in any vocational program

Special Skills and Personality Traits—Administrative skills, especially leadership and team building for staff interaction; thorough understanding of budgetary process and controls; enjoyment of the energy of youngsters and teens and patience with beginners

CAREER LADDER

```
┌─────────────────────────────────┐
│      Vocational School or        │
│    Culinary Academy Dean         │
└─────────────────────────────────┘

┌─────────────────────────────────┐
│    Vocational School Director    │
└─────────────────────────────────┘

┌─────────────────────────────────┐
│    Food Service Management       │
│            and/or                │
│      Culinary Arts Teacher       │
└─────────────────────────────────┘
```

Position Description

The director of a vocational culinary program may do some teaching, particularly in smaller schools, but the essential demands of the job are administrative. The director, consulting with both an advisory board and the teaching staff, develops and implements the class plans and curriculum; oversees program marketing and student admittance; hires the specialized teachers; manages the budget for the program, including capital equipment requests (which can be anything from a new standing mixer or walk-in refrigerator to computer software to manage inventory); oversees purchasing, cost controls, and menu pricing; and is the liaison between his or her school and other schools.

Some of the specialist teachers the director hires for the program teach food service management; food and beverage management; sanitation; nutrition and dietetics; dining room (teaching) chef; culinary arts and food production, including pastry and baking; butchering and charcuterie; garnishing and presentation. Throughout the school year, the director observes the teachers and judges their performance based on student success; when necessary, the director will work closely with a teacher to upgrade his or her teaching skills.

The school's fiscal year begins at least four months before its start with budget planning, plant maintenance inventory, capital equipment estimates and requests, and student census projections to determine the cost of teaching staff and supplies. Hiring is done if the program is expanding or if there are teachers leaving due to retirement or relocation. Once the director has submitted the budget, sometimes the next step is fighting for it with the higher administration at the school.

The director constantly reviews the food industry and vocational training programs to ensure that the program meets the needs of students who expect to earn their living from professional cooking. The director participates in professional organization conferences, trade shows, and seminars to stay current, and also, as time allows, attends restaurant and hospitality industry conferences to keep informed about the job market and what skills are being sought.

Within the community, the director develops an informal advisory relationship with the local restaurant owners, managers, and chefs, to guard against any real or imagined competition from the school's dining room program, and to involve them in counseling relationships with students.

Salaries

Salary figures for these positions are surveyed and published annually by CHRIE, (the Council on Hotel, Restaurant and Institutional Education), and an interested professional can call them for this information.

Employment Prospects

The availability of jobs is limited by the number of schools providing vocational food service training. At the present time there are hundreds of programs varying from four-year curricula that carry a baccalaureate or graduate degree to community college programs that confer a certificate upon completion of the course. The field is growing.

Advancement Prospects

Advancement may be internal, consisting of promotion from a teaching to administrative position, but there may be only one such job available per program. External advancement is as likely, i.e., becoming director in another school.

Best Geographical Location(s)

Community colleges with vocational culinary training are scattered throughout all parts of the country, but only one director job exists per school. Check the appendix listing of schools to determine those states with a density of schools.

Education and Training

Universities and colleges usually require an advanced degree—at least a master's—for a program director or department head, in addition to administrative experience in an educational program. Some programs, such as academies or vocational training education, prefer to hire from the food service industry, choosing an executive chef from a major hotel chain or a teacher who has been trained in an accredited culinary program.

Experience/Skills/Personality Traits

Administrative experience consisting of human resources management, budget planning and cost controls, and curriculum design are the three primary areas a director must master. Teaching skills are needed to the extent that the director may also teach in the program, and they are highly useful in hiring and reviewing other teachers.

Unions/Associations

The major professional association for culinary education programs is the Council on Hotel, Restaurant, and Institutional Education (CHRIE). Most schools with culinary vocational education at any level, from certificate-granting to graduate degrees, are institutional members of CHRIE.

Tips for Entry

1. Join and participate in one or more of the professional associations serving the restaurant and hospitality industries—Council on Hotel, Restaurant, and Institutional Education; American Culinary Federation; or the National Restaurant Association.
2. If you are teaching in a vocational program, volunteer to serve on the curriculum development committee.
3. Learn everything you can about school funding and budgeting peculiarities.

APPRENTICE PROGRAM CHEF

CAREER PROFILE

Duties: Responsible for supplying a three-year program of professional training for apprentices in a working restaurant kitchen, following a course of study provided by the American Culinary Federation, and integrating the apprentices into the kitchen work force with other chefs and cooks.

Alternate Title(s): Teaching Chef

Salary Range: $30,000 to $48,000

Employment Prospects: Limited

Advancement Prospects: Limited

Best Geographical Location(s) for Position: In urban areas with grand hotels having huge kitchen facilities for multiple restaurants, banquet service, and catering

Prerequisites:

Education or Training—Excellent culinary skills are needed to hold one of the top kitchen appointments

Experience—Excellent and extensive culinary background and any teaching experience

Special Skills and Personality Traits—Patience, and the ability to remember what it was like to be a kitchen novice

CAREER LADDER

```
┌─────────────────────────────┐
│      Executive Chef          │
└─────────────────────────────┘

┌─────────────────────────────┐
│   Apprentice Program Chef    │
└─────────────────────────────┘

┌─────────────────────────────┐
│           Chef               │
└─────────────────────────────┘
```

Position Description

The restaurant or hotel chef charged with supervising an apprentice training program is guided by requirements set up by the Educational Institute of the American Culinary Federation (ACFEI) and registered by the United States Department of Labor. There is a standard three-year course of instruction during which the apprentice works a 40-hour week as a full employee of the restaurant or hotel. The supervising chef uses the ACFEI Culinary Manual as an instruction guide.

Before an apprentice is accepted into the program under the direction of a supervising chef, he or she has passed a screening process of interviews and tests, and the first six months of training are probationary. The supervising chef has the job of integrating the apprentice into the work schedules of the restaurant as a productive employee and, at the same time, seeing that he or she spends the required hours in a succession of work stations learning soups, sauces, salads, meats, fish, poultry, game,

vegetables, desserts, baking, butchering, buffet presentation, recipe development, budgets and purchasing, supervising kitchen crews, being a good team member, and mastering display skills such as ice carving, tallow sculpturing, cake decorating, and garnishing.

There are requirements for the apprentice to complete a general education program simultaneously, and the supervising chef has to allow time for the student to attend a local community college for appropriate math, English, and science courses.

The chef who supervises the apprentice program usually has more than one candidate, possibly up to six at the same time, to be integrated into the restaurant schedule. This is quite unlike an entry-level employee who is being trained on premises and can be assigned to the salad station for an extended period of time because that's where someone is needed. The apprentice is moved to the next learning station regardless of where employees are really needed from day to day.

The restaurant chef usually has other standard duties beyond shepherding the group of apprentices, so time management for him or her becomes more essential; the supervising chef's primary job may be as executive chef or sous-chef, which involves a full day's work.

Hotels and large restaurants participating in the ACF apprentice program try to provide additional benefits for their charges—such as field trips to specialty farms, nearby wineries, the nearest fishing industry or processing plant—to broaden their knowledge of food and food preparation. There are local and regional competitions that apprentices are encouraged to enter, leading to the international culinary olympics contests, held every four years.

Salaries
Salaries for experienced chef/teachers range between $30,000 to $48,000 a year, depending on qualifications and geographic location. The chef assigned to supervise an apprentice program will be one of the highest paid in the establishment, but he or she probably won't receive extra pay for the assignment.

Employment Prospects
The ACF states that there are over 100 chefs' associations in the United States participating in the apprentice program. That indicates a great number of restaurants and hotels taking part in large cities.

Advancement Prospects
A successful chef/supervisor of restaurant apprentices may decide training is more fulfilling work than cooking and look for employment in one of the culinary academies.

Being a part of the apprenticeship program brings the supervising chefs into a network that opens information channels of available jobs in bigger, better, or higher paying establishments.

Best Geographical Location(s)
Major urban areas are more likely to have grand hotels and restaurants that can afford the space for an apprentice program among their staff.

Education and Training
Chef education and training can come from trade-tech and vocational schools, culinary academies, and restaurant kitchen work. The ACF sponsors a certification program for chefs that tests and rates the individual and grants a highly-respected certificate.

Experience/Skills/Personality Traits
Supervising apprentices, who range in age from 16 and older with a high school diploma or equivalent, calls on the combined skills of a chef and a teacher.

Unions/Associations
Some major urban areas have a restaurant workers union, but it does not necessarily extend to the kitchen. Professional associations for chefs include the American Culinary Federation (local chapters) and the National Restaurant Association (local chapters).

Tips for Entry
1. Contact the American Culinary Federation for information about apprentice programs in your area and follow up with queries about job openings that would include apprentice training responsibility.
2. If you are already employed as the managing chef or sous-chef in a restaurant and can afford space for an apprentice, talk to the restaurant owner about qualifying for the ACF program.

CULINARY ACADEMY INSTRUCTOR

CAREER PROFILE

Duties: Responsible for providing professional training in culinary skills and restaurant business management to adult students, preparing students for internships in fine dining kitchens and commercial catering companies, and eventual job placement

Alternate Title(s): Educator; Teacher

Salary Range: $50,000 to $75,000

Employment Prospects: Limited

Advancement Prospects: Good

Best Geographical Location(s) for Position: Wherever culinary academies are located, mostly in New York, California, Rhode Island, and Maryland

Prerequisites:

Education or Training—Professional culinary training

Experience—All teaching experience, including in-service training of kitchen workers; as much fine restaurant experience as possible

Special Skills and Personality Traits—Teamwork; patience with beginners; love of fine food and the ability to communicate that love

CAREER LADDER

```
┌─────────────────────────────────────┐
│          Academy Director            │
└─────────────────────────────────────┘

┌─────────────────────────────────────┐
│      Culinary Academy Instructor     │
└─────────────────────────────────────┘

┌─────────────────────────────────────┐
│            Academy Chef              │
└─────────────────────────────────────┘
```

Position Description

Instructors in culinary academies, who are training students for professional chefs' jobs in restaurants, are most often former chefs themselves. They offer students an intrinsic knowledge of what's involved in working in a restaurant kitchen and what the chef they work for will expect.

Schools for professional chefs move their students through the same stages that restaurant cooks go through—pantry, salads, stocks and sauces, soup, garde manger, meats, poultry, fish and shellfish, butchering, dairy products and eggs, sauté, roasting, braising, pastry—in segments lasting several weeks each. Additionally, there are classroom subjects to be taught—safety, sanitation, tools and equipment, ordering and inventory control, pricing menu items, employee training and management, and principles of running a business.

The academy's executive chef is responsible for all the courses taught (even though he or she may not teach all the subjects) and thus is responsible for supervising other teach-ers. Hiring the academy chefs is usually an assignment shared among the school's management staff and the chef.

Most culinary academies have at least one six-month period during the course when students cook off campus, working as interns in fine restaurants across the country. It is the executive chef's duty to turn out qualified cooks who are able to pull their own weight alongside longtime employees of the restaurant.

Culinary academy students start cooking for the public as soon as they have mastered a few basic skills. The school will have an open cafe or a dining room. A simple lunch menu can be produced by the class of first-year students; a more elaborate dinner menu is the work of advanced, second-year students.

Since the instructor's charge is to prepare professional workers for restaurants and catering businesses, the standards the students are learning are influenced by work ethics—such as showing up in a clean uniform, being sober, energetic, and ready to work. If a student fails in any of these respects it means expulsion. There is an enormous lore of cooking techniques that an academy has to teach, starting with how to care for the raw materials, knife skills, the preparation of basic components—stocks, vegetable aromatics, base sauces—before the student goes on to create and assemble classic recipes.

One aspect of culinary teaching is always being right: the students learn to do it the chef's way without argument. The next lesson may bring a different chef with a different style of béarnaise sauce or preparing meats for braising, and the students learn to do it a different way, still without argument. This is preparation for the real workplace, working for real chefs.

An important draw for students when they choose a school is the network of restaurants that will accept them for internships while they are training. The reputation of the school, the reputation of the academy staff, and the network the school has built of restaurant owner/chefs to participate in the internship program must be maintained to the highest standards. The final step is outplacement of students in challenging jobs after graduation.

Salaries

Salaries depend on whether the academy is a year-round institution and whether teaching is full-time or part-time. For a full-time, year-round executive chef, salary ranges from $50,000 to $75,000 a year. Degrees and advanced degrees are not influential with regard to salary; culinary training and work experience are the currency.

Employment Prospects

There is a growing number of culinary academies in the United States scattered across the country, and existing academies have added programs in other geographic areas, providing even more jobs.

Advancement Prospects

Culinary instructors play employment musical chairs as much as restaurant chefs (remember, they are the same "animal"). As soon as a chef/teacher takes a position at another school, there is a chance for other teachers to move up or move in.

Best Geographical Location(s)

The primary academies are in Hyde Park, New York, New York City, Providence, Rhode Island, Chicago, Illinois, and Napa, San Francisco, and Los Angeles, California; some are in large cities, some in rural areas.

Education and Training

Academy teachers are selected for their chef skills, including kitchen management and creativity with food. The more teaching experience—whether it is with staff in the restaurant or with professional students in a community college—the better chance a chef has for being hired.

Experience/Skills/Personality Traits

The culinary academy staff has to work as a team, passing students from one learning segment to another. The ability to work with beginners is essential, as is an interest in the students' progress.

Unions/Associations

Most schools are members of CHRIE, the Council on Hotel, Restaurant and Institutional Education; academy teachers are individual members as well.

Tips for Entry

1. Some academy instructors started as students in the same institution where they teach.
2. Local restaurant chefs are often in demand by small cooking schools to teach menu classes based on the restaurant's cuisine. A knack for teaching can be revealed this way, leading the chef to apply to a professional program for a job.
3. Write to all the academies for information about their standards for teachers. Be creative about describing your own experience in keeping with their stated criteria.

NUTRITION AND DIETETICS

UNIVERSITY NUTRITION COUNSELOR

CAREER PROFILE

Duties: Responsible for a service program of nutrition and health information and education for college and university students, working with a health team that includes medical doctors, psychiatrists, and nurses; trains students or interns to practice peer health education; produces pamphlets and reprints from journals and newsletters to provide responsible nutrition advice to students; performs outreach beyond the school community within budget limitations; continues his or her own education in nutritional studies for registration status

Alternate Title(s): Registered Dietitian

Salary Range: $30,000 to $55,000 for full-time employment

Employment Prospects: Good

Advancement Prospects: Limited

Best Geographical Location(s) for Position: Everywhere in the country at colleges and universities

Prerequisites:

Education or Training—A bachelor's degree in nutrition and dietetics from an accredited school and an American Dietetic Association–approved hospital internship; state registration; continuing education to validate registration

Experience—The required internship provides nutritional work in a wide range of health and wellness areas

Special Skills and Personality Traits—Sensitivity, insight, and a sense of humor in communicating with young adults and adolescents; a care and concern for the well-being of clients

CAREER LADDER

```
┌─────────────────────────────┐
│  Health Education Director   │
└─────────────────────────────┘


┌─────────────────────────────┐
│    Nutrition Counselor       │
└─────────────────────────────┘


┌─────────────────────────────┐
│      Nutrition Intern        │
└─────────────────────────────┘
```

Position Description

The nutrition counselor in a college or university provides information and education for students with special nutritional needs due to illness, stress, or physical disabilities. The structure of the health education program will vary greatly among institutions, but the work of the nutrition counselor will be much the same everywhere, requiring R.D. (Registered Dietitian) status. Most of the hottest health topics and biggest health problems are present in the youthful population: anorexia, bulimia, AIDS, cancer, high blood pressure, high cholesterol, and stress.

The health education program provides students with nutritional advice to deal with everything from eating disorders, midterm and breakup stress, sexually transmitted diseases, alcohol and drugs, to the "Freshman 15" (the expected 15-pound weight gain experienced by young women their first semester away from home). The R.D. usually has medical, nursing, and mental health professionals to work with in diagnosing student health needs; a student might start at any of those points and be referred to the nutrition counselor or the R.D. may refer the student for medical or psychiatric attention.

The balancing part of a nutritionist's work in health education is teaching. One way this can be done is by peer health education—giving students course credit for nutrition training and sending them out to speak in dormitories and college clubs about specific health concerns. If the college or university is one with an accredited nutrition and dietetics course, this is an ideal use of interns. Otherwise there may be premed, home economics, or public health majors who have a career interest in nutrition; they will be drawn to these programs and enjoy the interaction of teaching their peers.

Every R.D. reads constantly to keep up in the field of nutrition, following clinical studies in medical and nutritional journals and consumer newsletters on health and fitness. The nutrition counseling team assigns publications to its members to read, and has them circulate pertinent articles. Many articles make their way onto the hand-out rack, copied onto brightly colored paper to catch student interest. An article on how to be a healthy vegetarian, complete with simple recipes, will be sure to make it to the rack. Another popular item will be about frozen processed foods, with a listing of menu additions to encourage balanced nutrition despite a lifestyle that has scant time and money to spend on meals. Additionally, the R.D. will develop some handout pamphlets, arrange for printing, and oversee distribution; these will address any nutrition issues that become hot topics on campus (such as a localized epidemic of colds, irritable bowels, or eating disorders). A significant advantage the R.D. has in a college or university environment is the intelligence level of the student client; he or she is working with a highly educated segment of society, many of whom are pursuing a science education and quickly understand nutritional advice.

If the department budget can support community outreach, the health services department will develop programs to promote nutrition in surrounding communities, by participation in health fairs and presenting videos or talks at public schools and to adult service clubs. If the school has an adult extension program, the nutritional consultant may be asked to teach continuing education classes. Teaching a class would count toward the R.D.'s own continuing education credits required to maintain registration status.

Salaries

Salaries for full-time counseling and teaching will range between $30,000 and $50,000 a year, depending on the R.D.'s experience and job responsibilities.

Employment Prospects

Nutrition counseling is common in colleges and university health programs, but rare in public or private secondary schools (more likely a school nurse provides nutrition assistance). In lean financial times, the job is more likely to be cut to part-time status than to be eliminated.

Advancement Prospects

Promotion is limited by the size of the department, and often advancement takes the form of moving into a research position or transferring to a larger institution.

Best Geographical Location(s)

These jobs are available in every part of the United States, at public or private colleges and universities.

Education and Training

The counselor must be a registered dietitian (R.D.), which means he or she has graduated with a B.S. from a college or university having a dietetic and nutrition program accredited by the American Dietetic Association (A.D.A.), completed an internship of six months to a year cycling through the departments—cancer, renal, community medicine, pediatrics, food service—then passed the registration test administered by the A.D.A., and continued his or her education with 75 approved units of study over every five years.

Depending on the R.D.'s career goals, he or she may also have a master's degree in a related specialty, for example, counseling and education.

Experience/Skills/Personality Traits

The registration requirements for dietitians are specific in terms of education and internship, providing a foundation of experience in working with the range of nutritional needs.

Working with adolescents and young adults, many of whom are away from home and on their own for the first time in their lives, calls on a heightened sensitivity and insight into the stresses that translate into their nutritional distress, and a sense of humor and lightness in communicating to put an uncomfortable client at ease.

Dietetics and nutrition, is one of the "rescuing" professions, reaching out to care for those in need and providing emotional support along with the scientific knowledge to deal with health problems.

Unions/Associations

The Commission on Dietetic Registration of the American Dietetic Association is the recognized accrediting agency that coordinates undergraduate and dietetic internship programs and establishes and enforces standards and qualifications for dietetic certification. National membership in the A.D.A. automatically provides enrollment in the appropriate state dietetic association, a source for continuing education and networking.

Tips for Entry

1. Contact the national A.D.A. or the state chapter in your area for educational materials, recommended schools, and possible scholarship assistance.
2. If you are attending a college or university, make yourself known to the health education department and sign up for peer health education training, if available.
3. If your school does not have training for outreach, discuss any chance for an internship with the R.D. in charge.

RETIREMENT RESIDENCE DIETITIAN

CAREER PROFILE

Duties: Provides nutritional and satisfying meals to independent-living and assisted-living residents of a retirement residence as well as clinical nutrition to residents receiving nursing care; supervises all food service operations, hires and trains dining room manager, head chef, and lead cook; responsible for meeting all regulatory guidelines for aged care, and sanitation and public health requirements for food service facilities

Alternate Title(s): Director of Dining Services; Food Service Director; Resident Nutritionist

Salary Range: $32,000 to $55,000, plus benefits

Employment Prospects: Good and growing

Advancement Prospects: Limited

Best Geographical Location(s) for Position: Everywhere in the United States

Prerequisites:

Education or Training—A B.S. degree in nutrition from an accredited university, registered dietitian, food service management or business management course

Experience—Any food service job in an institutional setting, especially hospital or nursing care

Special Skills and Personality Traits—Empathy for the lifestyle of retired residents; a high value for the quality of food and diet; very organized and attentive to detail; leadership skills in managing the food service staff

CAREER LADDER

```
┌─────────────────────────────────────┐
│      Residence Administrator         │
└─────────────────────────────────────┘

┌─────────────────────────────────────┐
│   Retirement Residence Dietitian     │
└─────────────────────────────────────┘

┌─────────────────────────────────────┐
│          Staff Dietitian             │
└─────────────────────────────────────┘
```

Position Description

The registered dietitian in charge of dining services at a retirement residence facility needs the combined talents of a restaurant manager and a hospital food service manager with the additional duty of providing quality nutritional guidance as a clinical dietitian.

A typical retirement residence has three levels of food service depending on the degree of self-reliance of the residents. Those in independent living quarters can make coffee and prepare snacks in the kitchenettes of their apartments, but are provided up to three meals a day in a convivial dining room setting. Well over half of the residents fall in this category. As age takes its toll on residents' health, they move into assisted living quarters when they are no longer ambulatory or need special diets to control conditions such as diabetes, ulcers, diverticulitis, or stroke. Their food choices are as broad as the other dining room provides, and they still have control over their own diets. The third level of care provides full nursing and clinical nutrition services, and many residents are bound to wheelchairs and need assistance to feed themselves. Most of these patients have special menus that conform to their doctor's orders. Their nutritional needs are screened and monitored; as the body ages, nutritional absorption slows down and merely getting the right foods isn't always enough to maintain good health.

In the dining room and lounge, mealtime has the appearance of an upscale resort. The dining room manager knows the residents by name and ushers them informally to their tables and presents the day's menu. Throughout the year the menu changes to fit seasonally-available produce and fruits and to recognize holidays and special events, and it is based on a cycle (such as five weeks) to guard against monotony. Every change in the menu requires training in the kitchen to produce the new recipes.

Budget concerns strongly influence this kind of food service. Although most residential care centers are nonprofit entities, they must manage their operation without losing money. Residents are charged for food, lodging, and services; thus they are customers whose needs and preferences must be met. This means more than never running out of ice cream. Even though a menu is established for the season, there are frequent holiday breaks, seasonal specials, and theme dinners to import the gaiety of, say, a Hawaiian luau or a Cape Cod clambake. Dining services also cater private parties for the residents, family banquets for wedding anniversaries and birthdays, bridge luncheons for guests, and memorials following a death. This service is charged to a resident's account, providing extra income to the dining room which is helpful in times of tight budgets.

The lifestyle that elderly residents expect has to be maintained as well. This extends to redecorating the dining area periodically, matching the table service with cloths and napkins that are as pleasing as what they were used to in their own homes. To meet public health and other regulations, the kitchen equipment has to be up to date, efficient, easy to clean, and appropriate for the menu and the volume of meals being served.

Federal and state guidelines, such as Title 22, Title 19, and the Omnibus Budget Reconciliation Act (OBRA), strictly regulate many details of food service down to the volume of a serving of prune juice. Health department inspections are surprise visits with a checklist of every possible delinquency, from untreated grease to a refrigerator reading one or two degrees too high.

The food service director plans all menus, supervises the residence kitchen, and hires and fires the next level of managers, such as an assistant director, the chef or head cook, or a dining room manager. On a day-to-day basis the assistant director or the executive chef manages the kitchen staff, training everyone when a new menu comes into season and training new hires to meet the facility standards; a dining room manager trains and supervises the wait-staff and bussers. These two managers report to the director, keeping him or her informed of any emerging problems or ideas for service improvement, either in formal weekly meetings or, more likely, in informal conversation. There are human resource management demands as well. Between hiring and firing come training, motivation, work safety issues, and salary and benefits reviews. The food service director also has bookkeeping records to maintain and financial reports to produce.

Salaries

The size of the residence facility and the number of meals served daily influence the rate of pay for managers. Salaries range from $32,000 to $55,000 for a medium-sized facility serving about 750 meals a day.

Employment Prospects

Good and growing prospects mark this field because of our growing elderly population. It is expected that many middle-range hotels and motels across the country will be converted to residence facilities in the next decade because of their convenient locations, sports and exercise equipment, and dining room facilities.

Advancement Prospects

Advancement is limited within a single residence. Chains provide more jobs at the top level. A substitute form of promotion is by moving to a larger or more luxurious facility.

Best Geographical Location(s)

Retirement residence facilities are in every part of the United States, but they more numerous near major urban areas and in states with mild climates, especially those away from harsh winter weather.

Education and Training

The food service director in a retirement center usually must be a registered dietitian, with a degree in nutrition and dietetics from an accredited college. Because the job entails management responsibilities, many R.D.'s acquire an advanced degree such as an M.B.A., master of business administration.

Experience/Skills/Personality Traits

Any related food service experience in an institutional setting would be valuable preparation for this work, but hospital and nursing care experience is most useful. An understanding of how an older citizen's taste changes is critical, and empathy is needed to counter diet limitations imposed by illness with delicious alternative food choices. For example, if ice cream is too rich to digest, frozen yogurt may be an enjoyable treat.

This work requires a highly organized and detail-oriented individual to meet the strict health and sanitation requirements of food service, and one who is also very concerned with pleasing residents and motivating staff to maintain a smoothly functioning environment. The director needs a good palate and a thorough understanding of ingredients and recipes to maintain a high-quality menu program.

Unions/Associations

The American Dietetic Association is a national professional association of dietitians, dietetic technicians, and nutritionists. Their Commission on Dietetic Registration is the accrediting agency for coordinating internships and establishing certification.

Tips for Entry

1. With a nutrition and dietetics degree, take advantage of the networking opportunities in the local dietetic association to learn of jobs in residential facilities.

2. To find out whether nutrition and dietetics will be a good personal choice for you as a career, contact the administrators of any nearby retirement residences to ask about part-time, temporary, or volunteer work opportunities.

3. Discuss the occupational options available for both a registered dietitian and for a dietetic technician with the career counselor at the nearest college or university that is accredited by the A.D.A. to provide a degree in dietetics and nutrition.

FOOD SERVICE COMPANY DIETITIAN

CAREER PROFILE

Duties: Markets and administers food service management to health care facilities; provides input in hiring and firing decisions; supervises contracted services; guides and interacts with dietetic interns; and participates in ongoing research projects

Alternate Title(s): Registered Dietitian; Clinical Dietitian

Salary Range: $45,000 to $70,000, plus benefits and performance bonuses

Employment Prospects: Good and growing

Advancement Prospects: Excellent

Best Geographical Location(s) for Position: Anywhere in the United States where there are health care institutions

Prerequisites:
  Education or Training—College degree in nutrition and dietetics, a completed internship, and A.D.A. registration as an R.D.
  Experience—Work experience as a clinical dietitian and as a food service consultant
  Special Skills and Personality Traits—Familiarity with computer research systems; good listening skills; good formal and informal communication skills, including writing; ability to motivate others; good team player; leadership skills; basic understanding of financial management tools

CAREER LADDER

```
┌─────────────────────────────────┐
│    Regional Vice President       │
└─────────────────────────────────┘

┌─────────────────────────────────┐
│ Food Service Company Dietitian   │
└─────────────────────────────────┘

┌─────────────────────────────────┐
│      Staff Nutritionist          │
└─────────────────────────────────┘
```

Position Description

The executive dietitian in the health care and nutrition department of a large food service company is responsible for marketing and administering food service management to hospitals, institutions, and retirement residence facilities; oversees services provided to a client under the active administration of a clinical manager; develops research programs that will define future services and enhance established programs; guides and interacts with dietetics interns (students between the stages of college degree and A.D.A. registration examination); participates in the hiring and firing of registered dietitians, researchers, and support staff for the department; and travels incessantly throughout the region in performing these duties.

Hospital administrators hire a food service company to run the kitchen, patient tray service, cafeteria, and related

catering, and provide human resources administration for the employees performing food services at the institution. A hospital's primary concern is patient satisfaction, but allied to that must be cost containment and cost controls.

The food service company dietitian is part of the marketing team when the institution is looking for a change in the way they provide food service, whether it is a matter of changing food service providers or shifting from a hospital-run kitchen to a consultant/administrator-run kitchen. The dietitian meets with the nursing executives, physicians, and dining room and kitchen managers to survey the needs of the institution; then the dietitian develops a proposal for providing food service administration, makes a presentation to showcase the company services and recommendations, and finally bids to do the work for the institution. Other marketing staff of the food service company are part of the sales team with the dietitian.

The client, whether a hospital, nursing care home, mental health institution, or retirement residence, judges the company by the same standards they use to interview and hire their own employees. If those standards are met, the food service company will probably win the contract, subject to cost containment guarantees and the contract negotiations. Once the company has been hired, the executive dietitian works with the client to select and place the best possible clinical nutrition and food service managers in the kitchen.

The balancing part of an executive dietitian's job consists of ongoing research projects. Those might consist of a study of the growing field of home health care, clinical staffing guidelines for acute care facilities, work on the joint commission standards for health care services, and insurance/government reimbursement for intravenous nutrition formulas. Some of this involves literature searches for a developing study in medical libraries or through electronic data base sources; other projects lean heavily on conferencing to develop guidelines and field testing to produce a marketable program for clients.

Since all registered dietitians must complete six months to a year of an approved medical internship before they are eligible for the certification test, major health care food service companies provide intern opportunities to work in the field and develop their work skills in concert with their scientific education. These interns have their first work experience in nutrition and dietetics, cycling through the spectrum of nutritional health care work: cancer, diabetes, heart disease, stroke, etc. This is an invaluable chance to sample various kinds of nutrition work before choosing one's particular career path. These interns report to the executive dietitian and get the support of a mentor, a chance to test a variety of career choices and be assessed by the company (which will hire the best and the brightest when they have passed their registration examination).

The executive dietitian is involved in the hiring process and decisions, but doesn't always get to interact with incoming staff because of the work and travel demands of his or her own job.

Depending on the executive dietitian's preferred lifestyle, the best or the worst part of the job is traveling. As much as 50 percent to 70 percent of the dietitian's month may be spent out of town, meeting with clients and discussing new contracts.

Health care food service companies rely heavily on well-educated and well-trained registered dietitians to maintain the quality of their product. A significant feature of this is that the companies place a high regard on the dietetics and nutrition professions and are supportive of women in executive career paths.

Salaries

After five to 10 years of developing a career path at a major health care food service company, an executive dietitian who started at a salary of about $45,000 a year can expect to earn up to $70,000 a year plus full insurance and vacation/sick leave benefits. In addition, he or she will be eligible for an annual bonus based on regional performance and meeting or exceeding written annual objectives.

Employment Prospects

The health care professions are a growth industry due primarily to the aging of our population and a growing demand for quality medical care. There are many jobs available in these companies, and more are being developed all the time for well-educated registered dietitians.

Advancement Prospects

Promotion is dependent on continued education and job performance within the company, or by moving to a larger company for greater opportunities.

Best Geographical Location(s)

These jobs are everywhere in the United States, and most dense in areas with excellent medical treatment facilities or in states with mild seasonal climates that attract retired people.

Education and Training

To become a registered dietitian (R.D.), an individual must complete a college degree in nutrition and dietetics at a school accredited by the American Dietetic Association, serve a work internship in a medical facility (usually of between six months and a year duration), and pass the registration examination.

Experience/Skills/Personality Traits

An executive dietitian is a resource person for the company and for clients; this calls for real enjoyment in being well-informed. She or he has to be a good listener as well as a good communicator, with both informal and formal presentation skills and writing. Computer skills are vital, and understanding financial management is essential. Within the company the dietitian is a part of a team, requiring motivational and leadership skills as well as flexibility, persuasion, and leadership.

Unions/Associations

The American Dietetic Association offers membership to dietitians, dietetic technicians, and nutritionists. Their Commission on Dietetic Registration is the accrediting agency for coordinating undergraduate college programs, internships, and for establishing and enforcing standards and qualifications for dietetic certification.

Tips for Entry

1. Contact the local chapter of the A.D.A. to ask about scholarship programs.

2. Call local hospitals and health care institutions to ask whether they use a food service company and which one. Arrange to talk to the dietitian in charge for informal career counseling.

3. If your local college has programs in nutrition and dietetics, talk to the career counselor about local job opportunities while going to school.

HOSPITAL CLINICAL DIETITIAN

CAREER PROFILE

Duties: Links the patient's nutritional needs with the medical staff and the food service department; reviews patient records; keeps up with nutritional research; presents educational seminars for the hospital medical staff; reports to hospital administrator; may be the director of food service in some hospitals

Alternate Title(s): None

Salary Range: $25,000 to $45,000+, depending on highest degree and years of work experience

Employment Prospects: Very good

Advancement Prospects: Very good

Best Geographical Location(s) for Position: Anywhere in the country; the more hospitals in an area, the more jobs are available

Prerequisites:

Education or Training—A B.S. in nutrition, completed internship, and R.D. registration; a master's degree (M.S.) is often necessary for advancement.

Experience—Hospital experience in clinical dietetics will lead to promotion from within.

Special Skills and Personality Traits—Patience and caring; persuasive and informative to encourage patients to continue new diet regimes at home

CAREER LADDER

```
┌─────────────────────────────┐
│   Food Services Director    │
└─────────────────────────────┘

┌─────────────────────────────┐
│     Hospital Dietitian      │
└─────────────────────────────┘

┌─────────────────────────────┐
│      Staff Dietitian        │
└─────────────────────────────┘
```

Position Description

The head of dietetic services in a hospital is a connecting link between the food services department and the medical staff caring for a patient. The patient's special dietary needs may be a result of accident, trauma, or the immediate illness or surgery, but he or she may also need to maintain specialized dietary needs for a previous condition (diabetes, hypertension, obesity).

The dietitian reviews patient records and in some hospitals also goes on rounds with the medical staff. After reviewing the patient's history, the dietitian consults with the attending physician to recommend nutritional care tailored to the patient's needs, reviews the special diet or formula nutrition with the food service manager, and interacts with the nursing staff if necessary to see that nutritional intake is properly administered and tracked.

The dietitian is a constant researcher, reading nutrition studies and journals to keep up-to-date on nutrition for varied medical purposes, and he or she must interact constantly with the nutritional community and dietitians at other hospitals to exchange information and improve his or her professional skills.

Continuing nutrition education at the hospital for the rest of the hospital staff—nurses, doctors, therapists—is planned and produced by the hospital dietitian, either by teaching the classes or by scheduling outside experts to teach them.

In some hospitals the dietitian is also the food service manager, with the accompanying responsibility for providing all patient meals as well as running the hospital cafeteria for staff and visitors.

If the size of the hospital warrants, the dietitian may have a staff of registered dietitians who share the patient case load and monitor patient progress.

Salaries

With appropriate education, registration, and experience, a hospital dietitian can earn an annual income between $25,000 and $40,000. Some will earn $50,000 a year or more, depending on the size of the hospital or medical center, the size of staff to be supervised, and the annual budget for the program.

Employment Prospects

Hospitals provide nutrition services. In the past, hospitals charged for room and board; now the itemized bill to the patient is for nutrition services and is infinitely more expensive than three meals a day. Large hospitals, medical centers, trauma centers, and medical clinics have nutrition services for patients for a variety of physical ailments, and these are always staffed by highly-trained registered dietitians.

Advancement Prospects

Promotion up the line in a hospital staff with additional administrative and technical responsibilities is always available at a large medical center; otherwise, advancement comes by changing jobs to a larger hospital with more staff.

Best Geographical Location(s)

Hospital services are nationwide, in large cities and small towns. Higher-paying jobs are available in major medical centers.

Education and Training

A dietitian must have at least a bachelor's degree (B.S.) in nutrition, and have completed an internship, and passed the registration tests and requirements for an R.D. A master's degree (M.S.) is often necessary for advancement.

Experience/Skills/Personality Traits

The field of nutrition lends itself to specialization, but in a hospital nutrition and dietetics experience working with a variety of age groups and diseases will have direct application.

In addition to the professional skills and aptitude for dietary employment, a nutrition consultant must be patient and caring. It is extremely hard for anyone to substantially alter their everyday diet, even when his or her health is the catalyst for change. A dietitian must be aware and tolerant of this human condition. In the hospital situation, the patient has less freedom to rebel and make other choices, but the work of the dietitian is to train the patient to follow the most healthful regime to speed his or her return to good health; the dietitian must be an effective teacher.

Unions/Associations

The Commission on Dietetic Registration of the American Dietetic Association is the recognized accrediting agency for coordinated undergraduate and dietetic internship programs and for establishing and enforcing standards and qualifications for dietetic certification. The A.D.A. is a membership association of dietitians, dietetic technicians, and nutritionists. State membership associations are allied with the national organization.

The American Society of Hospital Food Service Administrators is a division of the national American Hospital Association that provides support for professionals who manage food and nutrition services in health care institutions.

Tips for Entry

1. Volunteer to help at your local hospital and ask to be assigned to any nutrition and food service assignments.
2. Contact the American Dietetic Association for information on schooling and jobs; join as a student member as soon as you are eligible.

SPORTS NUTRITIONIST

CAREER PROFILE

Duties: Trains athletes and competitive sports participants how to use nutrition to improve performance; assists undernourished athletes to attain normal growth and compete at a heavier weight; teaches injured athletes to adjust caloric input to maintain healing and avoid weight gain while immobilized

Alternate Title(s): Team Nutritionist

Salary Range: $25,000 to $50,000

Employment Prospects: Good

Advancement Prospects: Fair

Best Geographical Location(s) for Position: Both urban and rural areas with abundant sports activities

Prerequisites:

Education or Training—Bachelor's degree in nutrition plus registration by the American Dietetic Association or a master's degree from an accredited university

Experience—Advisory work with school teams as a nutritional aide; any experience working with children and teens to gain communication skills

Special Skills and Personality Traits—A thorough understanding and up-to-date knowledge of nutrition research; the teaching and persuasion skills to convince clients to change their lifestyle for health

CAREER LADDER

```
┌─────────────────────────────┐
│   Sports Health Director    │
└─────────────────────────────┘

┌─────────────────────────────┐
│     Sports Nutritionist     │
└─────────────────────────────┘

┌─────────────────────────────┐
│      Nutrition Intern       │
└─────────────────────────────┘
```

Position Description

A nutritionist usually works with athletic participants as a consultant for a variety of teams, schools, or athletic programs. The purpose of nutrition advice is to help the players achieve optimum health that improves their athletic skill.

Nutritional advice to athletes addresses more than just calories and fluids; increased carbohydrates need to be managed so they will enhance endurance, and special nutrients can improve a particular performance. Essentially, the athlete's health should be tip-top all the time, whether he or she is competing or not. The sports nutritionist provides guidance on every part of the player's diet, including high energy snacks to eat on the road and what foods are easy to bring to an out-of-town game that can be eaten in the hotel room without surrendering to the easily-accessible high-fat hamburgers and french fries.

It is not unusual for an athlete to be undernourished. Those who compete in sports that are grouped by weight often over-diet to maintain their place in a certain weight group when they should be growing and moving up to the next level. A sports nutritionist has a real training job here: to convince a successful competitor that going for the extra weight won't hurt performance.

A fit player who is injured, resulting in a loss of training practice, has to cut down on calories because the burn rate is slower during a sedentary period. A sports nutritionist has to teach the player what foods to choose during this time.

The sports nutritionist may also teach cooking classes to give athletes their independence from fast food by learning how to prepare simple, healthy and inviting meals consisting of soups and pasta dishes, salads, fruit desserts, and non-alcoholic beverages.

Salaries

A registered dietitian paid a salary as a direct employee of a sports program or freelancing as a consultant for several client companies will earn in the range of $25,000 to $50,000 a year. The R.D. may also work on the staff of a medical group specializing in sports medicine and will earn in the same range.

Employment Prospects

This is a growing field, as team sports have become an important part of school programs starting at younger and younger grades, and sports continue to be a lifestyle choice of adults into their senior years. Nutrition information is avidly sought by competitors to improve or gain an advantage.

Advancement Prospects

The rapid growth of private businesses in this field generates increasing opportunities for advancement.

Best Geographical Location(s)

These jobs are everywhere and in communities of all sizes, but the greatest number of jobs are where population density is high and fitness gyms are in abundant supply.

Education and Training

A nutrition consultant has to have at least a bachelor's degree in nutrition and be registered as a dietitian by the American Dietetic Association. A master's degree for advanced study in one specialty or another will lead to better-paying jobs or higher fees as a freelance consultant.

Experience/Skills/Personality Traits

A sports nutritionist is often involved with teaching clients to change their lifestyle—diet, sleep schedule, and training regime—to improve their health and thereby their performance. This takes persuasion, teaching skills, and a sure knowledge of the outcome to make the athlete's efforts successfully goal-oriented.

Unions/Associations

The American Dietetic Association (A.D.A.) is a national professional organization of dietitians, dietetic technicians and nutritionists that serves the public by promoting optimal nutrition, health, and well-being. Each state has a chapter association that provides educational meetings and association with other dietitians and nutritionists.

Tips for Entry

1. If you are a competing athlete in a school or athletic club, get acquainted with your nutrition consultant if there is one, and find out about qualified nearby colleges and opportunities for internships and work/study programs.
2. Look in the yellow pages for sports nutrition clinics and visit them to learn about their program and whether you can work at one of them while you're pursuing the necessary education.

CULINARY COMPUTER

WEBMASTER, CULINARY BUSINESS

CAREER PROFILE

Duties: Creating a business website custom-designed to the client's desires and educating the client in what is and is not doable, working to ensure that the final product pleases the client, selecting the appropriate software programs, assessing what computer hardware will be needed, proceeding with the detailed design, graphics components, and information about the client's business, providing consulting services as needed by the client and training any staff in the daily maintenance of the site

Alternate Title(s): Web Designer, Website Consultant

Salary Range: $36,000 to $90,000 and up or $20/hour to $45/hour

Employment Prospects: Exceptionally good

Advancement Prospects: Very good

Best Geographical Location(s) for Position: These jobs are nationwide and global. Any time the perfect client comes along, the webmaster can move to that location, or telecommuting may be an option.

Prerequisites:

Education or Training—As much computer training as possible, from all sources: a community college, university extension classes, university computer degree, and self-taught by reading and working with groups of computer savvy colleagues

Experience—Working as an assistant to a highly skilled designer is a good way to learn

Special Skills and Personality Traits—Content-oriented, curiosity about how things work, Net surfing, innovative and outgoing

CAREER LADDER

```
┌─────────────────────────────┐
│    Web Services Business    │
│        or Partnership       │
└─────────────────────────────┘

┌─────────────────────────────┐
│          Webmaster          │
└─────────────────────────────┘

┌─────────────────────────────┐
│      Computer Technician     │
└─────────────────────────────┘
```

Position Description

Culinary business owners are eager to have a company presence on the Internet. Web pages are also used by culinary organizations to promote conferences, build membership, and market section services. They are useful for cooking school schedules and sign-ups and for travel and tourism relating to culinary interests.

The webmaster's work for a company starts with website design. By interacting with the business owner to discuss in detail what the owner wants and how he or she visualizes the end product, the webmaster learns what the owner expects the website to accomplish for the business and identifies as much as possible the style, or the "look," the owner thinks will work best for the business. For this stage of the work—even more important than computer training and experience—the webmaster needs to have a strong background in graphic arts and prior design experience of any sort, from business logos to full-color layouts.

The webmaster may need to educate the client in aspects of Web design and uses. There are three kinds of websites:

one is an extension of the existing business or an expansion of the business to provide services to additional customers; second is a "portal site" which directs the Internet surfer to other websites for specific needs and generates income from these referrals of business; the last is an on-line store engaged in "e-tailing" as retailing.

The webmaster takes the information about the client and the business from this first consultation to work out various design options. Before another meeting, the webmaster will identify the software programs that will work best in developing the intended site. Knowledge of what programs to use comes from prior experience, but also from constant reading of computer trade magazines and by word of mouth from a network of colleagues. Design software is often available free of charge as a trial version to introduce it to buyers; use it for a few weeks or months, then it disappears like a puff of smoke with a message of "buy it or lose it." There are plenty of Web design "chat rooms" on the Internet, communities of webmasters picking each other's brains, sharing gains and losses, and bailing each other out.

When the start-up design parameters have been set, the webmaster assesses what computer hardware will be needed to proceed. This knowledge also results from the webmaster's prior experience, trade magazine reviews, and colleagues.

With agreement on (1) the design concept, (2) the type of site the owner has selected, and (3) the purchase and assembly of computer hardware components, the next stage is fine-tuning the design and getting it up on the Internet site. At this stage, the client can decide whether to retain the webmaster to develop and service the site further or to hire an in-house computer technician to take it over. The webmaster will train someone from the company if that is the client's preference. The relationship of the webmaster with the client is usually ongoing to some extent, regardless of which direction the client chooses. The webmaster is indefinitely available to the client for troubleshooting and problem solving, including design modifications as desired.

Salaries

A webmaster working full time for a single client/business will earn in the range of $36,000 to $90,000 and higher. As an outside consultant the webmaster will charge in the range of $20/hour to $45/hour or more.

Employment Prospects

This field is growing exponentially, and there is no indication it will diminish soon. Any computer-savvy culinary specialist who pursues this work will be welcomed by eager clients. The potential for this work is as creative as people want to be.

Advancement Prospects

An individual who combines culinary knowledge with graphic arts and Web design training can be an indispens-

able employee as part of an in-house team. That role can be transferred to larger companies with higher salaries, benefits, and perks.

Best Geographic Location(s)

Geographic location almost doesn't matter with computer specialists. Telecommuting for these artists goes beyond staying home in the suburbs instead of driving into the city. A webmaster can be across the country and still work in a hands-on manner on a Web design or maintenance project, consulting with the client electronically.

Education and Training

Community colleges and university extension programs have a full spectrum of computer training classes. Graphic design for computers is one of the regular offerings in extension catalogs, usually a series of long weekend (Friday evening, all day Saturday and Sunday) sessions.

Experience/Skills/Personality Traits

The essential attitude of a webmaster is to focus on content. Being flashy isn't valued in a webmaster; the core motto is "Content is King."

All experience with computer programs and programming is useful. Attention to detail is essential. Being a team player is invaluable in meeting the expectations of a client and in rounding up all the appropriate personnel within the firm who can contribute to the project. A willingness to occasionally work around the clock gets the work done in the shortest time for an impatient client. Perception to recognize other solutions, surfing websites to find unusual presentations, and constantly searching for fresh ways to capture customer attention are everyday work habits.

Unions/Associations

There are no professional societies or annual conferences for these specialists, but they create their own informal groups in Internet chat rooms.

Tips for Entry

1. Take any college or university short courses in Web design, and network with the other students about job openings or ideas for entry. Talk to the instructor of the course about job possibilities to pursue.
2. Develop a file on the latest technology available and pore over the major trade magazines for information about trends, new products, and eye-catching techniques.

ON-LINE CULINARY CATALOG DESIGNER

CAREER PROFILE

Duties: Designing a website for selling merchandise, consulting with the client to define what message to display and to itemize general categories of merchandise to be sold, preparing sample layouts and programs, working with the client's merchandise manager, contracting with selected vendors for hardware and software, conforming the computer with the installation, and training the client's staff in how to maintain the catalog, remaining available to the client for troubleshooting and any additional training

Alternate Title(s): Catalog Programmer

Salary Range: $36,000 to $90,000 and up or $20/hour to $45/hour

Employment Prospects: Extremely good, and growing

Advancement Prospects: Very good

Best Geographical Location(s) for Position: Anywhere. Telecommuting is well accepted for this work

Prerequisites:

Education or Training—As much computer training as possible, especially in the design and use of graphics, plus experience as an assistant to an experienced catalog designer will provide a quick start to these jobs

Experience—All computer experience is useful, especially graphic design

Special Skills and Personality Traits—Knowledge of retail processes and some familiarity with the merchandise being sold, organized

CAREER LADDER

```
┌─────────────────────────────┐
│      Client/Company         │
│     Marketing Manager       │
└─────────────────────────────┘

┌─────────────────────────────┐
│   Online Catalog Designer   │
└─────────────────────────────┘

┌─────────────────────────────┐
│    Computer Technician      │
│          and/or             │
│      Graphic Designer       │
└─────────────────────────────┘
```

Position Description

Culinary catalogs on the Internet cover a wide variety of products. The most common are those for specialty food items, cookware, and cookbooks.

Designing a website for selling merchandise and service starts with consultation between the company's sales manager or owner and an Internet site designer. Their first concern is to define the message they want to display and to itemize the general categories of what they want to sell. The designer then develops some alternative ways to present the message and the material and comes back to the owner with examples of how it can be done and how it will look. This step can be done on paper, but it is more appropriate for the designer to develop screen images of his or her suggestions, presenting them on a conference room large screen where every detail can be scrutinized by clients who decide if they like the design or not.

When this preliminary design has been presented by the designer and approved by the client, the next step is deciding on the Internet "location" for the site. It can be a unique, independent catalog address or one that is partnered with other related companies by establishing links within their website and submitting to the existing search engine.

The catalog designer will work closely with a merchandise manager (or services manager) inside the company. That person will decide what items, how many, and what variety will be displayed in the catalog at any time. Developing a healthy respect for each other and learning what means of communication works best between them is essential.

The designer is responsible for contracting with selected vendors (those that will be the link connections to the new catalog) and customizing the new catalog to work smoothly on their sites. If the catalog is intended to stand alone, the designer identifies the hardware and software to order and install and then sets up the catalog for the client.

A separate step is necessary to identify the method of payment that will be accepted, the mysterious labyrinth that puts the box on the customer's computer screen with the message about a "secure server" and gives the option to "continue" with the selection of purchases. This is handled by the designer, and when it is established the client will have the ultimate approval responsibility.

Finally, of course, there is entering the graphic images to illustrate the merchandise, the text descriptions of each item, and pricing. This data is updated constantly, and double-checked for accuracy.

Maintenance of the site is ongoing. These dynamic sites must keep up with the latest technology. They are interactive and must maintain a comfortable communication style.

Salaries

An on-line culinary catalog designer working full time for a single client/business will earn in the range of $36,000 to $90,000 and higher. As an outside consultant the webmaster will charge in the range of $20/hour to $45/hour or more.

Employment Prospects

As the buying public has become comfortable with shopping on the Internet, this field has grown steadily, and the trend is sure to continue. There is ample work for newcomers entering this computer design field.

Advancement Prospects

Designers have the option of staying with a growing company, one that will add more and more catalogs to their business, or of moving to larger companies or more upscale companies with higher-end merchandise.

Best Geographic Location(s)

This is a career field in which telecommuting has been commonplace from the beginning. It is simply a matter of the employer allowing the designer to work at home in the adjoining community, the next state, or completely across the country.

Education and Training

There is unlimited variety of education and training available for computer specialists. A Web search brings up hundreds of choices. Training in the use of computer graphics is essential. Working with an experienced catalog designer will be a valuable quick start to learning the ropes.

Experience/Skills/Personality Traits

As with almost all computer-related careers, exercising constant curiosity is one of the best ways to train yourself and to stay motivated. As noted in the webmaster profile, the essential attitude is to focus on content. Being flashy isn't valued—the core motto is "Content is King."

Unions/Associations

Internet chat rooms full of computer catalog designers and other computer specialists, are the on-line substitute for a professional association for these workers.

Tips for Entry

1. Surf the Net looking for on-line catalogs that you like. At the foot of the home page, there is usually a credit for the site designer. Contacting that company for information and advice might turn up a mentor.
2. If the local community college has catalog design and graphic design classes, talk to the teachers for any suggestions.

CULINARY ASSOCIATION DATABASE MANAGER

CAREER PROFILE

Duties: Customizing the organization's membership list to produce a directory of members, creating systems to automatically format the data for mailing labels, generating membership dues renewal forms, training members to maintain it or negotiating with the organization for a retainer fee to do it for them, working to develop professional sections for specialized services, providing guidance to the organization about ways they can manipulate computer records to streamline communication and prepare for future growth

Alternate Title(s): Records Manager, Computer Consultant

Salary Range: $12/hr to $18/hr

Employment Prospects: Limited

Advancement Prospects: Poor

Best Geographical Location(s) for Position: As with other computer-related occupations, this work can be done from a remote location. Lively culinary organizations usually spring up in locations where there is an active restaurant business and available vocational training programs for cooks.

Prerequisites:

Education or Training—Computer training in reports design and using available database programs; graphics design classes, covering principles of relationships and layout

Experience—Any work that has involved getting data from many sources to consolidate in one document will be useful

Special Skills and Personality Traits—Attention to detail and communication skills to listen to what the culinary group thinks they need and translating that into records they can use

CAREER LADDER

```
┌─────────────────────────────────┐
│      Management Services         │
│   Business Owner or Executive    │
└─────────────────────────────────┘

┌─────────────────────────────────┐
│       Database Manager           │
└─────────────────────────────────┘

┌─────────────────────────────────┐
│      Word Processing and         │
│      Graphics Technician         │
└─────────────────────────────────┘
```

Position Description

Small culinary organizations (associations, guilds, societies) with either a broad-based membership (open to everyone who earns income in the culinary field) or limited (pastry chefs, food writers, whatever) can keep their membership information on paper until they reach a membership level of about 35, and then they think about putting it all on one computer. Prior to this point, the membership chairman has some data, the program chairman has other data, and the newsletter editor may use cut-and-paste skills to put the news together.

Usually there is at least one culinary member who can set up a database, but when the membership begins to grow that person may not want to use precious time that could be producing income. Two alternatives face the organization: either pay the skilled member an hourly rate for the work or hire an outside company that does this sort of work for many groups.

The work starts with customizing the membership list. By the time the membership is large enough to need a data processor, members are clamoring for a membership directory so that they have everyone's phone numbers and email addresses in one package. This can be as simple as name, address, phone, fax, and email, or it can also include a statement written by each member about his or her business or work, a statement intended to market their services among the group to members who don't know them very well.

Once that file is defined and filled in with all members, it is easy to produce mailing labels for meeting notices and newsletters. Depending on the organization's policy for membership dues—all due at the beginning of the year, or sprinkled through the year based on what month the member originally paid dues—the file can produce a flyer tailored to each member that includes a statement for dues and a form for updating the membership directory.

Those are the minimal needs of a small group. If the organization is in a large city and if it is a broad-based group, the membership could reasonably grow to several hundred or to more than a thousand. This is the time when the group again has to decide whether to keep its own records or to out-source the job.

With unwieldy size, the organization may decide to break into sections: one for chefs and caterers, one for restaurant owners and managers, one for writers, and so forth. The original database, if it was developed on software that had expansion capabilities, could still do the job. If the original data keeper doesn't want to continue then the group needs to look for a freelance computer technician to set up a consulting contract with them, probably at hourly rates.

This is also the time when the group may decide to incorporate as a trade association or as a not-for-profit corporation. The computer consultant may have the experience to shepherd the organization through that process and continue to keep their membership and operating records. If this person is a culinary professional, although that is not a necessary qualification, it will be easier for the group to work with him or her, simply because they will speak a common language.

Salaries
This is usually freelance hourly work that brings between $12/hour and $18/hour depending on the complexity of the organization's structure.

Employment Prospects
There are few of these culinary-related job projects in any given area, but the person who gets the work can also become the record keeper for other unrelated groups. It is a type of freelance work that any computer-savvy person can handle.

Advancement Prospects
As the group becomes larger, they may agree to pay an increase in freelance fees. If the group combines with other similar groups elsewhere, the person handling one membership roll can market himself or herself to the rest of the associations.

Best Geographic Location(s)
There is no reason this work cannot be done outside the geographic home of the organization, but while the group is small it makes more sense to have a local data processor.

Education and Training
Anyone with reasonable word processing skills who is able to use Quicken accounting software (or any similar program) can handle this work. Training in data management and financial bookkeeping is useful.

Experience/Skills/Personality Traits
As is common with any record-keeping work, attention to detail is vital. Setting up the paper trail from various officers of the organization is critical in the beginning; then it must be maintained. With any freelance work, the person hired should be friendly, flexible, and always on time with supplying the documents and records the organization requests.

Unions/Associations
Unless this freelance work mushrooms into a full-fledged management company (and that is not impossible) there are no peer group associations, nor are any needed for this level of involvement.

Tips for Entry
Consider every group that you belong to as a possible customer for this work.

WRITING AND PUBLISHING

COOKBOOK AUTHOR

Duties: Submits a book proposal leading to a contract with a cookbook publisher; writes the book and tests all recipes; submits the manuscript and revises it according to the editor's suggestions; checks galleys; prepares index; participates in publicity tour to sell the book

Alternate Title(s): Cookbook Writer

Salary Range: $5,000 to $10,000 for a first book with a limited press run; more for succeeding books based on royalties for number of books sold and larger print runs

Employment Prospects: Limited

Advancement Prospects: Good, steady

Best Geographical Location(s) for Position: Anywhere

Prerequisites:
    Education or Training—Good education, especially good writing skills
    Experience—Food writing for a magazine, newspaper, or cooking classes is helpful, especially recipe writing.
    Special Skills and Personality Traits—Accuracy, thoroughness, and the ability to restrain imagination beyond the ability of readers to follow

CAREER LADDER

```
┌─────────────────────────────────┐
│        Cookbook Author          │
└─────────────────────────────────┘

┌─────────────────────────────────┐
│       Cookbook Test Cook        │
└─────────────────────────────────┘
```

Position Description

The author of a cookbook may start assembling recipes while teaching cooking classes, developing recipes for a cooking specialty (such as desserts or cooking for teens), researching in a foreign country with an exotic cuisine (such as Morocco or India), or just cooking at home to raves from family and friends.

The first step in writing a published cookbook is the hardest: signing a book contract with a good publisher. Contact with other cookbook authors can be invaluable in providing connections with agents (who sell the book idea to a publisher) and editors (who sell the book idea to their publishing house). Without that connection, the only way to reach the publisher is "over the transom," by sending an unsolicited manuscript or book proposal to known publishers of cookbooks—and being very lucky.

Getting a contract is based on a written proposal for the cookbook, consisting of (1) some description of the overall concept and why it will be seized with enthusiasm by eager

cooks, (2) an outline of the recipes by chapters, (3) one or two sample recipes carefully selected to make the agent/editor/reader salivate while reading them, and (4) an objective statement of the author's background and credentials, which makes him or her the only likely person in the world to produce this particular work. The proposal should be double-spaced, with one-inch margins on all four edges, and its pages should be numbered; it must be clean, clear, and concise. Getting a contract can take a year or more from the time the agent starts selling the project. During this time, the successful selling and negotiation of the contract is up to the agent, and the author goes on with his or her other activities.

With a book contract in hand and a deadline looming, it is time to write every recipe and its introduction, test every recipe and retest it for better flavor, texture, appearance, or ease of cooking techniques. Testing recipes can be very expensive because the very best ingredients have to be used every time the dish is prepared. (Then, there's the question of what to do with all the extra food if the author doesn't have a gang of ravenously hungry teenage boys in the house or the neighborhood.)

Some cookbook writers hire an assistant to help with shopping, ingredient preparation, cooking, and clean-up. As each recipe reaches perfection, the author wants to get right to the word processor to describe the process, and having someone to put the kitchen in order is a luxury.

After the manuscript has been shipped to the editor, and has traveled back and forth to accommodate the editor's revisions, it is accepted for publication. At this point there is still more work to be done. An art director is designing the book, but selection of a food stylist and photographer may rest with the author. During the food shoots, the author may elect to be on the set, watching to be sure that the food is cooked precisely to his or her writing and that the presentation and pictures reflect the very best of each dish.

When the book is set in type, a set of the galleys is sent to the writer to check for any errors. This is not the time to rewrite a recipe or add or delete anything. This is hands-off-the-goods, proof-only time. And it has to be done promptly, as sales of the book may depend on publishing the book on schedule.

The index is among the last items to be finished, and most book contracts provide for the author to supply it working from the galleys, but if the author doesn't want to do it, the publisher will hire an indexer (often at the author's cost).

When the book is released, the publisher plans its promotion and publicity. If the publisher doesn't provide these, the author should, using every culinary connection possible. This may include a multiple-city tour for the author to appear at bookstores and, more likely, at trendsetting cooking schools to demonstrate one or two of the recipes, sign books, and be interviewed by the local food editor and/or television news.

Salaries

Authors receive royalties based on the number of copies of the book sold, commonly 7 to 15 percent of the book's retail price. Advances against the royalties may be a part of the contract; often one-half of the advance is paid when the contract is signed and the balance when the manuscript is accepted. A first cookbook will probably have a print run of 3,000 copies; if the retail price is $19.95, soft cover, that means about $4,000 to $9,000 to the author (deducting the publicity copies, author's copies, and agent's copies). As a cookbook author continues to produce popular books, the press run gets bigger and the advance gets bigger, and there may even be royalty payments in future years. (Keep in mind your agent will usually keep 15 percent of your earnings!)

Employment Prospects

Cookbook writing is freelance work, with the exception of working as a writer/editor for a publisher's series such as Williams-Sonoma, or sponsored by a culinary academy such as the Culinary Institute of America (CIA). In some of these cases the author/editor does not get royalties, but is paid a salary or an hourly wage for the term of work—this is called "work for hire."

Advancement Prospects

One successful cookbook leads to another. It also leads to traveling the teacher circuit to cooking schools and enhances the fee paid for teaching a class, and an opportunity for testing student interest in the next cookbook idea.

Best Geographical Location(s)

A cookbook can be written anywhere. A certain geographic background that supports an expertise (such as southern or midwestern cooking) can prove beneficial when writing a specialized cookbook.

Education and Training

Clear and lucid writing reflects a good education, even if it doesn't include a college degree. Thoughtfully reading good writers and seeing the stylistic ways they make their point is a means of self-training to write.

Experience/Skills/Personality Traits

Prior recipe writing experience for a newspaper, magazine, or cooking classes is certainly helpful.

A cookbook writer must be precise and careful, listing every ingredient, describing every step of the preparation, and guiding the reader to success in the kitchen.

Unions/Associations

The International Association of Culinary Professionals (IACP) numbers most of the current crop of successful cookbook authors among its membership. Their annual meeting is an excellent opportunity to meet other authors and influential professionals in the food industry.

Tips for Entry

1. Ask the food editor of your local newspaper if any successful cookbook authors live in the area, and contact the author about working as a test cook on his or her current book. This could lead you to a relationship with an agent, an editor, and a mentor—and possibly a contract!

2. Most public libraries maintain an up-to-date reference book section, and there should be one or more books of sources for writers. Find one with a list of literary agents who specialize in culinary writing. The IACP also maintains a list of literary agents who are members. Write your most bewitching letter to one or more agents, extolling your skills and describing the engrossing books you are ready to write.

COOKBOOK EDITOR

CAREER PROFILE

Duties: Works with a submitted manuscript to bring out the voice of the writer; reads proposals; selects promising book ideas; presents ideas to acquisitions committee; negotiates book contracts; reviews manuscripts; supervises rewrites and editing; works with graphics and marketing departments to bring books to the public

Alternate Title(s): Senior Editor

Salary Range: $24,000 to $85,000+

Employment Prospects: Limited

Advancement Prospects: Good

Best Geographical Location(s) for Position: Mostly in New York City, but some publishing houses are in other areas.

Prerequisites:

Education or Training—A good general education and familiarity with fine literature; college major of English, communications or journalism; love of good food and a basic knowledge of ingredients and cooking

Experience—Any publishing experience

Special Skills and Personality Traits—Sensitivity to the writer's intent, ability to lead a writer without rewriting him or her

CAREER LADDER

```
┌─────────────────────────────┐
│      Cookbook Editor        │
└─────────────────────────────┘

┌─────────────────────────────┐
│       Senior Editor         │
└─────────────────────────────┘

┌─────────────────────────────┐
│     Editorial Assistant     │
└─────────────────────────────┘
```

Position Description

The work of a cookbook editor is to bring out the voice of the writer at its best. An editor does not rewrite but rather identifies areas in the manuscript that can be improved by rewriting or reorganizing and works with the author to accomplish it. The extent to which the editor is involved in the final work can range from minor enhancements to an unacknowledged collaboration; the norm is at the side of enhancement.

Every published cookbook starts with a written proposal. This is the editor's basic tool for first assessing the value of the cookbook idea and the author's style. The editor presents it to a more senior editor or directly to the publisher's acquisitions committee. Once it is approved, the editor contacts the author or the literary agent and proceeds to make an offer and negotiate a contract for the book. The author may be asked to provide more writing samples or a different structure to the recipe lists. At this point the book is being shaped by the synergy of the author's food knowledge and the editor's marketing knowledge. Once the contract is signed, the deadline for submission of the manuscript is determined, and the work is in the hands of the author until the due date.

In the meantime, the editor is available to answer the writer's questions and may want to see some of the work in batches to make sure the book is developing as it was intended. An editor may be working on 20 to 30 books in various stages of completion at once. The editor may start some of the advance work for publishing the cookbook by consulting the design department on the layout of the book, on whether to use photographs or line drawings as illustrations, and on the cover and the jacket designs.

After the manuscript is submitted the editor goes to work on the submitted text. Some questions might be, "What does this term mean?", "What is happening during this assembly?" or "How is this going to look?" These questions fed back to the author may cause a major rewrite or just a bit of fine tuning.

The editor's relationship with the writer is crucial to the work being done on the manuscript. Regardless of the friendship, respect, or admiration the writer may feel toward the editor, when the work is being judged and changes are being encouraged, the only relationship that will serve the process is trust. It is the editor's job to engender trust; nothing less works.

From the time the manuscript is submitted until the work is accepted according to contract terms, many months may pass and many revisions may happen. The art department will begin work on the layout, illustrations, and the cover, providing some of these to the marketing department for inclusion in catalogs and mailings. The editor's work is to keep everything moving on schedule toward publication date. The marketing department may be scheduling personal appearances by the author. A trade show presentation may be part of the marketing effort. It usually takes about a year from the manuscript submission until publication.

Salaries

Editors' salaries range widely depending on the publishing house, the years of experience, the editor's ability to bring in new, successful authors, and the level of responsibility within the editorial structure of the house. A book editor in the first year or two of full responsibility for a project would earn between $24,000 and $30,000 a year. A senior editor, supervising junior editors as well as handling his or her own writers, can earn $85,000 a year and up.

Employment Prospects

Some editors known for their cookbook lists are general editors, also working with fiction, biography, current events, poetry, and self-help work. As they develop a reputation for cookbooks, more query letters, proposals, and literary agent submissions will be addressed directly to them. "Wannabe" editors start at the front desk, reading query letters and proposals that come in unsolicited.

Advancement Prospects

Some editors move from house to house during their career; others stay with one publisher, rising through the editorial ranks. Some editors have a legendary reputation for mentoring their assistants. Those jobs are rare and highly sought after.

Best Geographical Location(s)

Most book publishers are clustered in New York City, but there are a few sprinkled in other places. Consult *Literary Market Place* for names and addresses of publishers, as well as the types of books they publish.

Education and Training

An editor should have an excellent general education background and a critical familiarity with clear writing. Training in vocational programs is listed under communications and journalism. There are summer institutes given annually at Radcliffe, Denver, Stanford, and Harvard universities for people interested in work in publishing.

Experience/Skills/Personality Traits

All editorial experience is useful, from the high school paper to the university literary journal. Magazine and newsletter editing, in-house journals for any company, public relations writing and editing provide a background for book editing.

Well-trained communications skills, either gained in college classes or fine-tuned in the workplace, are essential for an editor. The human relationship between writer and editor is the editor's most valuable asset in working with the manuscript and to elicit the best work from every writer.

Hands-on knowledge of food and cooking may not be necessary for editing cookbooks since seeing lapses and recognizing questions in the text are the essentials of editing. The editor does need a clear sense of the reader—the customer for the book—to ensure that the product will have sufficient appeal.

Unions/Associations

There are a few professional associations for book editors (see Appendix IV). Cookbook editors can join one of the networks of culinary organizations to connect with professionals in other lines of food work.

Tips for Entry

1. Take an entry-level job, usually receptionist or editorial assistant, at a publishing house that maintains a good cookbook list, and let your food background be known to cookbook editors on staff. You'll be in line for the next editor's assistant slot.
2. Attend marketing book fairs such as the annual Book Exposition of America, every spring (usually over Memorial Day weekend); meet and talk to editors about job possibilities, but don't get in their way while they are talking to book dealers about their lists—that's what they're there to do.
3. Review the cookbook selection in your public library and at bookstores to identify prominent cookbook publishers; write to them about job opportunities and recommendations for education and training.

FOOD EDITOR

CAREER PROFILE

Duties: Responsible for the style and content of all food pages in a print publication or for radio, TV, or cable programs; writes, edits, and selects illustrations; represents the publication or media to the community; hires and supervises staff writers and assistants

Alternate Title(s): None

Salary Range: $35,000 to $80,000+

Employment Prospects: Limited

Advancement Prospects: Limited

Best Geographical Location(s) for Position: Magazine publishers are clustered in a half dozen states; newspapers and TV are in every part of the country.

Prerequisites:

Education or Training—A good general education with an emphasis on English, communications, home economics, or nutrition

Experience—Any writing or editing work is helpful

Special Skills and Personality Traits—A thorough knowledge of food ingredients, cuisines, products, chefs, nutrition, and trends

CAREER LADDER

```
┌─────────────────────────────┐
│      Managing Editor        │
└─────────────────────────────┘

┌─────────────────────────────┐
│        Food Editor          │
└─────────────────────────────┘

┌─────────────────────────────┐
│        Staff Writer         │
└─────────────────────────────┘
```

Position Description

The food editor for a newspaper, magazine, or other print publication sets the style and the tone of the food section. This consists of subject matter, source of material, language, and difficulty of producing the recipes. Even before these can be determined, the food editor must have a clear picture of his or her reader—level of income, level of education, and lifestyle. For *Vogue* those answers are high income, university and advanced degrees, culture-seeking, and well-traveled. For a factory-town weekly newspaper the answers may be moderate to low income, high school and community college degrees, family activities including sports, popular entertainment, and home improvements. There is a significant difference in the types of food of interest to readers for each publication.

The food editor determines the subject or focus of each edition; assigns articles to staff writers if there are any or writes the articles himself or herself if it's a one-person department; plans or approves the make-up of the pages; edits all written material submitted; chooses any wire-service material to be added; decides on illustrations or photographs and works with the artist or photographer and food stylist to produce them; sends the editorial copy to the printer; and turns his or her attention to the next edition.

The food editor is also a representative to the community. For a daily newspaper, this means building a profile in the community, being recognized and speaking out on community matters affecting food. For a national magazine, it means participating in symposiums and workshops that question and influence public policy and personal choices.

Depending on the size of the food section, the food editor is also an administrator, managing the staff of the department, setting schedules, reviewing performances, recommending promotions and salaries, and nurturing the professional development of the individual writers.

Salaries

A food editor will earn within the range of $35,000 to $80,000 and up a year, depending on the circulation size of the publication, and to some extent the location of the editorial offices.

Employment Prospects

There are a limited number of food editors for magazines, although many fashion and lifestyle magazines do have a food section and an editor. There are many more newspaper food editors, although not all smaller or weekly magazines have a food section. The stable of food editors in the United States is quite small, probably under 1,000, and they network constantly, so they are all known to each other; this leads to most food editor jobs being passed along by word of mouth rather than by employment ads.

An increasing number of food related sites on the Internet has created jobs for food editors that have never before existed. The increasing number of on-line newsletters for food writers would be a good place to start a search for those jobs.

Advancement Prospects

Food editors find advancement by moving from one publication to another, finding a larger opportunity for their work and a higher salary in a new location.

Best Geographical Location(s)

Most food magazines and other publications with food departments are clustered on the East Coast, but some are sprinkled around the country in Vermont, Iowa, California, and New Mexico. Newspapers are spread broadly throughout the United States.

Education and Training

Editing skills are taught in communications and journalism departments in colleges and universities. Additionally, an editor needs a good command of written English and a thorough knowledge of grammar. Some publications require their editor to be a graduate home economist, but less so now than in the past.

Experience/Skills/Personality Traits

An editor with a staff of writers needs the instincts and skills of a teacher to bring out the best in a writer's piece. To successfully assign stories to the staff, the editor has to know the individual strengths and the personal interests of each writer.

The editor has to know a lot about food, ingredients, trends, chefs, cookbook authors and others who are influential in the food world, local products, and nutrition- and diet-related health matters; this knowledge has to be constantly honed to stay current.

Unions/Associations

The Association of Food Journalists limits its membership to full-time employees of daily newspapers. At various times they have allowed associate memberships; it is always subject to change.

Food writers and editors are welcome to membership in the International Association of Culinary Professionals.

Tips for Entry

1. Check with your local community college for journalism and editing courses that will prepare you for a newspaper or magazine writing job.
2. Contact the food editor of your local newspaper about any possibility of assisting at editorial duties to learn aspects of the work.
3. If your local paper doesn't have a food section, contact the managing editor with a proposal to develop one.

FOOD WRITER

CAREER PROFILE

Duties: Develops sources and conducts research to write stories and articles about food, recipes, products, and personalities for print in newspapers, magazines, and for radio, TV, and cable

Alternate Title(s): Food Journalist

Salary Range: $29,000 to $50,000

Employment Prospects: Good

Advancement Prospects: Limited

Best Geographical Location(s) for Position: Major urban areas

Prerequisites:

Education or Training—A good liberal arts education with emphasis on writing, English literature, and grammar or a home economics degree

Experience—Any writing or editing experience is beneficial; computer experience, especially word processing, is essential

Special Skills and Personality Traits—Both a love and a knowledge of food and the food industry and the ability to communicate this enthusiasm; curiosity; cooking skills

CAREER LADDER

```
┌─────────────────────────────┐
│         Food Editor         │
└─────────────────────────────┘

┌─────────────────────────────┐
│         Food Writer         │
└─────────────────────────────┘

┌─────────────────────────────┐
│      Research Assistant     │
└─────────────────────────────┘
```

Position Description

A food writer may be either a newspaper, magazine, or broadcast journalism staff writer or a freelancer to any of those markets. Although food writing usually contains recipes, there is also writing about prominent individuals, exotic ingredients, basic techniques, restaurants, and personal accounts relating to food.

Subject matter is usually assigned to a staff writer based on the design and layout of the coming issue. Writers are selected for specific assignments based on their writing experience and food knowledge, and are given guidance as to length and point of focus by the editor or through the editorial meeting to plan the issue.

The writer decides on the lead to use, checks facts in available books, on the Internet, or by calling appropriate sources, plans the article, and writes the text for submission to the editor for approval. The text is returned to the writer if the editor wants more information, a different focus, or rewriting until it is acceptable.

Food writing that contains recipes relies on the writer for accurate ingredient lists and trustworthy descriptions of the steps for preparation. It is the food writer's responsibility to test all the recipes included in his or her articles; testing often brings to light a step or an admonition that the writer wouldn't otherwise include.

In the case of freelancing, the writer first submits a query letter to the editor, outlining the idea and sources for the article, and when it has been accepted by the editor and scheduled for publication, the writer proceeds with the story idea.

Freelance writing is an excellent entry device for newcomers. It appeals to former staff writers who may want to work fewer hours or to current staff writers who want do a larger volume of work to earn extra income.

Salaries

A staff writer or a freelance writer can earn in the range of $29,000 to $50,000 a year and up.

Employment Prospects

The local newspaper of most large to small towns usually has a one-day-a-week food section that is prepared either from locally-produced articles or cut and pasted off the wire services, or a combination of both. There are several dozen popular food magazines for recreational cooks and trade magazines for professionals; all of them have staff writers and most of them accept outside work. Cities that have a higher than average number of fine restaurants often have independent tabloids that review and critique the eateries, attracting restaurant and gourmet advertising; those same areas may have a market for food material on local radio and television.

Advancement Prospects

While it is possible to move up the ladder from writer to editor, a lot depends on the age of the current editor and his or her plans for retirement or moving to another job.

Best Geographical Location(s)

Major urban areas with more than one large daily newspaper and cities where food magazines are headquartered, such as New York City, Chicago, and Los Angeles, have the greatest number of food jobs locally.

For freelance writers, where to live is purely a matter of personal preference, but it helps to have an active food community nearby to provide story ideas and sources.

Education and Training

A writer needs a good liberal arts education with a heavy emphasis on writing and communication skills. A journalism major or a combination of journalism and home economics is very attractive to magazine editors who hire general staff.

A stint of at least a couple of years working for a nurturing editor is the best training.

Experience/Skills/Personality Traits

Any writing experience is valuable. A writer should maintain a portfolio of published articles from any source to show to an interested editor, whether applying for a job or querying for a freelance article.

Computer skills in word processing are almost mandatory by now. Newspapers are fully computerized, as are major magazines. Cooking skills are valuable, especially for writing recipes and testing them for articles. A vast knowledge about food and cooking will help with any food writing.

Knowledge of food and the food industry, and enthusiasm for the subject (especially if the writer has an infectious style), are the two characteristics that herald credibility in food writing. Curiosity is a writer's beacon, leading on to new information.

Unions/Associations

The only membership group specifically for food writers is the Association of Food Journalists for newspaper food editors, but regional culinary associations usually have a sampling of members who are regular contributors to local and nationwide publications.

Tips for Entry

1. Call your local daily or weekly newspaper, no matter how small, and ask whether they take unsolicited material; even if this is unpaid work, it allows a writer to assemble a portfolio for future work.
2. If you have the qualifications to belong to the local food society, or if you belong to one of the crossover associations such as the American Institute of Wine and Food (A.I.W.F.), offer to write for the member newsletter, either an occasional article or a regular column.

LITERARY AGENT

CAREER PROFILE

Duties: Making the best possible match for a food writer and a book concept with an editor working for a successful publishing house, presenting the idea to one or more editors, selecting appropriate publishing offers, negotiating contracts with input from writer, providing a strong shoulder to the writer during the creative time to write the book

Alternate Title(s): Book Agent

Salary Range: 15 percent of author's earnings from the book

Employment Prospects: Limited

Advancement Prospects: Fair

Best Geographical Location(s) for Position: New York is a major publishing center, but agents may work from anywhere.

Prerequisites:
  Education or Training—Good liberal arts education
  Experience—Working with editors and publishers
  Special Skills and Personality Traits—Love of language and appreciation for clear communication, good judgment for writer's ideas in view of current book publishing trends

CAREER LADDER

```
┌─────────────────────────────┐
│   Literary Agency Owner      │
└─────────────────────────────┘

┌─────────────────────────────┐
│       Literary Agent         │
└─────────────────────────────┘

┌─────────────────────────────┐
│      Agent's Assistant       │
└─────────────────────────────┘
```

Position Description

A literary agent is a skilled marketer for food writers, using his or her up-to-the minute knowledge about publishing houses, editors with a strong interest in food writing, and upcoming trends in cooking and ingredients to make the best possible match for a food writer and a book concept with an editor working for a successful publishing house. The success of the relationship between the writer and the client depends on the trust and respect that each has for the talent and skill of the other.

In the process of transforming the concept into a published work, a process that may take two years or more, the agent has many roles to fulfill. For the writer/client the agent is a cheerleader, a mirror of reality, a judge of craft, a financial guide. The relationship is usually initiated by the writer, who asks colleagues about their agents and seeks references on particular agents who are well known, or by a chance encounter at a conference or other culinary get-

together. This means that the agent needs to be out in the culinary world, going to conferences, writer's workshops, and major book fairs, getting around to see and be seen.

Once the writer and the agent have connected, as soon as the writer has a book concept the agent considers worth selling, it is the agent's work to present the idea—or, better yet, a fully developed book proposal—to appropriate editors in appropriate publishing houses, those that have a proven interest in similar books. This may mean sending the proposal to several editors simultaneously, to see how many are interested and how many want to make a deal on the book. It is the agent's job to get the highest price, the terms most advantageous to the writer, and keep the writer involved and informed as the process unfolds. The details of the contract undergo a steely-eyed review by both the agent and the author until a deal is made and the contract is approved and signed by both sides.

The agent provides counsel and a strong shoulder through the writing and publishing process. No agent's job is over the day the contract is signed; the agent doesn't earn income unless the book is published and sells to readers.

Salaries

The agent earns 15 percent of everything the author receives for the book under the contract—the advance against future royalties upon contract signing, the second advance when the manuscript is finished and accepted by the editor and publisher, and semiannual royalties as long as the book is in print and continuing if a second edition is printed. This can be very minimal income in the early years of a book agent's business. Most independent agents operate at a deficit for the first 18 months, at least.

Employment Prospects

Agents who work on salary or a "draw" at established agencies can afford this start-up phase and eventually reach a point where they are earning what they need as income; in the case of a very eager and energetic agent, this point may also be 18 months.

The field of independent agents is enormously overcrowded. Many publishers are shrinking staff. Proficient editors merely move from the buying side of the table to the selling side to continue using their well-honed skills.

Advancement Prospects

With writers under contract who are very successful—bestselling authors—the agent's income can reach a very high level. Writers want to be associated with successful agents, and writers are likely to switch agents to be under contract with a "winner." Winner is an appropriate term, because there are some major award programs just for culinary writing (Beard House and the International Association of Culinary Professionals [IACP] are two) and being listed as the agent for one or more of the winners is a big boost for an agent's reputation.

Best Geographic Location(s)

New York City is where the action is. Publishing houses are headquartered there, and the media buzz often starts there as well. However, an agent can live anywhere in the country and make periodic trips to New York to meet publishers, eat breakfast, lunch, and dinner with editors, and come home with contracts in process for the book proposals in hand. The current evolution of business communication with email, fax, phones, and overnight delivery companies has made location a matter of preference instead of necessity. Many writers would rather have their agents living close enough to meet somewhere convenient to both for work sessions.

Education and Training

No specific education or training is required to set up a literary agency business. Most agents have a good liberal arts education and work experience as writers and editors in a vast realm of companies: magazines, newspapers, and advertising or public relations firms.

Experience/Skills/Personality Traits

A love of language and an appreciation for the clear communication of knowledge are the agent's most essential tools. An agent must be an equally good judge of the proposed book concept and of the writer. The first involves keeping in touch with book-buying and book-publishing trends to know how to present the idea to a publisher; the second requires an ability to assess whether the writer has the commitment to creatively and diligently produce the manuscript on time.

The pleasure in marketing, making a sale, setting up a value for goods—even if these are not among the original traits that literary agents bring to this work, they are the heart of the work. Being able to engender trust from colleagues is another essential trait, because the writer is counting on the agent to choose the most skilled editor and publishing house for the work at hand, elicit the best offer in terms of advances, and make a personality match with the writer.

The agent must understand the legal language of contracts and know where the editor's offer can be bettered for the writer. Sometimes the advance is structured in an uncommon way; sometimes the book's graphics, photographs, and design features can be guaranteed to please the writer's initial idea of the "look" of the final book.

Unions/Associations

Literary agents who specialize in culinary writing meet many of their future clients at large events such as the annual conferences of the IACP or Women Chefs & Restaurateurs, and at trade shows such as the Fancy Food Show sponsored by the National Association for the Specialty Food Trade (NASFT).

The Authors Guild and the National Writers Union are two membership organizations that many agents join.

Tips for Entry

1. Look for a literary agency in your area, although these are most common in New York City, Chicago, and Los Angeles, and take an entry-level job, preferably working with agents who specialize in culinary writing.

2. Since writing and editing seems to be the most common experience that agents have, working in these jobs will be good experience while pursuing the dream of becoming an agent.

FOOD HISTORIAN

CAREER PROFILE

Duties: Conducts original research on food and cooking in former times; assembles documentation consisting of photographs, old cookbooks and recipe collections, or cooking tools from another time; provides authenticity to museum exhibits, historic villages, and cookbooks; consults for TV and movie writers and directors

Alternate Title(s): None

Salary Range: Hourly rate for freelancing around $200 an hour and from $500 to $3,000 a day. College and university teaching posts pay $30,000 and $60,000 a year

Employment Prospects: Limited

Advancement Prospects: Limited

Best Geographical Location(s) for Position: Anywhere, but expect to travel

Prerequisites:

Education or Training—For college or university teaching or to get research grants, a degree in history is needed, with at least a master's or working on a Ph.D.; additional credentials include a résumé and portfolio of jobs completed

Experience—Working on historical projects as a researcher or assistant

Special Skills and Personality Traits—Organizational skills for cataloging; good memory; curiosity; thoroughness

CAREER LADDER

```
┌─────────────────────────────┐
│   Historic Project Curator   │
└─────────────────────────────┘

┌─────────────────────────────┐
│       Food Historian         │
└─────────────────────────────┘

┌─────────────────────────────┐
│     Assistant Historian      │
└─────────────────────────────┘
```

Position Description

Research historians are treasure seekers who call on their imaginations to unearth fresh raw materials for their current projects. These can be as dissimilar as the archives in a small-town library or newspaper where a plant or a mill was a dominant employer to the oral histories gleaned from elderly residents. Other sources are local historic societies, early books written about the area, and the artifacts of the plant or mill. A food historian is hired to contribute research to publications, to historic villages and landmarks, and to museum projects that must be historically accurate with regard to food and food preparation.

Regardless of the eventual product, the food historian works from original sources to understand, document, and replicate the cuisine and food preparation of the particular time or place. The original sources that are available are archives of old photographs, early documents such as cookbooks, receipt books (as they were sometimes called), and diaries and personal accounts of lives and times.

Historians learn their research skills during college and university years, writing and contributing to historical papers. A food historian needs to have the same general education as a historian in any other field. When a book or a museum show presents itself as historically authentic, the research sources must be professionally documented even though they may not be listed or posted.

Some of the questions a historian must answer are about the kitchen tools that were used, how refined the raw ingredients were, and what local factors led to specific types of seasoning. In pioneer days, food had to be either eaten while it was fresh or preserved by pickling or smoking because there was no refrigeration. A food historian can prepare a historic food very close to the way it originally tasted. In a historic village it might be cooked exactly that way, with authentic kitchen tools. For a historic cookbook, the food preparation presented by the historian would be brought up-to-date by the author or editor using modern milled flours instead of stone ground, commercial yeasts instead of wild spores, food processors and microwaves instead of a few knives and a reflector in the fireplace.

For a museum or a historic village, a model might be built to give a visual picture of yesteryear. Many historians do this work themselves; others hire a model maker. For a cookbook illustration, the historian might provide old photographs or construct an elaborate classic dish, such as *croquembouche* or meats presented in pastry or aspic, grandly decorated, to photograph alongside the dish in modern form.

Salaries

Most food historians work on a freelance basis, contracting for a specific job such as a cookbook, development of a historic site, or consulting to a museum for a single show. A freelance historian contracts for services on an hourly or daily rate with an estimate of the total time the project will take. Hourly rates are around $200 an hour. Daily rates range from $500 to $3,000 a day plus expenses for interpretive performances or presentations at historic villages or fairs.

Colleges and universities provide employment for all manner of historians; a food historian is likely to be on the faculty of one with a strong culinary program, either food technology or home economics. College and university salaries for research historians range between $30,000 and $60,000 a year.

Employment Prospects

Employment prospects for food historians are limited, but it is a field that attracts only a few practitioners. The extent to which one is able to develop a reputation has a direct connection with the number, type, and variety of jobs that are offered. In university teaching and research, with advanced degrees, a food historian will qualify for teaching posts.

Advancement Prospects

For a freelancer, the mark of advancement is being able to charge a high rate for services. In educational and museum posts, advancement may not be available with the current employer, and advancement is a matter of seeking the same position in a larger and wealthier institution.

Best Geographical Location(s)

It makes very little difference where a food historian lives, with the possible exception of New York City, which provides business and social access to editors and publishers. The work involves travel to the site of original sources for research, after which the writing can be done wherever home and computer terminal are located.

Education and Training

As a freelancer, the portfolio and résumé that result from years of practice are viewed as equivalent to education, but not as a substitute. A food historian must have a graduate history degree from an accredited institution (at least an M.S.; ideally a Ph.D.) for a teaching post. Academic experience (senior projects, dissertations) in historic research is essential because it trains the individual in accepted practices that historians use through their lifetime.

Experience/Skills/Personality Traits

Any experience working with a trained researcher or historian as an assistant, intern, or volunteer is an opportunity to learn field practices. A lot of the historian's work is cataloging, working with original sources, and keeping records for finding the same fact faster the second time around. A good memory is invaluable. Curiosity and thoroughness are primary traits for researchers.

Unions/Associations

History is also termed folklore; the American Folklore Society has a Foodways section. Based at Bowling Green State University in Bowling Green, Ohio, they publish a semiannual digest that contains articles and lists upcoming conferences, exhibits, newsletters, book notes, and articles in related publications.

Tips for Entry

1. Make the acquaintance of a local food historian and offer to work as a volunteer or apprentice in exchange for training.
2. Check your local library for food history books, and request they requisition (or get on inter-library loan) additional food histories from your state library system. Reading will acquaint you with the historians and give you a clear sense of differing points of view and focuses.
3. Call your local museums, including botanic gardens (edible herbs), natural history (local game birds, fish, and mushrooms), and fine arts to identify any local experts who may welcome an assistant.

FOOD PHOTOGRAPHER

Duties: Consults with the art director about photographic subjects to illustrate advertising, packaging, cookbooks, magazines, or press kits; hires food stylist and sets up shoot, working with art director to provide appropriate photography

Alternate Title(s): None

Salary Range: From $15,000 to $65,000+, but most photographers are self-employed

Employment Prospects: Good and growing

Advancement Prospects: Good

Best Geographical Location(s) for Position: Major urban areas where advertising agencies are headquartered, and any major food-producing area

Prerequisites:
    Education or Training—Art school with emphasis on photography
    Experience—Work with established photographers
    Special Skills and Personality Traits—Both a team worker and a leader to get the best out of the client and the staff

```
┌─────────────────────────────────┐
│      Food Photographer          │
└─────────────────────────────────┘

┌─────────────────────────────────┐
│    Photographer's Assistant     │
└─────────────────────────────────┘
```

Position Description

A food photographer is a trained commercial photographer who specializes in food images. The work is primarily illustrative, providing pictures for newspaper and magazine advertising, product packages, food magazine contents, and cookbooks.

The photographer is hired by the art director of an advertising agency or a magazine, or the cookbook author. The photographer usually selects the food stylist who will cook and arrange the food to be photographed. The photo studio used by the photographer must be equipped with excellent appliances, counter space, and lighting. It should have a general collection of props—dishes, glassware, linens, and knickknacks that set off a plate arrangement. (Often the food stylist will provide the necessary props; in large urban areas there are prop stylists who work as freelancers and prop stores that rent equipment and trinkets by the day.)

The day of the shoot the food photographer is responsible for guiding all the work to be done. A full day's work,

10 to 12 hours at a stretch, will produce no more than four main shots of a food and wine subject or eight to nine small close-ups. The art director, the photographer, and the stylist consult to get a clear understanding of the image to be produced. With the constant help of an assistant, the photographer sets up the camera and lights, selects the appropriate lens, assembles the props, and prepares to take a Polaroid picture to check the arrangement before actual shooting. While the stylist is cooking, the photographer works with a dummy plate to design the background. This can consist of painting the surface, selecting color features to go with the food, and locating props into the picture.

As soon as the food is ready, the arranged ingredients are set into the scene, and the photographer takes a Polaroid shot to match the way the camera is set up. If the art director is satisfied with the first picture, the photographer's team completes the image. It is just as likely everyone will see changes they want made, to heighten color, to make something looser or more dense, or to increase or decrease one of the ingredients so it does or doesn't dominate. When the food stylist has recreated the dish, the process starts again with the Polaroid and on to the final camera image. These steps are repeated for each shot planned for the day.

On days when no shooting is scheduled, the rest of the photographer's work has to be attended to. Film is developed, either by the photographer in his or her own darkroom or by a trusted photo lab. Prints are delivered to the client. Bills for the job are made up and sent to the client. The studio has to be cleaned and readied for the next job.

The photographer is always perfecting his or her portfolio; it contains samples of work to show a client when the photographer is interviewed for jobs. It has to be up-to-date, because food styles and trends influence what the consumer finds appealing and attractive. The photographer's job is to lure consumers to read the copy in a food advertisement, pick the package off the supermarket shelf, or buy the cookbook because one particular dish looks so delicious.

To get jobs, a food photographer makes constant calls to art directors and magazine editors, and if there is some interest for an upcoming job, the portfolio is sent over for consideration, usually followed by a personal interview. A well-established photographer might make 40 cold calls to produce 10 interview appointments leading to two to four jobs. A beginner would make as many as 100 calls to get 10 interviews leading to only one job.

Salaries

Food photography pays well for a talented, trained beginner and pays generously for a well-established veteran. A full day of a shoot will cost the client from several hundred to several thousand dollars a day. Occasionally a shoot will go over to a second day, but overall a month will have only 10 to 12 day-long shoots, leaving the alternate days for cleanup and making marketing calls. A photographer can earn from $15,000 to $65,000+ a year, but most are self-employed and also have the costs of owning a business—paying salaries, rent, insurance, buying equipment, and marketing expenses.

Employment Prospects

There is an immense volume of food photography being done for print purposes, and more for film, video, and websites. Every food client wants the very best photos to sell the product.

Advancement Prospects

Advancement is based largely on skill and appeal in the marketplace, allowing the good photographer to raise his or her fees.

Best Geographical Location(s)

Major urban areas with a strong culinary publishing presence, New York City, Chicago, Seattle, San Francisco, are where major advertising agencies that handle large food accounts are located. Another source of work is food magazines, and they work with top photographers anywhere in the country, but give most of the work to local studios.

Education and Training

Graduate training in photography from one of the top schools is invaluable. Self-trained photographers struggle to succeed to any great extent. A degree in fine arts, while not essential, trains the student's eye for defining the components of a picture.

Experience/Skills/Personality Traits

During and after schooling, working with established photographers provides an apprenticeship. Working for more than one photographer as an assistant exposes the newcomer to various styles and points of view. A professional food photographer has to be a good team player; the client, the art director, the food stylist, and the photographer work as a team for the long hours of a shoot.

Unions/Associations

There are two major professional associations for food photographers. The APA, Advertising Photographers of America, and ASMP, American Society of Magazine Photographers, both provide a network for peer contacts, business forms and guidance, and educational programs on the local chapter level.

Tips for Entry

1. Find a food photographer in your area and ask about any opportunities to work in his or her studio.
2. Study food photography in the major magazines (both in ads and in articles) to develop a sense of current styles.
3. Photography for articles is usually credited; decide who are your favorite photographers and follow their work.

FOOD STYLIST

CAREER PROFILE

Duties: Shops, cooks, and arranges food for photography, both still and film; provides props; arranges for extra equipment needed for location shoots; interacts with photographer, art director, and client

Alternate Title(s): None

Salary Range: $25,000 to $120,000+

Employment Prospects: Limited

Advancement Prospects: Limited

Best Geographical Location(s) for Position: Major urban areas and cities where major food and wine publications are headquartered

Prerequisites:

Education or Training—Culinary training and/or art school

Experience—Work for top restaurants and caterers

Special Skills and Personality Traits—Patience, artistry, curiosity, and physical stamina

CAREER LADDER

```
┌─────────────────────────────┐
│      Art Director           │
└─────────────────────────────┘

┌─────────────────────────────┐
│      Food Stylist           │
└─────────────────────────────┘

┌─────────────────────────────┐
│    Stylist's Assistant      │
└─────────────────────────────┘
```

Position Description

A food stylist cooks and arranges food for film and video photography: food product advertisements in magazines, restaurant commercials on television, recipe illustrations in cookbooks, sumptuous buffet displays in movies, cover photographs for newspaper food sections, and mail-order catalog arrangements. The stylist may work as a freelance specialist hired by the photographer or be on the staff of a food publication. Once the photographic job is defined, the stylist is responsible for all ingredient shopping, props, cooking, arrangement, and staying at the studio until the shoot is satisfactory to the photographer and the client.

Food stylists work excruciatingly long hours on a shoot; 10-hour days are normal and many run longer. Often the food to be photographed must be prepared over and over again because the art director or the photographer wants something changed after a Polaroid test shot, or because the food has gone cold and limp as time dragged on.

To photograph a lip-licking hamburger, the stylist may go through as many as eight dozen hamburger buns, grilling or toasting to achieve the right color and moving sesame seeds with a tweezers and glue for a better-looking arrangement. Pounds and pounds of hamburger patties might be used to get just the right look of thickness, adding the visual appearance of juiciness by painting on food color—even adjusting the crusty edge with a blow torch!

When the food stylist is hired for a specific shoot, he or she has an opportunity to interact with the client or the cookbook writer, helping to choose what dishes or combinations of ingredients will be used and how the picture will be arranged or garnished. Even with a cookbook, if the text has not yet been typeset for publication, a food stylist may suggest some additions or changes in a particular recipe to make the picture more appealing. After a first discussion, the stylist knows what specific pictures or film are going to be shot on the scheduled date. Shopping is the stylist's job, not just for ingredients but also for props. A stylist has a collection of plates, bowls, glasses, placemats, silverware, and accessories, and often the photographer, if he or she specializes in food photography, does as well. Additionally, in some cities there are prop rental stores where the stylist can select a few alternative pieces to try in the picture.

Depending on how extensive the job is, the stylist may call one or more assistant cooks to help in preparing for the shoot and to work at the studio during the shoot. Whatever steps can be prepped ahead of time are done the day before and taken to the studio.

In addition to the tweezers and glue, a stylist's bag of tricks includes bamboo skewers, T-pins, cotton-tipped picks, dental floss, scissors, X-Acto knives, paint brushes, needles and thread, that blow torch, eyedroppers, Photoflo (a detergent to simulate bubbles on a wine glass), food color vials, rulers, and a few Band-Aids for accidents. Dental floss will cut yeast bread to look like rolls. The needle and thread sews things together, like lemons or raw poultry.

Most photographer's work is done in studios, and those who regularly do food illustration have a working kitchen with a commercial stove, ovens, refrigerator, and well-lighted work surfaces for the stylist. For a location shoot, there may be heavy equipment that must be rented—freezers, refrigerators, folding tables, or pounds of ice.

Salaries
Food stylists may earn up to $1,000 a day for a 10-hour shoot and $150 an hour overtime. This can translate into an annual income of $25,000 to $120,000 depending on the amount of work done in a year. Stylists on the staff of a food magazine or a newspaper earn annual salaries in the same range, but work full time and may have other cooking/testing work to do.

Employment Prospects
There are very few salaried jobs for food stylists, and they are primarily for the print media at magazines. Most of the freelance work is for food photographers, advertising agencies, and cookbook publishers.

Advancement Prospects
Advancement consists of shifting from being an assistant to being a stylist, or as a freelance stylist being in sufficient demand to be able to raise his or her fees.

Best Geographical Location(s)
Major urban areas with publishing companies, major advertising agencies, and food-dominant regions such as the California wine country have substantial work for food stylists.

Education and Training
Professional culinary training and/or art training both contribute positively to an individual's skill at food styling. The Minneapolis chapter of Home Economists in Business (HEIB) holds a biannual week-long workshop in food styling, but it is not for beginners; some of the top food stylists in the country attend as students.

Experience/Skills/Personality Traits
Any work experience for top restaurants or caterers, especially working with buffets and garnishing, is valuable. Art school is good training for arrangement, texture, color, and lighting aspects of a picture.

Patience is invaluable, especially when the same steps have to be repeated over and over, hours into the day's work. A useful trait is curiosity about new ingredients, new products, table accessories, and the willingness to constantly browse in specialty stores and supermarkets to keep current. Good physical health along with a high level of energy and exceptional stamina are essential for putting in the long working hours on a shoot.

Unions/Associations
Home Economists in Business is associated with the American Association of Family & Consumer Sciences. The Minneapolis chapter holds a week-long training workshop in food styling every other year.

The International Association of Culinary Professionals is a broad-based membership organization of food professionals, including food stylists; they hold an annual meeting and can connect you with regional food organizations.

Tips for Entry
1. Study the top food magazine illustrations to learn current trends in styling.
2. If your city has an advertising council with a good membership base of local agencies representing major food accounts, contact the chairperson to learn what local photographers specialize in food; then call and get acquainted.
3. Contact the local chapter of the photographers association, either Advertising Photographers of America or Professional Photographers of America, to meet members who specialize in food photography.

RECIPE DEVELOPER

CAREER PROFILE

Duties: Defines new recipe ideas; develops the specific dishes; writes promotional recipes for food advertising, magazine articles, product packages, industry recipe collections and cookbooks

Alternate Title(s): Product Consultant

Salary Range: $24,000 to $63,000

Employment Prospects: Good, especially at the entry level

Advancement Prospects: Good

Best Geographical Location(s) for Position: Urban areas where food processing and food product companies are headquartered, and where major food magazines are published. Some freelance work can be done anywhere, using your home kitchen.

Prerequisites:

Education or Training—College degree in home economics, specializing in foods and nutrition

Experience—Similar work for a food publication, or working for a freelance food consultant

Special Skills and Personality Traits—Creativity; artistry; knowledge of food chemistry; patience; consistency; self-confidence

CAREER LADDER

```
┌─────────────────────────────┐
│     Test Kitchen Manager     │
└─────────────────────────────┘

┌─────────────────────────────┐
│      Recipe Developer        │
└─────────────────────────────┘

┌─────────────────────────────┐
│        Assistant Cook        │
└─────────────────────────────┘
```

Position Description

Most large food processing companies and major food brokers have test kitchens where they develop recipes using their own products. Food magazines and lifestyle magazines do some creative recipe development, as well as hire freelance cooks to submit food articles. Additionally, public relations firms working for a number of food product companies often maintain a test kitchen for recipe development. There are also consulting firms who work for a number of food companies that are too small to have their own test kitchens and hire the consultant to do recipe development. The resulting recipes are used on packaging, in advertising, and in customer service brochures. The premise is that consumers who are attracted by a luscious picture of a dish that uses the company's product are likely to put that product in their shopping cart.

Recipe development work is imaginative and creative. The recipe developer works with a shopping basket that must contain the employer's product, but the accompanying ingredients are as broad as the cook can conceive, using his or her own palate memory of flavors that go together well, using food chemistry knowledge of what will and won't work in the cooking, and using a confident knowledge of current tastes and trends in food.

In an average day's work, the recipe developer may have in mind several ideas and work from broad, descriptive notes that he or she has reviewed with the marketing director or the test kitchen director. A shopping basket full of flavor-compatible ingredients to combine with the company's product is brought in, and the tester goes to work creating dishes to appeal to today's cook: working wives, single parents, and cooks with a limited time for food preparations because of the demands of work, family, or vocational interests. The recipes must be simple to prepare, use few ingredients, meet nutritional standards of low fat and low sodium, and photograph appealingly to sell the product. Sometimes the recipes are a variation on a classic dish, like scaloppine substituting low-fat turkey for more expensive veal, or an ethnic twist to a common dish, like a teriyaki coating to chicken strips on a salad tossed with toasted sesame seeds.

As the recipes begin to develop and emerge from the cooking stage, tasters on the staff are alerted to wake up their taste buds to judge the new dishes. As many as five or six people from the consumer affairs department and the marketing staff converge to taste and evaluate, making suggestions to the cook. Each recipe may go through several evolutions before it satisfies everyone. At each step the recipe developer makes notes on methods and techniques used to accomplish a particular flavor or effect, and the key ingredient must always be showcased.

It is the recipe developer's job to write the recipe in the style of the company's brochures and ads, controlling the final flavor and appearance of the dish. Some of the restrictions that govern recipe development are making sure that all ingredients are available throughout the country, that the dish is not dependent on an alcohol ingredient (unless the client is a spirits producer), and that it can be produced with standard kitchen equipment. Most test kitchens do not contain state-of-the-art professional appliances because recipe developers are designing for home cooks, who may have older equipment.

Recipes are tested and retested, often by another employee without an extensive culinary background, just to confirm they can be successfully recreated by the average home cook. The purpose of these recipes is to sell product, not to train exotic cooks. As a recipe moves from the creative process to its commercial destination, the recipe developer works with the designers in the marketing department, the food stylist and photographer in the photo studio, and the consumer affairs staff who will be fielding customer questions after the recipe has been issued.

Salaries

For full-time work in a test kitchen, salaries are excellent, in the range of $24,000 to $63,000 a year. Part-time or freelance employees are paid a rate based on their experience, training, and talent. Hourly rates range from $10 to $25, with higher rates for hot-shot chefs or media stars.

Employment Prospects

Major food companies are constantly looking for talented cooks to work on creative projects. Job prospects are usually in larger urban areas where food processing and production companies have their headquarters. These companies often recruit at state colleges and schools with respected culinary programs.

Advancement Prospects

A creative recipe developer can move upward within a company to test kitchen manager, director of publications, or even marketing director. Sometimes the advancement removes the employee from the kitchen, and such a promotion, while it brings a higher salary, may be unwelcome. Another direction for advancement is to move away from corporate security to starting one's own business, consulting for a variety of smaller food production companies. A successful consultant can live almost anywhere and travels extensively to meet with clients, returning to the test kitchen with each new assignment.

Best Geographical Location(s)

Urban areas where food processing corporations cluster provide the widest job opportunities for recipe developers. Editorial offices of major food publications with test kitchens are primarily on the East Coast, with only a few in the Midwest and on the Pacific coast.

Education and Training

Most test kitchens prefer to hire graduate home economists, because they can rely on a given level of education, particularly in food chemistry. In recent years, some food companies have experimented by hiring trained chefs to develop new recipes.

Experience/Skills/Personality Traits

A recipe developer needs a creative palate, an active imagination, and a clear vision of what is currently popular to be able to spin off new ideas and flavors. Infinite patience is desirable when a particular recipe has to be tested a dozen times or more before it passes the review. A scientific knowledge of how cooking works (food chemistry), is essential to prevent false starts. The eye of an artist to bring together appealing color and texture combinations is critical.

Unions/Associations

This work is almost exclusively the arena of graduate home economists. Two professional organizations are instrumental in keeping their members up to date: the American Association of Family and Consumer Sciences (AAFSC) and Home Economists in Business (HEIB). Many job opportunities are circulated by word of mouth at local monthly meetings or annual national conventions of these two groups.

Tips for Entry

1. Before entering a college home economics program, it's a good idea to talk with the job placement officer at the school. Learn whether they are placing their graduates in the kind of job you want, if they are primarily training secondary school home economics teachers, or if they are well-known for some other career path. The right school with the right job placement goals is the best first step.

2. Apply for an internship at least once during your college years; sell yourself to a food product company that meets your vision of a perfect job. You will be working closely with the recipe developer in the test kitchen and can learn first hand if this is the right career for you.

3. Enter recipe contests, especially those that stress originality, and utilize the publicity from winning to get in the front door of a food product company.

RECIPE TESTER

CAREER PROFILE

Duties: Tests recipes exactly as written to assist the food editor or recipe developer to identify omissions or unclear directions before printing.

Alternate Title(s): Test Kitchen Cook

Salary Range: $18,000 to $30,000

Employment Prospects: Fair; minimum opportunities for the work

Advancement Prospects: Good, by advancing on the career ladder

Best Geographical Location(s) for Position: Major urban areas where food magazines and cookbooks are edited and published; large cities where the daily newspaper runs a weekly food section

Prerequisites:

Education or Training—High school diploma; excellent reading and comprehension skills; basic cooking knowledge

Experience—Widely varied home cooking background. Entry level will not require prior work experience.

Special Skills and Personality Traits—Extreme accuracy and precision; a personal comfort level about asking questions

CAREER LADDER

```
┌──────────────────────────────┐
│   Recipe Developer/Writer     │
└──────────────────────────────┘

┌──────────────────────────────┐
│        Recipe Tester          │
└──────────────────────────────┘

┌──────────────────────────────┐
│    Test Kitchen Assistant     │
└──────────────────────────────┘
```

Position Description

A recipe tester provides a second opinion and confirmation that a given recipe is written accurately and leads to the exact flavor, texture, and appearance that the recipe writer desires. The tester is a stand-in for the home cook who will read and want to make the recipe with the best possible results.

Working for a cookbook writer, a newspaper food editor, a food magazine, or a corporate test kitchen, the tester takes the written recipe, shops for the ingredients, and prepares the dish using ordinary home equipment. The writer of the recipe is available to the tester while the work is being done in order to answer questions: "1 tiny package raisins—do you mean the lunchbag packages?" And the writer will add in the ounces in the package for identification. What about this: "1 tart apple, cored and diced—shouldn't it be peeled?" "Sorry to bother you, but it calls for '$\frac{1}{2}$ teaspoon thyme'—that seems like such a lot, did you mean fresh instead of dried?"

This is the point where accidental omissions are caught: A veal stew recipe calls for 8 small scallions, tops chopped but not bottoms—the veal pieces are floured and seasoned, sauteed in butter with the scallion tops. But the bottoms are never, ever, mentioned again.

It is not the tester's job to rewrite the recipe or to make substitutions in either ingredients or techniques to bring it closer to his or her own taste. The tester's job is to cook the dish with perfect accuracy to the way it is written so the writer can decide on any changes. Often a tester will be asked to prepare a dish twice to test whether butter or margarine make a difference in the final taste; if not, both can be listed as alternative ingredients.

Salaries

A recipe tester may be a salaried employee at a magazine or large newspaper or a freelance, hourly worker for a cookbook author. Depending on experience in this work, a tester can earn between $9 and $14 an hour; higher pay comes with seniority.

Employment Prospects

Wherever there is a test kitchen, there is a probability of work for a recipe tester. In addition to the food department in newspapers and magazines, food brokers and processors with a wide range of products, fast-food restaurant chains, and cookbook writers have the most need for recipe testing. Most of these opportunities exist in urban areas. The exception is testing a cookbook, which should be done in a home kitchen to match the book users' conditions and equipment.

Advancement Prospects

Recipe testing is work that relies on an even level of skill over years of work; because of this, raises in pay tend to be minimal, based on cost-of-living increases. The opportunity for advancement is to move into a more skilled and related job, such as recipe writing or development; these jobs pay a higher rate and are more valuable to the publication.

Best Geographical Location(s)

Major urban areas where food magazines are edited and where food processing companies have their corporate offices and test kitchens provide the best opportunities for recipe testers. Next best is any urban area whose daily newspaper has a test kitchen or where regional magazines with food sections are produced.

Education and Training

A high school diploma is sufficient for this work, providing good reading and comprehension skills. A tester needs a knowledge of basic cooking skills: sauté, roast, bake, braise, fry, etc. The tester's cooking skills should be equivalent to those of the intended reader of the recipe; that may require advanced techniques if the publication is an upscale one.

Experience/Skills/Personality Traits

Reading and comprehension skills must be excellent. A full gamut of cooking skills is valuable but not essential to start. A recipe tester must have a high degree of accuracy and precision, cooking to the letter of the written recipe, making no presumptions, and asking questions whenever there seems to be no clear direction.

Unions/Associations

Union membership depends on whether the employing company is a union shop; some newspapers are, as are some processing plants.

Regional culinary associations provide local contacts with food writers and editors, a network that provides word-of-mouth information about available jobs and promotions.

Tips for Entry

1. Call and talk to the food editor of your local newspaper to learn whether they test recipes before printing; if not, offer to do the work on a freelance basis.
2. Locate the nearest regional culinary association and attend one or two meetings to meet food writers and authors who might steer you to testing work.

APPENDIXES

APPENDIX I
CULINARY SCHOOLS AND ACADEMIES

The following list includes accredited institutions only, but should not be considered an exhaustive directory of culinary schools and academies. Check your area for additional possibilities. All websites listed were current at the time the book was being written. If a site is no longer active, try typing the institution name into a search engine to find the address.

ALABAMA

Bishop State Community College
Carver Campus
414 Stanton Street
Mobile, AL 36617
www.bscc.cc.al.us
wdaniels@bscc.cc.al.us

Faulkner State Community College
3301 Gulf Shores Parkway
Gulf Shores, AL 36542
www.faulkner.cc.al.us
on-site request/contact form

Jefferson State Community
2601 Carson Road
Birmingham, AL 35215
www.jscc.cc.al.us
pputnam@jscc.cc.al.us

Lawson State Community College
3060 Wilson Road SW
Birmingham, AL 35221
www.ls.cc.al.us
dharris@cougar.ls.cc.al.us

Wallace State Community College
P.O. Box 2000
Hanceville, AL 35077-2000
www.wallacestatehanceville.edu

ALASKA

University of Alaska—Fairbanks
P.O. Box 757480
Fairbanks, AK 99775-7480
www.uaf.edu
fyapply@uaf.edu

ARIZONA

Art Institute of Phoenix
School of Culinary Arts
2233 W. Dunlap Avenue
Phoenix, AZ 85021-2859
www.aipx.aii.edu
denglert@aii.edu

Phoenix College
1202 W. Thomas Road
Phoenix, AZ 85013
www.pc.maricopa.edu
fischer.donna@a1.pc.maricopa.edu

Pima Community College
4905 B East Broadway Boulevard
Tucson, AZ 85709-1120
www.pima.edu
COAdmissions@pimacc.pima.edu

Scottsdale Community College
9000 E. Chaparral Road
Scottsdale, AZ 85256-2626
www.sc.maricopa.edu
ruby.miller@sccmail.maricopa.edu

Scottsdale Culinary Institute
8100 E. Camelback Road
Suite 1001
Scottsdale, AZ 85251
www.scicefs.com
fredp@scicefs.com

ARKANSAS

Ozarka College
P.O. Box 10
218 College Drive
Melbourne, AR 72556
www.ozarka.edu
rtankersley@ozarka.edu

CALIFORNIA

American River College
4700 College Oak Drive
Sacramento, CA 95841
www.arc.losrios.cc.ca.us
recadmis@mail.arc.losrios.cc.ca.us

Art Institute of Los Angeles
School of Culinary Arts
2900 31st Street
Santa Monica, CA 90405-3035
www.aila.artinstitutes.edu
on-site request/contact form

California Culinary Academy
625 Polk Street
San Francisco, CA 94102
www.baychef.com
admissions@baychef.com

California School of Culinary Arts
1416 El Centro Street
South Pasadena, CA 91030
www.scsa.com
pam@scsca.com

California State Polytechnic University—Pomona
3801 W. Temple
Pomona, CA 91768
www.csupomona.edu
uac@csupomona.edu

Chaffey College
5885 Haven Avenue
Rancho Cucamonga, CA 91701
www.chaffey.cc.ca.us
cburkhart@chaffey.cc.ca.us

Chapman University
1 University Drive
Orange, CA 92866
www.chapman.edu
on-site request/contact form

Chinatown American Cooks School
1450 Powel Street Box C
San Francisco, CA 94133

City College of San Francisco
50 Phelan Avenue
San Francisco, CA 94112
www.ccsf.cc.ca.us
mmanzo@ccsf.org

Columbia College
11600 Columbia College Drive
Sonora, CA 95370
columbia.Yosemite.cc.ca.us
westr@yosemite.cc.ca.us

**Culinary Institute of America—
 Greystone**
2555 Main Street
St. Helena, CA 94574
www.ciachef.edu
admissions@culinary.edu

Cypress College
9200 Valley View Boulevard
Cypress, CA 90630
www.lib.cypress.cc.ca.us
chefmike@speed.net

Diablo Valley College
321 Golf Club Road
Pleasant Hill, CA 94523
www.dvc.edu
admissions@dvc.edu

Laney College
900 Fallon Street
Oakland, CA 94607
laney.peralta.cc.ca.us
jgreenspan@peralta.cc.ca.us

Los Angeles Trade-Tech College
400 W. Washington Boulevard
Los Angeles, CA 90015
www.lattc.cc.ca.us
Doris_R._Martinez@laccd.cc.ca.us

Orange Coast College
2701 Fairview Boulevard
Costa Mesa, CA 92628
www.occ.ccd.edu
kclark@mail.occ.cccd.edu

Oxnard College
4000 S. Rose Avenue
Oxnard, CA 93033
www.oxnard.cc.ca.us
ocinfo@vcccd.cc.ca.us

San Joaquin Delta College
5151 Pacific Avenue
Stockton, CA 95207
www.deltacollege.org
questions@sjdccd.cc.ca.us

Santa Barbara City College
721 Cliff Drive
Santa Barbara, CA 93109-2394
www.sbcc.net
craven@sbcc.net

Santa Rosa Junior College
1501 Mendocino Avenue
Santa Rosa, CA 95401
www.santarosa.edu
rosa_turner@garfield.santarosa.edu

COLORADO

Art Institute of Colorado
School of Culinary Arts
200 E. Ninth Avenue
Denver, CO 80203
www.aic.artinstitutes.edu
browninb@aii.edu

Colorado Mountain Culinary Institute
P.O. Box 10001SG
Glenwood Springs, CO 81602
www.coloradomtn.edu
JoinUs@coloradomtn.edu

Cooking School of the Rockies
637 S. Broadway
Suite H
Boulder, CO 80303
www.cookingschoolrockies.com
on-site request/contact form

Culinary Institute of Colorado Springs
TISO Division, PPCC
5675 S. Academy Boulevard
Colorado Springs, CO 80906
www.ppcc.cccoes.edu
rob.hudson@ppcc.cccoes.edu

Johnson & Wales University at Vail
616 W. Lionshead Circle
Vail, CO 81657
www.jwu.edu
admissions@jwu.edu

Pueblo Community College
900 W. Orman Avenue
Pueblo, CO 81004
www.pcc.ccoes.edu
admissions@pcc.ccoes.edu

Warren Occupational Technical Center
13300 W. 2nd Place
Lakewood, CO 80228-1256
www.jeffco.k12.co.us
dgomes@jeffco.k12.co.us

CONNECTICUT

Connecticut Culinary Institute
230 Farmington Avenue
Farmington, CT 06032
www.ctculinary.com
ct.culinary.inst@snet.net

Gateway Community Technical College
60 Sargent Drive
New Haven, CT 06511
www.gwctc.commnet.edu
gateway_ctc@commnet.edu

**Institute of Gastronomy & Culinary
 Arts**
University of New Haven
300 Orange Avenue
West Haven, CT 06516
Bubbles@charger.newhaven.edu

**Manchester Community Technical
 College**
60 Bidwell Street
Manchester, CT 06040
www.mcc.commnet.edu
admissions@mail.mcc.com

**Naugatuck Valley Community-
 Technical College**
750 Chase Parkway
Waterbury, CT 06708
www.nvctc.commnet.edu
nvctc@nvctc5.commnet.edu

Norwalk Community Technical College
188 Richards Avenue
Norwalk, CT 06854-1655
nctcadmit@commnet.edu

DELAWARE

Delaware Technical Community College
P.O. Box 610
Georgetown, DE 19947
www.dtcc.edu/owens
on-site request/contact form

FLORIDA

**Academy/American Culinary Arts
 Program**
3131 Flightline Drive
Lakeland, FL 33811
www.theacademy.net

**Art Institute of Fort Lauderdale—
    School of Culinary Arts**
1799 SE 17th Street
Fort Lauderdale, FL 33316
www.aifl.edu
on-site request/contact form

Atlantic Vocational Technical Center
4700 NW Coconut Creek Parkway
Coconut Creek, FL 33066
www.sunsentinel.com/browardeducator/
    aeatla1.htm

**Charlotte County Vocational Technical
    Center**
18300 Toledo Blade Boulevard
Port Charlotte, FL 33948-3399
www.ccps.k12.fl.us/Schools/TechCenter
richard_santello@ccps.k12.fl.us

Daytona Beach Community College
1200 W. International Speedway Boulevard
Daytona Beach, FL 32114
www.dbcc.cc.fl.us
lunac@dbcc.cc.fl.us

Florida Culinary Institute
2400 Metro Centre Boulevard
West Palm Beach, FL 33407-9985
www.floridaculinary.com
mikes@floridaculinary.com

Gulf Coast Community College
5230 West US Highway 98
Panama City, FL 32401
www.gc.cc.fl.us
on-site request/contact form

Hillsborough Community College
P.O. Box 22127
Tampa, FL 33622
www.hcc.cc.fl.us
on-site request/contact form

**Institute of the South for Hospitality &
    Culinary Arts**
Florida Community College at Jacksonville
4501 Capper Road
Jacksonville, FL 32218
rwolf@fccj.org

**Johnson & Wales University at North
    Miami**
College of Culinary Arts
1701 NE 127th Street
North Miami, FL 33181
www.jwu.edu
admissions@jwu.edu

Marchman Technical Education Center
7825 Campus Drive
New Port Richey, FL 34653
Corbin61@aol.com

Mid Florida Technical Institute
2900 W. Oakridge Road
Orlando, FL 32809
Mft.ocps.k12.fl.us

**Pensacola Junior College Culinary
    Management Program**
1000 College Boulevard
Pensacola, FL 32504
www.pjc.cc.fl.us
on-site request/contact form

**Pinellas Technical Education Center—
    Clearwater**
6100 154th Avenue
N. Clearwater, FL 33516
168.213.60.5/FTEC2.htm
Cbyerly@ptecclw.pinellas.k12.fl.us

**Pinellas Technical Education Center—
    St. Petersburg**
901 34th Street S.
St. Petersburg, FL 33711
168.213.60.5/FTEC2.htm
Cbyerly@ptecclw.pinellas.k12.fl.us

**Robert Morgan Vocational Tech
    Institute**
18180 SW 122nd Avenue
Miami, FL 33177

Sarasota County Technical Institute
4748 Beneva Road
Sarasota, FL 33583
www.saratosa.k12.fl.us/SCTI/scti/
    culinary.html

Southeast Institute of Culinary Arts
Collins at Del Monte Avenue
St. Augustine, FL 32094-9970
www-satc.stjohns.k12.fl.us/culinaryarts
infoplz@fcti.org

South Florida Community College
600 W. College Drive
Avon Park, FL 33825
www.sfcc.cc.fl.us
meyedi1033@sfcc.cc.fl.us

**Southeastern Academy's Culinary
    Training Center**
233 Academy Drive, Box 421768
Kissimmee, FL 34742-1768
sea_admis@southerncollege.org

Valencia Community College
P.O. Box 3028
Orlando, FL 32802
www.valencia.cc.fl.us
On-site request/contact form

GEORGIA

Art Institute of Atlanta
6600 Peachtree Dunwoody Road
Atlanta, GA 30326
www.aia.artinstitutes.edu
on-site request/contact form

Atlanta Area Technical School
1560 Stewart Avenue SW
Atlanta, GA 30310

Augusta Technical Institute
3116 Deans Bridge Road
Augusta, GA 30906
WCritten@admin1.augusta.tec.ga.us

East Central Technical Institute
P.O. Box 1069
Fitzgerald, GA 31750
www.eastcentral.tec.ga.us
info@ecti.org

Savannah Tech Institute
5717 White Bluff Road
Savannah, GA 31405
www.savannah.tec.ga.us

HAWAII

Kapiolani Community College
4303 Diamond Head Road
Honolulu, HI 96816
www.leahi.kcc.hawaii.edu

Leeward Community College
96-045 Ala Ike
Pearl City, HI 96782
www.lcc.hawaii.edu

Maui Community College
310 Kaahamanu Avenue
Kahului, HI 96732
Mauicc.Hawaii.edu
Karen.Tanka@mauicc.hawaii.edu

IDAHO

Boise State University
1910 University Drive
Boise, ID 83725
www.idbsu.edu
kbrandt2@boisestate.edu

ILLINOIS

College of Dupage
425 22nd Street
Glen Ellyn, IL 60137
www.cod.edu
protis@cdnet.cod.edu

College of Lake County
19351 W. Washington
Grayslake, IL 60030-1198
www.clc.cc.il.us
info@clc.cc.il.us

Cooking and Hospitality Institute of Chicago
361 W. Chestnut Street
Chicago, IL 60610-3050
www.chicnet.org
chic@chicnet.org

Elgin Community College
1700 Spartan Drive
Elgin, IL 60123
www.elgin.cc.il.us
admissions@elgin.cc.il.us

French Pastry School, Inc.
1153 W. Grand Avenue
Chicago, IL 60622
www.frenchpastryschool.com
Jpfeif0927@aol.com

Joliet Junior College
1216 Houbolt Avenue
Joliet, IL 60431-8938
www.jjc.cc.il.us

Kendal College
2408 Orrington Avenue
Evanston, IL 60201
www.kendall.edu
on-site request/contact form

Lexington College
10840 S. Western Avenue
Chicago, IL 60643-3294

Lincoln Land Community College
5250 Shepherd Road
Springfield, IL 62794
www.llcc.cc.il.us
jay.kitterman@llcc.cc.il.us

Triton College
2000 Fifth Avenue
River Grove. IL 60171
www.triton.cc.il.us
triton@triton.cc.il.us

William Rainey Harper College
1200 W. Algonquin Road
Palatine, IL 60067-7398
www.harper.cc.il.us
question@harper.cc.il.us

INDIANA

Ivy Tech State College—East Chicago
410 E. Columbus Drive
East Chicago, IN 46312
www.ivy.tec.in.us
msiddiqu@ivy.tec.in.us

Ivy Tech State College—Fort Wayne
3800 N. Anthony Boulevard
Fort Wayne, IN 46805
www.ivy.tec.in.us/FortWayne

Ivy Tech State College—Gary
1440 E. 35th Avenue
Gary, IN 46409
www.gar.ivy.tec.in.us

Ivy Tech State College—Indianapolis
One W. 26th Street
Indianapolis, IN 46208
www.ivy.tec.in.us/Indianapolis

Vincennes University
1002 North First Street
Vincennes, IN 47591
www.vinu.edu
vuadmit@indian.vinu.edu

IOWA

Des Moines Area Community College
2006 S. Ankeny Boulevard
Ankeney, IA 50021
www.dmacc.cc.ia.us
webmaster@dmacc.cc.ia.us

Indian Hills Community College
525 Grandview
Ottumwa, IA 52501
www.ihcc.cc.ia.us

Iowa Lakes Community College
3200 College Drive
Emmetsburg, IA 50536
www.ilcc.cc.ia.us
info@ilcc.cc.ia.us

Iowa Western Community College
2700 College Road,
Box 4C
Council Bluffs, IA 51502
icc.cc.ia.us
On-site request/contact form

Kirkwood Community College
6301 Kirkwood Boulevard SW
Cedar Rapids, IA 52406
www.kirkwood.cc.ia.us

KANSAS

American Institute of Baking
1213 Bakers Way
Manhattan, KS 66502

Johnson County Community College
12345 College Boulevard
Overland Park, KS 66210-1299
www.jccc.net
jhaas@jccc.net

KENTUCKY

Elizabethtown Technical College
505 University Drive
Elizabethtown, KY 42701
brenda.harrington@kctes.org

Jefferson Community College
109 E. Broadway
Louisville, KY 40202
www.jcc.uky.edu

Kentucky Technical College
Davies County Extention
1901 Southeastern Parkway
Owensboro, KY 42303
www.owecc.net/otc
Beth.Vanfleet@kctcs.net

Sullivan College—National Center for Hospitality Studies
3101 Bardstown Road
Louisville, KY 40205
www.sullivan.edu
admissions@sullivan.edu

West Kentucky Technical College
Blandville Road
P.O. Box 7408
Paducah, KY 42001
www.wkytech.com
nancy.mcmurtry@kctcs.net

LOUISIANA

Bossier Parish Community College
2719 Airline Drive N.
Bossier City, LA 71111
www.bpcc.cc.la.us

Chef John Folse Culinary Institute
Nicholls State University
P.O. Box 2014, NSU
Thibodaux, LA 70301
www.server.nich.edu
nichweb@mail.nich.edu

Culinary Arts Institute of Louisiana
427 Lafayette Street
Baton Rouge, LA 70802
www.caila.com
school@caila.com

Delgado Community College
615 City Park Avenue
New Orleans, LA 70119-4399
www.dcc.edu
enroll@dcc.edu

Louisiana Technical College—Lafayette
1101 Bertrand Drive
Lafayette, LA 70506-4909
www.ltcl.lafayette.tec.la.us

**New Orleans Regional Technical
   Institute**
980 Navarre Avenue
New Orleans, LA 70124-2710

**Sidney N. Collier Vocational Technical
   Institute**
3727 Louisa Street
New Orleans, LA 70126

MAINE

Southern Maine Technical College
2 Fort Road
South Portland, ME 04106
www.ctech.smtc.mtcs.tec.me.us
adms@smtc.net

MARYLAND

Baltimore International College
17 Commerce Street
Baltimore, MD 21202
www.bic.edu
on-site request/contact form

**International School of Confectionery
   Arts, Inc.**
9209 Gaither Road
Gaithersburg, MD 20877
www.notterschool.com
esnotter@aol.com

L'Academie de Cuisine
5021 Wilson Lane
Bethesda, MD 20814
www.rockmanroy.com

MASSACHUSETTS

Berkshire Community College
1350 West Street
Pittsfield, MA 01201-5786
www.cc.berkshire.org
admission@mail.cc.berkshire.org

Boston University
121 Bay State Road
Boston, MA 02215
www.bu.edu
admissions@bu.edu

Bristol Community College
777 Elsbree Street
Fall River, MA 02720
www.bristol.mass.edu
jcaressi@bristol.mass.edu

The Cambridge School of Culinary Arts
2020 Massachusetts Avenue
Cambridge, MA 02140
www.cambridgeculinary.com
info@cambridgeculinary.com

**Essex Agricultural & Technical
   Institute**
562 Maple Street
Hathorne, MA 01833
www.agtech.org
admin@agtech.org

Holyoke Community College
303 Homestead Avenue
Holyoke, MA 01040
www.hcc.mass.edu
tgill@hcc.mass.edu

Newbury College
129 Fisher Avenue
Brookline, MA 02146
www.newbury.edu
info@newbury.edu

MICHIGAN

Baker College Culinary Arts
1903 Marquette Avenue
Muskegon, MI 49442
www.baker.edu
jacobs_k@muskegon.baker.edu

Grand Rapids Community College
143 Bostwick Avenue NE
Grand Rapids, MI 49503-3295
www.grcc.cc.mi.us
admit@grcc.cc.mi.us

Henry Ford Community College
5101 Evergreen Road
Dearborn, MI 48128
www.henryford.cc.mi.us
AskTheExpert@henryford.cc.mi.us

Macomb Community College
14500 E. 12 Mile Road
Warren, MI 48093
www.macomb.cc.mi.us
answer@macomb.cc.mi.us

Monroe County Community College
1555 Rainsville Road
Monroe, MI 48161
www.monroe.cc.mi.us
rdaniels@mail.monroe.cc.mi.us

Northern Michigan University
1401 Presque Isle Avenue
Marquette, MI 49855
www.nmu.edu
admiss@nmu.edu

Northwestern Michigan College
1701 E. Front Street
Traverse, MI 49684
www.nmc.edu
r_kucera@nmc.edu

Oakland Community College
27055 Orchard Lake Road
Farmington Hills, MI 48334
www.occ.cc.mi.us

Schoolcraft College
18600 Haggerty Road
Livonia, MI 48152-2696
www.schoolcraft.cc.mi.us
continued@schoolcraft.cc.mi.us

Washtenaw Community College
4800 E. Huron River Drive
Ann Arbor, MI 48106-0978
www.washtenaw.cc.mi.us
admissions@wccnet.org

MINNESOTA

**Art Institutes International—
    Minnesota**
Culinary Arts
15 S. Ninth Street
Minneapolis, MN 55402-3137
www.aim.artinstitutes.edu
buechnej@aii.edu

Brown Institute—Le Cordon Bleu
1440 Northland Drive
Mendota Heights, MN 55120
www.brown-institute.com
info@brown-institute.com

Hennepin Technical College
9000 Brooklyn Boulevard
Brooklyn Park, MN 55445
www.htc.mnscu.edu
info@htc.mnscu.edu

**Northwest Technical College—
    Moorhead**
1900 28th Avenue South
Moorhead, MN 56560
www.ntconline.com
info@mail.ntc.mnscu.edu

**South Central Technical College—
    Mankato Campus**
1920 Lee Boulevard
North Mankato, MN 56001
www.sctc.mnscu.edu

**St. Cloud Technical College Culinary
    Arts**
1540 Northway Drive
St. Cloud, MN 56303-1240
www.sctcweb.tec.mn.us
dmw@cloud.tec.mn.us

St. Paul Technical College
235 Marshall Avenue
St. Paul, MN 55102
www.stpaul.k12.mn.us

MISSISSIPPI

Hinds Community College
3925 Sunset Drive
Jackson, MS 39213
www.hinds.cc.ms.us
info@hinds.cc.ms.us

Mississippi University for Women
Culinary Arts Institute
Box W-1639
Columbus, MS 39701
www.muw.edu
on-site request/contact form

MISSOURI

**St. Louis Community College—
    Forest Park**
5600 Oakland Avenue
St. Louis, MO 63110
www.stlcc.cc.mo.us/fp
on-site request/contact form

MONTANA

**University of Montana—College of
    Technology in Missoula**
909 South Avenue West
Missoula, MT 59801-7910
www.cte.umt.edu
wwyatt@selway.umt.edu

NEBRASKA

Central Community College
P.O. Box 1024
Hastings, NE 68092
www.cccneb.edu
on-site request/contact form

Metropolitan Community College
P.O. Box 3777
Omaha, NE 68103-0777
www.mccneb.edu

**Southeast Community College—
    Lincoln Campus**
8800 O Street
Lincoln, NE 68520-9989
www.college.sccm.cc.ne.us
mmurphy@sccm.cc.ne.us

NEVADA

**Community College of Southern
    Nevada**
3200 E. Cheyenne Avenue, Z1A
North Las Vegas, NV 89030
www.ccsn.nevada.edu
admrec@ccsn.nevada.edu

Truckee Meadows Community College
7000 Dandini Boulevard
RDMT-207
Reno, NV 89512-3999
www.tmcc.edu
on-site request/contact form

NEW HAMPSHIRE

McIntosh Culinary
23 Cataract Avenue
Dover, NH 03820
www.mcintoshcollege.com
bryang@mcintoshcollege.com

**New Hamphire College—Culinary
    Institute**
2500 North River Road
Manchester, NH 03104
www.nhc.edu
bringerme@nhc.edu

**New Hampshire Community Technical
    College—Berlin**
2020 Riverside Drive
Berlin, NH 03570
www.berl.tec.nh.us
berlin4u@tec.nh.us

NEW JERSEY

Atlantic Cape Community College
5100 Black Horse Pike
Mays Landing, NJ 08330-2699
www.atlantic.edu
accadmit@atlantic.edu

Bergen Community College
400 Paramus Road
Paramus, NJ 07652
www.bergen.cc.nj.us

**Culinary Education Center
    of Monmouth County**
Brookdale Community College
765 Newman Springs Road
Linroft, NJ 07738-1597
www.brookdale.cc.nj.us
cberg@brookdale.cc.nj.us

Hudson County Community College
162 Sip Avenue
Jersey City, NJ 07306
www.hudson.cc.nj.us
rkahrmann@mail.hudson.cc.nj.us

Middlesex County College
2600 Woodbridge Avenue
P.O. Box 3050
Edison, NJ 08818-3050
www.middlesex.cc.nj.us
admissions@middlesex.cc.nj.us

Salem County Vocational Technical Schools
800 Salem-Woodstown Road
Woodstown, NJ 08098
www.salemettc.org
ettc@willie.salem.cc.nj.us

NEW MEXICO

Albuquerque Technical Vocational Institute
525 Buena Vista SE
Albuquerque, NM 87106
www.tvi.cc.nm.us
on-site request/contact form

Santa Fe Community College
P.O. Box 4187
Santa Fe, NM 87502-4187
www.santa-fe.cc.nm.us
on-site request/contact form

NEW YORK

Adirondack Community College
640 Bay Road
Queensbury, NY 12804
www.sunyacc.edu
info@acc.sunyacc.edu

Alfred State College—Culinary Arts
Upper College Drive
Alfred, NY 14802
www.alfredtech.edu
admissions@alfredtech.edu

Culinary Institute of America
1946 Campus Drive
Hyde Park, NY 12538-1499
www.ciachef.edu
on-site request/contact form

Erie Community College, City Campus
121 Ellicott Street
Buffalo, NY 14203-2698
www.sunyerie.edu
on-site request/contact form

French Culinary Institute
462 Broadway
New York, NY 10013-2618
www.frenchculinary.com
on-site request/contact form

Fulton-Montgomery Community College
Route 67
Johnstown, NY 12095
www.fmcc.suny.edu
ahanabur@fmcc.suny.edu

Jefferson Community College
Outer Coffeen Street
Watertown, NY 13601
www.sunyjefferson.edu
admissions@ccmgate.sunyjefferson.edu

Mohawk Valley Community College
1101 Floyd Avenue
Rome, NY 13440
www.mvcc.edu
admissions@www.mvcc.edu

Monroe Community College
1000 East Henrietta Road
Rochester, NY 14623
www.monroe.cc.edu
on-site request/contact form

New York City Technical College
300 Jay Street
#N220
Brooklyn, NY 11201-2983
www.nyctc.cuny.edu
connect@citytech.cuny.edu

New York Institute of Technology
211 Carleton Avenue
Central Islip, NY 11722
www.nyit.edu
admitme@nyit.edu

New York Restaurant School
75 Varick Street
16th Floor
New York, NY 10013
www.nyrs.artinstitutes.edu
nyrsadm@aii.edu

New York University
22 Washington Square South
New York, NY 10012-1172
www.nyu.edu
admissions@nyu.edu

Paul Smith's College of Arts & Sciences
Routes 30 & 86
P.O. Box 265
Paul Smiths, NY 12970-0265
www.paulsmiths.edu
sorgulp@paulsmiths.edu

Schenectady County Community College
78 Washington Avenue
Schenectady, NY 12305
www.sunysccc.edu
on-site request/contact form

State University of New York (SUNY)—Cobleskill
Champlin Hall
Cobleskill, NY 12043
www.cobleskill.edu
admwpc@cobleskill.edu

Sullivan County Community College
1000 LeRoy Road
Box 4002
Loch Sheldrake, NY 12759
www.sullivan.suny.edu
admissions@sullivan.suny.edu

Westchester Community College
75 Grasslands Road
Valhalla, NY 10595
www.sunywcc.edu
info@sunywcc.edu

NORTH CAROLINA

Alamance Community College
1247 Jimmie Kerr Road
P.O. Box 8000
Graham, NC 27253-8000
www.alamance.cc.nc.us
schombed@alamance.cc.nc.us

Asheville Buncombe Technical Community College
340 Victoria Road
Asheville, NC 28801
www.asheville.cc.nc.us
admissions@asheville.cc.nc.us

Cape Fear Community College
411 N. Front Street
Wilmington, NC 28401
www.capefear.cc.nc.us
vmason@capefear.cc.nc.us

Central Piedmont Community College
P.O. Box 35009
Charlotte, NC 28235
www.cpcc.cc.nc.us

Guilford Technical Community College
1601 High Point Road
P.O. Box 309
Jamestown, NC 27282
technet.gtcc.cc.nc.us

Wake Technical Community College
9101 Fayetteville Road
Raleigh, NC 27603
www.wake.tec.nc.us

OHIO

**Cincinnati State Technical &
    Community College**
3520 Central Parkway
Cincinnati, OH 45223
sheldonj@cinstate.cc.oh.us

Columbus State Community College
550 E. Spring Street
Columbus, OH 43215
www.colstate.cc.oh.us

Cuyahoga Community College
2900 Community College Drive
Cleveland, OH 44115
www.tri-c.cc.oh.us
on-site request/contact form

Hocking College
3301 Hocking Parkway
Nelsonville, OH 45764
www.hocking.edu

The Loretta Paganini School of Cooking
Lakeland Community College
8613 Mayfield Road
Chesterland, OH 44026

Owens Community College
P.O. Box 10000
Oregon Road
Toledo, OH 43699-1947
www.owens.cc.oh.us
admissions@owens.cc.oh.us

Sinclair Community College
444 W. Third Street
Dayton, OH 45402
www.sinclair.edu
on-site request/contact form

OKLAHOMA

**Oklahoma State University—School of
    Technology**
4th & Mission
Okmulgee, OK 74447
www.osu-okmulgee.edu

Pioneer Technology Center
2101 North Ash
Ponca City, OK 74601
www.pioneertech.org

OREGON

Linn-Benton Community College
6500 SW Pacific Boulevard
Albany, OR 97321
www.lbcc.cc.or.us
admissions@gw.lbcc.cc.or.us

Western Culinary Institute
1201 SW 12th Avenue
Suite 100
Portland, OR 97205
www.westernculinary.com
on-site request/contact form

PENNSYLVANIA

**Art Institute of Philadelphia—School
    of Culinary Arts**
2300 Market Street
Philadelphia, PA 19103
www.aiph.artinstitutes.edu
cabrellm@aii.edu

Bucks County Community College
275 Swamp Road
Newton, PA 18940
www.bucks.edu
admissions@storm.bucks.edu

**Community College of Allegheny
    County—Monroeville**
595 Beatty Road
Monroeville, PA 15146
www.ccac.edu
Admissions@ccac.edu

**Community College of Allegheny
    County—Pittsburgh**
808 Ridge Avenue
Jones Hall, Room 012
Pittsburg, PA 15212
www.ccac.edu

Drexel University
3141 Chestnut Street
Nesbitt College
Philadelphia, PA 19104
www.drexel.edu
admissions@drexel.edu

Harrisburg Area Community College
One HACC Drive
Harrisburg, PA 17110-2999
www.hacc.edu
admit@hacc.edu

Hiram G. Andrews Center
727 Goucher Street
Johnstown, PA 15905
www.hgac.org
bceryak@dli.state.pa.us

Indiana University of Pennsylvania
105 Ackerman Hall
Indiana, PA 15701
www.iup. edu
admissions-inquiry@grove.iup.edu

International Culinary Academy
555 Grant Street
Pittsburgh, PA 15219
www.icacademy.com
on-site request/contact form

JNA Institute of Culinary Arts
1212 S. Broad Street
Philadelphia, PA 19146
www.culinaryarts.com
admissions@culinaryarts.com

**Mercyhurst College North East—
    The Culinary & Wine Institute**
16 West Division Street
North East, PA 14628
www.mercyhurst.edu
jtheeuwe@mercyhurst.edu

Northamptom Community College
3835 Green Pond Road
Bethelem, PA 18107
www.nrhm.cc.pa.us

Pennsylvania College of Technology
One College Avenue
Williamsport, PA 17701-5799
www.pct.edu
on-site request/contact form

Pennsylvania Culinary
717 Liberty Avenue
Pittsburgh, PA 15222
www.paculinary.com
on-site request/contact form

School of Culinary Arts
Yorktowne Business Institute
West 7th Avenue
York, PA 17404
www.yorkchef.com
on-site request/contact form

The Restaurant School
4207 Walnut Street
Philadelphia, PA 19104
www.therestaurantschool.com
info@therestaurantschool.com

**Westmoreland County Community
    College**
Armbrust Road
Youngwood, PA 15697
www.westmoreland.cc.pa.us
admissions@westmoreland.cc.pa.us

RHODE ISLAND

Johnson & Wales University
8 Abbot Park Place
Provindence, RI 02903
www.jwu.edu
on-site request/contact form

SOUTH CAROLINA

Greenville Technical College
P.O. Box 5616, Station B
Greenville, SC 29606-5616
www.greenvilletech.com
on-site request/contact form

Horry-Georgetown Tech College
2050 Highway 501 East
Conway, SC 29526
www.hor.tec.sc.us
admissions@hor.tec.sc.us

Johnson & Wales University
701 East Bay Street
PCC Box 1409
Charleston, SC 29403
www.jwu.edu
on-site request/contact form

Trident Technical College
7000 Rivers Avenue
P.O. Box 118067, HT-P
Charleston, SC 29423-8067
www.trident.tech.sc.us
admissions@trident.tec.sc.us

SOUTH DAKOTA

Mitchell Technical Institute
821 N. Capitol
Mitchell, SD 57301
www.mti.tec.sd.us
DoescherR@mti.tec.sd.us

TENNESSEE

Opryland Hotel Culinary Institute
2800 Opryland Drive
Nashville, TN 37214
www.vscc.cc.tn.us/opryland
dstarks@oprylandhotels.com

TEXAS

Art Institute of Houston
1900 Yorktown
Houston, TX 77056
www.aih.aii.edu
on-site request/contact form

Del Mar College
101 Baldwin Boulevard
Corpus Christi, TX 78404
www.delmar.edu
reqinfo@camino.delmar.edu

El Centro College
Main & Lamar States
Dallas, TX 75202
www.ecc.dcccd.edu

El Paso Community College
919 Hunter Drive
El Paso, TX 79915
mjlinney@aol.com

Galveston College
4015 Avenue Q
Galveston, TX 77550
www.gc.edu
web@gc.edu

Houston Community College System
Culinary Services
Houston, TX 77004
www.hccs.cc.tx.us
pile_w@hccs.cc.tx.us

Odessa College
201 W. University
Odessa, TX 79764
www.odessa.edu
dnesmith@odessa.edu

San Jacinto College—Central
8060 Spencer Highway
Pasadena, TX 77505
www.sjcd.cc.tx.us
lpring@central.sjcd.cc.tx.us

San Jacinto College—North
5800 Uvalde
Houston, TX 77049
www.sjcd.cc.tx.us
gmessi@sjcd.cc.tx.us

St. Phillips College
1801 Martin Luther King Drive
San Antonio, TX 78203
www.accd.edu/spc
on-site request/contact form

Texas State Technical College
3801 Campus Drive
Waco, TX 76705
www.tstc.edu/waco.html
hjones@tstc.edu

UTAH

Salt Lake Community College
4600 S. Redwood Road
Salt Lake City, UT 84130
www.slcc.edu
maysa@slcc.edu

Utah State University
Dept. of Nutrition & Food Science
1200 E. 750 North
Logan, UT 84322-8700
www.usu.edu
admit@cc.usu.edu

Utah Valley State College
800 West University Parkway
Orem, UT 84058-5999
www.uvsc.edu
brownan@uvsc.edu

VERMONT

New England Culinary Institute
250 Maine Street
Montpelier, VT 05602
www.neculinary.com
on-site request/contact form

VIRGINIA

Johnson & Wales
2428 Almeda Avenue
Suite 316
Norfolk, VA 23513
www.jwu.edu
admissions@jwu.edu

J. Sargeant Reynolds Community College
P.O. Box 85622
Richmond, VA 23285-5622
www.jsr.cc.va.us
on-site request/contact form

Northern Virginia Community College
8333 Little River Turnpike
Annadale, VA 22003-3796
www.nv.cc.va.us
nvcorkh@nv.cc.va.us

Stratford College
School of Culinary Arts
7777 Leesburg Pike
Suite 100
Falls Church, VA 22043-2403
www.stratford.edu
admissions@stratford.edu

WASHINGTON

Art Institute of Seattle
School of Culinary Arts
2323 Elliot Avenue
Seattle, WA 98121-1642
www.ais.artinstitutes.edu
aisadm@aii.edu

Bellingham Technical College
3028 Lindberg Avenue
Bellingham, WA 98225
www.beltc.ctc.edu
beltcadm@belltc.ctc.edu

North Seattle Community College
9600 College Way North
Seattle, WA 98103-3599
www.gonorth.org
hsccinfo@sccd.ctc.edu

Renton Technical College
3000 NE Fourth Street
Renton, WA 98056
www.renton-tc.ctc.edu
cdanielson@rtc.ctc.edu

Seattle Central Community College
1701 Broadway
Mailstop 2BE2120
Seattle, WA 98122
seattlecentral.org
admiss@sccd.ctc.edu

Skagit Valley College
2405 College Way
Mount Vernon, WA 98273
www.svc.ctc.edu
admissions@skagit.ctc.edu

South Seattle Community College
6000 16th Avenue SW
Seattle, WA 98106-1499
www.sccd.ctc.edu/south
advisorsouth@sccd.ctc.edu

Spokane Community College
1810 N. Greene Street
Spokane, WA 99207
www.scc.spokane.cc.wa.us

WEST VIRGINIA

West Virginia Northern Community College
College Square
Wheeling, WV 26003
www.northern.wvnet.edu
vwright@northern.wvnet.edu

WISCONSIN

Blackhawk Technical College
6004 Prairie Road
P.O. Box 5009
Janesville, WI 53547
www.blackhawk.tec.wi.us
lbrown@blackhawk.tec.wi.us

Fox Valley Technical College
1825 N. Bluemound Drive
Appleton, WI 54913
www.foxvalley.tec.wi.us
info@foxvalleytech.com

Madison Area Technical College
3550 Anderson Street
Madison, WI 53704
www.madison.tec.wi.us
admissions@madison.tec.wi.us

Milwaukee Area Technical College
700 W. State Street
Milwaukee, WI 53233
www.milwaukee.tec.wi.us
on-site request/contact form

Moraine Park Technical Institute
235 N. National Drive
Fond du Lac, WI 54935
www.moraine.tec.wi.us
on-site request/contact form

Southwest Wisconsin Technical College
Culinary Management
1800 Bronson Boulevard
Fennimore, WI 53809
www.southwest.tec.wi.us
kkreul@southwest.tec.wi.us

Waukesha County Technical College
800 Main Street
Pewaukee, WI 53072
www.waukesha.tec.wi.us

PUERTO RICO

Instituto de Educación University
Barbosa Avenue
#404
Hato Rey, PR 00930

Instituto del Arte Moderno, Inc.
Avenida Monserrate FR-5
Villa Fontana
Carolina, PR 00983-3912

APPENDIX II
BIBLIOGRAPHY

Books related to food and the culinary arts are too numerous to include them all in this appendix. The following list of titles offers many excellent sources for fundamental information, and many of the books will serve as outstanding springboards for further reading.

BUSINESS

Ketterer, Manfred. *How to Manage a Successful Catering Business.* 2nd ed. New York: John Wiley & Sons, Inc., 1991.

Lawrence, Elizabeth. *The Complete Caterer: A Complete Guide to the Craft and Business of Catering.* Rev. New York: Doubleday, 1992.

Murphy, Martha Watson. *How to Start and Operate Your Own Bed & Breakfast.* New York: Henry Holt and Company, 1999.

Rainsford, Peter, and David H. Bangs, Jr. *The Restaurant Start-Up Guide.* Chicago, Ill.: Upstart Publishing Company, 1997.

———. *The Restaurant Planning Guide.* Chicago, Ill.: Upstart Publishing Company, 1996.

Rogak, Lisa Angowski. *The Upstart Guide to Owning and Managing a Bed & Breakfast.* Chicago, Ill.: Upstart Publishing Company, 1995.

Vivaldo, Denise. *How to Open and Operate a Home-Based Catering Business.* Old Saybrook, Conn.: The Globe Pequot Press, 1993.

Wemischner, Robert, and Karen Karp. *Gourmet to Go: A Guide to Opening and Operating a Specialty Food Store.* New York: John Wiley & Sons, Inc., 1997.

CAREERS

Bolles, Richard Nelson. *What Color Is Your Parachute? A Practical Manual for Job Hunters and Career Changers.* Berkeley, Calif.: Ten Speed Press, 2000.

Donovan, Mary. *Careers for Gourmets and Others Who Relish Food.* Lincolnwood, Ill.: Career Horizons, 1992.

Echikson, William. *Burgundy Stars: A Year in the Life of a Great French Restaurant.* New York: Little, Brown and Company, 1995.

Kaplan, Dorlene, ed. *The Guide to Cooking Schools 2001.* Coral Gables, Fla.: Shaw Guides, 2000.

Kleeman, E. J., and J. A. Voltz. *How to Turn a Passion for Food into Profit.* New York: Rawson, Wade Publishers, Inc., 1979.

Peterson's. *Peterson's Culinary Schools.* Princeton, N.J.: Peterson's, 1999.

Ruhlman, Michael. *The Soul of a Chef: The Journey Toward Perfection.* New York: Viking, 2000.

Sims-Bell, Barbara. *Food Work: Jobs in the Food Industry.* Santa Barbara, Calif.: Advocacy Press, 1994.

CATERERS

Cracknell. H. L., and G. Nobis. *The New Catering Repertoire,* Vol. 1, *Aide-Mémoire du Chef.* New York: Van Nostrand Reinhold, 1989.

Janericco, Terrance. *Soups for the Professional Chef.* New York: Van Nostrand Reinhold, 1988.

CHEFS

Bergeron, David Paul. *Professional Vegetarian Cooking.* New York: John Wiley & Sons, Inc., 1999.

Cracknell, H. L., and R. J. Kaufmann. *The Complete Guide to the Art of Modern Cookery* (1st translation into English of *Le Guide Culinaire*). New York: John Wiley & Sons, Inc., 1979.

Dawn, Davis. *If You Can Stand the Heat: Tales from Chefs & Restaurants.* New York: Penguin Books, 1999.

Dornenburg, Andrew, and Karen Page. *Becoming a Chef.* New York: John Wiley & Sons, Inc., 1999.

———. *Culinary Artistry.* New York: Van Nostrand Reinhold, 1996.

Lerousse, David Paul. *The Professional Garde Manger: A Guide to the Art of Buffet.* New York: John Wiley & Sons, Inc., 1996.

Peterson, James. *Essentials of Cooking.* New York: Artisan, 2000.

Ruhlman, Michael. *The Making of a Chef: Mastering Heat at the Culinary Institute of America.* New York: Henry Holt and Company, 1997.

Soltner, André, with Seymour Britchky. *The Lutèce Cookbook.* New York: Alfred A. Knopf, 1995.

Trotter, Charlie, and Paul Clarke. *Lessons in Excellence.* Berkeley, Calif.: Ten Speed Press, 1999.

Wenzel, William, and George Wenzel. *Wenzel's Menu Maker.* New York: John Wiley & Sons, Inc., 1997.

Willan, Anne. *La Varenne Pratique.* New York: Crown Publishers, Inc. 1989.

CLASSIC COOKING

Child, Julia, L. Bertholle, and S. Beck. *Mastering the Art of French Cooking.* New York: Alfred A. Knopf, 1966.

Child, Julia, and Simone Beck. *Mastering the Art of French Cooking.* Vol. 2. New York: Alfred A. Knopf, 1975.

Escoffier, Auguste. *Ma Cuisine.* New York: Bonanza Books, 1984.

Pépin, Jacques. *La Technique (The Fundamental Techniques of Cooking: An Illustrated Guide).* New York: Pocket Books/Simon & Schuster, 1976.

Saulnier, Louis. *Le Répertoire de La Cuisine.* English Ed. New York: Barron's Educational Series, 1976.

COMMUNITY

Shore, Bill. *Revolution of the Heart.* New York, Riverhead Books, 1995.

DIRECTORY

James Beard Foundation. *2000–2001 Directory of Food and Beverage Professionals.* New York: James Beard Foundation, 2000.

FOOD SAFETY

Lolun, Joan K., C.F.E., *The HACCP Food Safety Manual.* New York: John Wiley & Sons, Inc., 1995

Mortimore, Sara, and Carol Wallace. *HAACP: A Practical Approach.* 2nd ed. Gaithersburg, Md.: Aspen Publications, 1998.

National Restaurant Association. *Serving Safe Food Certification Coursebook.* Chicago, Ill.: The Educational Foundation of the National Restaurant Association, 1995.

HISTORY

Counihan, C., and P. Van Esterik, eds. *Food and Culture: A Reader.* New York: Routledge, 1997.

Kiple, K. F., and C. O. Kriemhild. *The Cambridge World History of Food.* Vol. I and II. New York: Cambridge University Press, 2000.

Sonnenfield, Albert (English ed.). *Food: A Culinary History* (Jean-Louis Flandrin and Massimo Montanari, eds.). New York: Columbia University Press, 1999.

Spang, Rebecca. *The Invention of a Restaurant: Paris and Modern Gastronomic Culture.* Cambridge, Mass.: Harvard University Press, 2000.

Trubek, Amy. *Haute Cuisine.* Philadelphia University of Pennsylvania Press, 2000.

INSTITUTIONAL COOKING

Fowler, S., B. B. West, and G. Shugart. *Food for Fifty.* New York: John Wiley & Sons, Inc., 1971.

Gisslen, Wayne. *Professional Cooking.* 4th ed. New York: John Wiley & Sons, Inc., 1999.

Holden, Chet. *Cooking for Fifty: The Complete Reference and Cookbook.* New York: John Wiley & Sons, Inc., 1993.

LITERARY PLEASURE

Berkeley, Ellen Perry, ed. *At Grandmother's Table.* Minneapolis, Minn.: Fairview Press, 2000.

Capon, Robert Farrar. *The Supper of the Lamb: A Culinary Reflection.* New York: Farrar, Straus & Giroux, 1989.

Colwin, Laurie. *Home Cooking: A Writer in the Kitchen.* New York: Harperperennial Library, 2000.

———. *More Home Cooking: A Writer Returns to the Kitchen.* New York: Harperperennial Library, 2000.

Fisher, M. F. K. *The Art of Eating: Consider the Oyster; The Gastronomical Me; Serve It Forth; How to Cook a Wolf; An Alphabet for Gourmets.* London: Picador, Pan Books, 1983.

Fisher, M. F. K., trans. *Brillat-Savarin's "The Physiology of Taste or Meditations on Transcendental Gastronomy."* New York: Harcourt Brace Jovanovich, 1971

Rosenblum, Mort. *A Goose in Toulouse and Other Culinary Adventures in France.* New York: Hyperion, 2000.

Thorne, John. *Simple Cooking,* New York: Viking Penguin, Inc., 1987.

Wechsberg, Joseph. *Dining at the Pavillion.* Boston: Little Brown & Co., 1962.

PASTRY CHEFS

Amendola, Joseph. *The Bakers' Manual.* 4th ed. New York: Van Nostrand Reinhold, 1993.

———. *Understanding Baking.* 2nd ed. New York: Van Nostrand Reinhold, 1992.

Friberg. Bo. *The Professional Pastry Chef.* 3rd ed. New York: Van Nostrand Reinhold, 1996.

Gisslen, Wayne. *Professional Baking.* 3rd ed. New York: John Wiley & Sons, Inc., 2000.

Maclauchlan, Andrew. *The Making of a Pastry Chef.* New York: John Wiley & Sons, 1999.

REFERENCE

American Home Economics Association. *Handbook of Food Preparation (of the Food and Nutrition Section).* 9th ed. Dubuque, Iowa: Kendall/Hunt Publishing Company, 1993.

Arndt, Alice. *Seasoning Savvy: How to Cook with Herbs, Spices, and Other Flavorings.* New York: The Haworth Press, 1999.

Bickel, Walter. *Hering's Dictionary of Classical and Modern Cookery.* 13th English ed. Giessen, Germany: Virtue, 1994.

Corriher, Shirley O. *Cook Wise: The Hows & Whys of Successful Cooking.* New York: William Morrow and Company, Inc., 1997.

Davidson, Alan. *The Oxford Companion to Food.* Oxford University Press, 2000.

Herbst, Sharon Tyler. *Food Lover's Tiptionary.* New York: Hearst Books, 1994.

Lang, Jennifer Harvey, ed. *Larousse Gastronomique.* New York: Crown Publishers, 1988.

McGee, Harold. *On Food and Cooking: The Science and Lore of the Kitchen.* New York: Scribners, 1984.

WINE

Cass, Bruce, and Jancis Robertson. *The Oxford Companion to the Wines of North America.* New York: Oxford University Press, 2000.

Kolpan, S., B. H. Smith, and M. A. Weiss, *Exploring Wine: The CIA's Complete Guide to the Wines of the World.* New York: John Wiley & Sons, Inc., 1996.

Lukacs, Paul. *American Vintage, The Rise of American Wine.* New York: Houghton Mifflin Company, 2000.

Robinson, Jancis. *The Oxford Companion to Wine.* Oxford University Press, 1999.

WOMEN

Cooper, Ann. *A Woman's Place Is in the Kitchen.* New York: Van Nostrand Reinhold, 1998.

Russell, Beverly. *Women of Taste: Recipes & Profiles of Famous Women Chefs.* New York: John Wiley & Sons, Inc., 1997.

Stillman, Julie. *A Celebration of Women Chefs: Signature Recipes from Thirty Culinary Masters.* Berkeley, Calif.: Ten Speed Press, 1999.

WRITERS

Allen, Gary. *The Resource Guide for Food Writers.* New York: Routledge, 1999.

Linford, Jenny. *Writing About Food.* London: A & C Black (Publishers) Limited, 1996.

Literary Market Place. New Providence, N.J.: R. R. Bowker, published annually.

Strunk, William, Jr., and E. B. White. *The Elements of Style.* 4th ed. Boston: Allyn & Bacon, 2000.

University of Chicago Press. *The Chicago Manual of Style.* 14th ed. Chicago, Ill.: University of Chicago Press, 1993.

Whitman, Joan, and Simon, Dolores. *Recipes into Type.* New York: HarperCollins, 1993.

APPENDIX III
MAGAZINES AND PERIODICALS

There are many fine periodicals published about the culinary arts and for those working in the food and beverage industry; new titles appear regularly. They are often a good source of information about job opportunities and trends in the industry. The following list includes some of the more useful publications with specific information about their contents and subscription rates.

AIB Research Technical Bulletin
American Institute of Baking
1213 Bakers Way
Manhattan, KS 66502
(913) 537-4750
Monthly newsletter. 16 pages. Subscription: $30/year. Sample: $3. American Institute of Baking publication contains nutrition information, current ingredient trends, products, equipment and processing, technical information, and large-quantity recipes. Good choice for professional bakers or food service personnel.

Art Culinaire
40 Mills Street
P.O. Box 9268
Morristown, NJ 07960
(201) 993-5500
Fax: (201) 993-8779
Quarterly hardcover magazine. 80 pages. Subscription: $59/year. Provides concepts and techniques for use by professionals in their kitchens but can easily be adapted to home kitchens.

Art of Eating
Box 242
Peacham, VT 05862
Editor: Edward Behr
Fax: (802) 592-3400
Quarterly newsletter. 16–22 pages. Subscription: $30/year. $55/two years. Historic, scientific food and wine essays by one of the country's finest food writers, according to *The New York Times*. Usually an issue addresses a single subject in depth. Illustrated with photographs. Recommended for the serious cook/food historian. A must for food professionals.

Baking Update
Lallemand, Inc.
1620 Prefontaine
Montreal, QC H1W 2NB
Canada
(514) 255-7747
Fax: (514) 255-6861
Quarterly newsletter. $10/2 years. Publisher is parent of American Yeast Sales, producers and distributors of Eagle instant and fresh yeast. For professional bakers. Features technical articles dealing with all aspects of baking. No recipes.

Baking with the American Harvest
626 Santa Monica Avenue
#526
Santa Monica, CA 90401
(310) 399-8680
Editor: Cindy Mushet
Quarterly newsletter. 12 pages. Subscription: $24/year. Sample copy: $4.50. "Celebrates the joys of baking, pastry & dessert making in their many forms." In-depth articles, recipes, history, explanation of ingredients and techniques, and the science of why it all works.

Bread
P.O. Box 841
Green Bay, WI 54305-0841
(920) 432-3514
Email: michelle@baywave.com
Editor: Michele Kennedy
Bimonthly journal. Subscription: $14.95/year. Sample copy: $2. Covers historic and current bread baking techniques, recipes, product and book reviews. Provides help on the business as well as the art of baking.

Cater Source Journal
P.O. Box 14776
Chicago, IL 60614
(800) 932-3632
Monthly newsletter. $139/year. Free sample copy. The publication of the catering industry offers tips, tactics, tools, templates, strategies, and winning business ideas.

Cheesemakers' Journal
85 Main Street
P.O. Box 85
Ashfield, MA 01330
(413) 628-3808
Fax: (413) 628-4061
Email: info@cheesemaking.com
Editor: Robert L. Carroll
Quarterly. 12 pages. $25/year. Focus on home cheese making. Reviews new books about cheese, includes cheese recipes and informative articles on the history of dairying. Listings of conferences and workshops and a classified section. The definitive guide for cheese lovers.

Chef
Talcott Communications
20 N. Wacker Drive
#1865
Chicago, IL 60606-3112
(312) 849-2220
Fax: (312) 849-2184
Nine issues per year. Subscription: $24/year. Trade publication for the food service professional, particularly chefs. News, trends, ideas, interviews, marketing, managing, restaurant design and pastry making. Some recipes.

Cooking for Profit
104 S. Main Street
7th Floor
Fond du Lac, WI 54935
Subscriptions: P.O. Box 267
Fond du Lac, WI 54936-0267
Monthly magazine. Subscription: $25/year.
Food service magazine for chefs,
caterers, or anyone entering the business. Covers food trends, management
techniques, and the latest kitchen
equipment news.

Cook's Illustrated
Boston Common Press
17 Station Street
P.O. Box 569
Brookline, MA 02147-0569
Subscriptions: P.O. Box 59046
Boulder, CO 80323-9046
Bimonthly magazine. No advertising.
$24.95/year. $4/issue. Professional
shortcuts, lots of how-tos with step-by-step illustrations, brutally honest
reviews of cookware, food products
and cookbooks, and, of course,
recipes. A natural look and feel plus
meaty contents.

Culinary Online
Culinary Software Services
1630 30th Street
Suite 300
Boulder, CO 80301
(800) 447-1466
www.culinary-online.com
Ten issues a year. Subscription: $29/year.
Recently revamped and now an electronic newsletter delivered in Adobe
Acrobat format. Sample: Free. Billed
as "a culinarian's guide to the Internet." Good resource for finding Web
resources including sites, recipes, discussion groups, etc.

Culinary Trends
6285 East Spring Street
Suite 107
Long Beach, CA 90808-9927
(310) 496-2558
Fax: (310) 421-8993
Quarterly magazine. $21.60/year. For
culinary professionals and anyone
aspiring to be one. Food service publication that addresses the basics of food
and its presentation. Appeals to culinary creativity and updates readers on
trends that shape the industry. Food
photos look like plated artwork. Also
features recipes.

Fine Cooking
The Taunton Press
63 South Main Street
P.O. Box 5506
Newtown, CT 06470-9905
Bimonthly magazine. Subscription: $26/
year. Step-by-step instructions and
numerous photos show the reader how
to master techniques. Unusual recipes,
Tidbits column, Shortcuts, Q&A column, Basics, Flavorings/Food Science,
Reviews. Wonderful photographs.

Food Arts
Food Arts Publishing, Inc.
387 Park Avenue South
New York, NY 10016
(212) 684-4224
Fax: (212) 684-5424
Ten issues a year. Subscription: $30/year.
A magazine for the food professional:
food and beverage directors, chefs and
restaurateurs. Lots of contest information here, mostly for professionals
chefs, but some for nonprofessionals
with cash awards and vacations. Also
articles on wine, event listings like
cook-offs, chef's festivals, wine fairs,
and fancy food shows. Professional
chef–created (intricate) recipes, some
with step-by-step photos. Nice food
service magazine.

Food History News
1061 Main Road
Isleboro, ME 04848
(207) 734-8140
Editor: Sandra L. Oliver
Quarterly newsletter. 10 pages. Subscription: $15/year; $18/year internationally.
"Dedicated to the three hundred years of
American food history from the early
17th century through the early 20th century in North America." Provides a
unique forum for news, information,
and debate about the study and preparation of historic food. Reports on work in
living history sites, museums, and traditional scholarship. Calendar of food
events. Historic recipes. Recommended
for serious culinary enthusiasts, food
professionals, and historians.

*Foodtalk: Newsletter for People Who
    Enjoy Food for the Mind as Well as
    the Table*
P.O. Box 6543
San Francisco, CA 94101
(415) 386-3067

Editor: Elaine Douglas Cahn
Quarterly newsletter. 8 pages. $18/year.
Sample copy: $3.50. Deals with the
background of food, history, ceremony, folklore, ritual, habit, etc.
Also features interviews with food
professionals. Book reviews. Rare
food-related background material for
people interested in more than just
recipes.

Foodwatch Newsletter
Smithson Associates
6800 Galway Drive
Edina, MN 55439
(612) 944-9454
(708) 366-4599
Editors: Eleanor Hanson and Linda
    Smithson
Bimonthly newsletter. Eight pages. Subscription: $48/year. Sample issue free
to qualified professionals. Tracks contents of 19 consumer magazines and
10 major newspapers to report on and
analyze current and future food trends.
Essential for food writers, public relations firms, food manufacturers, trade
associations, and other culinary professionals.

Fork, Fingers & Chopsticks
Four Winds Food Specialists
P.O. Box 70015
Sunnyvale, CA 94086
(408) 735-8847
Fax: (408) 735-8610
Website: http://www.eatethnic.com
Quarterly newsletter. $32/year. "Supporting
Food, Nutrition and Health Professionals in Multicultural Settings." Well-referenced information and recipes
featuring many cultures. Highly recommended for its outstanding and often
unusual content.

International Cookbook Revue
S.P.A., Lagasca, 27-1-E,
Madrid, 28001 Spain
34-1-575 93 50
Fax: 34-1-575 99 62
New York office: 645 Fifth Avenue
Suite 703
New York, NY 10022
(212) 753-6849
Fax: (212) 753-6948
Quarterly magazine. $39/year. Slick,
beautifully designed journal for food
and wine lovers, featuring cookbook
reviews, publishing and culinary news.

Loaded to the gills with reviews of cookbooks and interviews with cookbookish people including the authors, publishers, and sellers of same.

Journal of Culinary Practice
Food Products Press
10 Alice Street
Binghamton, NY 13904-1580
(607) 722-5857
Fax: (607) 722-1424
Quarterly publication. Subscription: $28/year. Research-based articles on food preparation and cooking, including techniques and applications for quantity food preparation and food service management.

Nation's Restaurant News
425 Park Avenue
New York, NY 10022
(212) 756-5000
E-mail: NRNMAIL@aol.com
http://www.nrn.com/main.html
Weekly trade magazine. Subscription: $39.95 a year for qualified professionals.

National Culinary Review
American Culinary Federation
P.O. Box 3466
San Bartoia Drive
St. Augustine, FL 32085
Monthly magazine. Membership dues include subscription. Otherwise, $35/year. The official magazine of the American Culinary Federation, a non-profit organization founded in 1929 for chefs and cooks. Its purpose is to promote education among culinarians at all levels. The magazine covers food, nutrition and industry issues, preparation techniques, recipes, and events.

Pastry Art & Design
Haymarket Group, Ltd.
45 W. 34th Street
Suite 600
New York, NY 10001
Subscriptions: P.O. Box 333
Mt. Morris, IL 61054-8089
Bimonthly magazine. $30/year. Devoted to pastry professionals. In addition to professional recipes, includes baking and dessert book reviews as well as regular departments: Tools of The Trade, Shop Talk & Cutting Edge, up-to-the minute news for the pastry chef. For the serious home baker as well.

Simple Cooking
P.O. Box 8
Steuben, ME 04680
(207) 546-2115
Editor: John Thorne
Bimonthly newsletter. Eight pages. Subscription: $24/year. Copy: $4. Binder hole-punched. A quality food letter with recipes, thoughtful essays on food and cooking, food, book, and product reviews.

Wine Spectator
387 Park Avenue South
New York, NY 10016
(212) 684-4224
Fax: (212) 684-5424
Subscriptions: P.O. Box 50463
Boulder, CO 80323-0463
(800) 395-3364.
Twenty issues per year. $40/year. Established 1976. Magazine featuring fine dining and wine, cooking and entertaining, world travel and the arts, unusual shopping and collectibles.

Word of Mouth: Food & The Written Word
P.O. Box 42568
Portland, OR 97242-0568
Editor: Johan Mathiesen
Bimonthly. 12 pages. Subscription: $22/year. Newsletter features recipes, cookbook reviews, food facts, anecdotes, and food history articles. Good essays. A very tasty and tasteful read.

APPENDIX IV
CULINARY ORGANIZATIONS, PROFESSIONAL SOCIETIES, TRADE ASSOCIATIONS, AND GENERAL MEMBERSHIP GROUPS FOR FOOD AND WINE ENTHUSIASTS

Many organizations offer excellent networking and training opportunities. The following list includes those dedicated to specific branches of the food and beverage industry, general culinary groups, and groups whose work is often related to the culinary arts.

Advertising Photographers of America (APA)
APA National Headquarters, Los Angeles Chapter
333 S. Beverly Drive, Suite 216
Beverly Hills, CA 90212-4314
(800) 272-6264
www.apanational.org
office@apa-la.org

American Association of Family and Consumer Sciences (AAFCS)
1555 King Street,
Alexandria, VA 22314
(800) 424-8080; (703) 706-4600
Fax: (703) 706-4663
www.aafcs.org
info@aafcs.org

American Cheese Society (ACS)
c/o Laura Jacobs-Welch,
P.O. Box 303
Delavan, WI 53115-0303
(262) 728-4458
Fax: (262) 728-1658
www.cheesesociety.org
ljwelch@elknet.net

American Culinary Federation (ACF)
10 San Bartola Drive
St. Augustine, FL 32086
(800) 624-9458
(904) 824-4468
Fax: (904) 825-4758
www.acfchefs.org
acf@adfchefs.net

American Dietetic Association (ADA)
216 West Jackson Boulevard
Chicago, IL 60606-6995
(800) 877-1600; (312) 899-0040
www.eatright.org
education@eatright.org

American Folklore Society, Foodways Sections (AFS)
4350 North Fairfax Drive, Suite 640
Arlington, VA 22203
(703) 528-1902
Fax: (703) 528-3546
www.afsnet.org
rsmariga@aaanet.org

American Home Economic Association (AHFA)
See American Association of Family and Consumer Sciences (AAFCS)

American Hospital Association (AHA)
Chicago Headquarters (CH)
One North Franklin
Chicago, IL 60606-3440
(312) 422-3000
Fax: (312) 422-4796
www.aha.org

American Hospital Association (AHA)
Washington Office (WO)
325 Seventh Street NW
Washington, DC 20004
(800) 424-4301; (202) 638-1100
Fax: (202) 626-2345
www.aha.org

American Hotel & Motel Association, (AH&MA)
1201 New York Avenue NW, #600
Washington, DC 20005-3931
(202) 389-3100
Fax: (202) 289-3199
www.ahma.com
infoctr@ahma.com

American Institute of Baking (AIB)
1213 Bakers Way, P.O. Box 3999
Manhattan, KS 66505-3999
(800) 633-5137; (785) 537-4750
Fax: (785) 537-1493
www.aibonline.org

American Institute of Wine & Food (AIWF)
304 West Liberty Street, Suite 201
Louisville, KY 40202
(502) 992-1022
www.aiwf.org

American Society for Enology and Viticulture (ASEV)
P.O. Box 1855
Davis, CA 95617-1855
(530) 753-3142
Fax: (530) 753-3318
www.asev.org
society@asev.org

American Society for Healthcare Food Service Administrators (ASHFSA)
One North Franklin
Chicago, IL 60606
(312) 422-3870
Fax: (312) 422-4581
www.ashfsa.org

**American Society of Interior Design
(ASID)**
ASID Headquarters
608 Massachusetts Avenue NE
Washington, DC 20002-6006
(202) 546-3480
Fax: (202) 546-3240
www.asid.org

**American Society of Magazine
Photographers (ASMP)**
150 North Second Street
Philadelphia, PA 19106
(215) 451-2767
Fax: (215) 451-0880
www.asmp.org
membership@ASMP.org

Association of Food Industries (AFI)
5 Ravine Drive, P.O. Box 545
Matawan, NJ 07747
(732) 583-8188
Fax: (732) 583-0798
www.afius.org
info@afius.org

Association of Food Journalists (AFJ)
Carol DeMasters, Executive Director
38309 Genesee Lake Road
Oconomowoc, WI 53066
(262) 965-3251
www.afjonlin.com
carolafj@execpc.com

**Association of Fundraising
Professionals (AFP)**
(formerly National Society of Fund
    Raising Executives [NSFRE])
1101 King Street, Suite 700
 Alexandria, VA 22314
(703) 684-0410
Fax: (703) 684-0540
www.nsfre.org
nsfre@nsfre.org

The Authors Guild
31 East 28th Street, 10th Floor
New York, NY 10016
(212) 563-5904
Fax: (212) 564-5363
www.authorsguild.org
staff@authorsguild.org

Chaîne des Rotîsseurs USA (CHAINE)
444 Park Avenue South, Suite 301
New York, NY 10016-7321
(212) 683-3770
Fax: (212) 683-3882
www.chaine-des-rotisseurs.com

**COPIA American Center for Wine,
Food, and the Arts**
1700 Soscol Avenue, Suite 1
Napa, California 94559-1315
(707) 257-3606
Fax: (707) 257-8601
Fax: (707) 265-9008
www.americancenter.org
mail@theamericancenter.org

Direct Marketing Association (DMA)
1120 Avenue of the Americas
New York, NY 10036-6700
(212) 768-7277
Fax: (212) 302-6714
www.the-dma.org

Food Marketing Institute (FMI)
655 15th Street NW
Washington, DC 20005
(202) 452-8444
Fax: (202) 429-4519
www.fmi.org
fmi@fmi.org

Home Economists in Business (HEIB)
5008-16 Pine Creek Drive,
    Blendonview Office Park
Westerville, OH 43081-4899
(614) 890-4342
Food Stylist's Workshop (biannual)
7227 West Fish Lake Road
Maple Grove, MN 55311
(612) 420-4552
Fax: (612) 420-2469

Institute of Food Technologies (IFT)
221 North LaSalle Street, Suite 300
Chicago, IL 60601-1291
(312) 782-8424
Fax: (312) 782-8348
www.ift.org
info@ift.org

**International Association of Culinary
Professionals (IACP)**
304 West Liberty Street, Suite 201
Louisville, KY 40202
(502) 581-9786
Fax: (502) 589-3602
www.iacp.com.www.iacp-online.org
iacp@hqtrs.com

**International Council on Hotel,
Restaurant & Institutional
Education (CHRIE)**
3205 Skipwith Road
Richmond, VA 23294-4442
(804) 747-4971
Fax: (804) 747-5022
www.chrie.org
info@chrie.org

James Beard Foundation
167 W. 12th Street
New York, N.Y. 10011
(800) 36BEARD or (212) 675-4984
www.jamesbeard.org
jbeard@pipeline.com

**Meeting Professionals International
(MPI)**
4455 LBJ Freeway, Suite 1200
Dallas, TX 75244-5903
(972) 702-3000
Fax: (972) 702-3070
www.mpiweb.org
feedback@mpiweb.org

**National Association for the Specialty
Food Trade, Inc., (NASFT)**
120 Wall Street, 27th Floor
New York, NY 10005
(212) 482-6440
www.specialty-food.com,
    www.fancyfoodshow.com

**National Association of Catering
Executives (NACE)**
5565 Sterrett Place, Suite 328
Columbia, MD 21044
(410) 997-9055
Fax: (410) 997-8834
www.nace.net

**National Association of College and
University Food Service (NACUFS)**
1405 South Harrison Road, Suite 305,
    Manly Miles Building, MSU
East Lansing, MI 48824-5242
(517) 332-2494
Fax: (517) 332-8144
www.nacufs.org
webmaster@nacufs.org

**National Kitchen & Bath Association
(NKBA)**
687 Willow Grove Street
Hackettstown, NJ 07840
(908) 852-0033
Fax: (908) 852-1695
www.nkba.org
feedback@nkba.org

National Restaurant Association (NRA)
1200 17th Street NW
Washington, DC 20036
(202) 331-5900
www.restaurant.org
info@restaurant.org

National Writer's Union (NWU)
13 Astor Place
New York, NY 10003
(212) 254-0279
Fax: (212) 254-0673
www.nwu.org
nwu@nwu.org

**North American Farmers' Direct
 Marketing Association (NAFDMA)**
62 Whiteloaf Road
Southampton, MA 01073
(888) 884-9270
Fax: (413) 529-2471
www.nafdma.com

**Professional Photographers of America
 (PPA)**
229 Peachtree Street NE, Suite 2200
Atlanta, GA 30303
(800) 786-6277
Fax: (404) 614-6400
www.ppa.com
csc@ppa.com

**Rountable for Women in Food Service
 (RWF)**
335 North River Street, Suite 203
Batavia, IL 60510
(800) 898-2849; (630) 482-2458
Fax: (630) 482-2145
www.rwf.org
national@rwf.org

Share Our Strength (SOS)
733 15th Street NW, Suite 640
Washington, DC 20005
(800) 969-4767
Fax: (202) 347-5868
www.strength.org

Slow Food Arcigola
Via Mendicità Istruita 14
12042 Bra (cn), Italy
Tel.: +39 (0)172419611
Fax: +39 (0)172421293
U.S.: 1(877) 756-9366
www.slowfood.com
international@slowfood.com

Society of Wine Educators (SWF)
1200 G Street NW, Suite 360
Washington, DC 20005
(202) 347-5677
Fax: (202) 347-5667
www.wine.gurus.com
vinatage@erols.com

Women Chefs & Restrauteurs (WCR)
304 West Liberty Street, Suite 201
Louisville, KY 40202
(502) 581-3033
Fax: (502) 589-3602
www.chefnet.com
wcr@hqtrs.com

**Women's National Book Association
 (WNBA)**
160 Fifth Avenue
New York, NY 10010
(212) 675-7805
Fax: (212) 989-7542

INDEX

Boldface page numbers denote main entries.